ANTI

IMPERIALISM

a guide for the movement

Edited by Farah Reza

ANTI-IMPERIALISM
a guide for the movement

Published March 2003
Bookmarks Publications,
1 Bloomsbury Street,
London WC1B 3QE.

ISBN 1 898876 96 7

Designed by Noel Douglas
noel@movementoftheimagination.org
Typeset by Phil Whaite
Printed by Bath Press

ACKNOWLEDGEMENTS

Many thanks to the following people for their assistance in the production of this book: John Charlton, Peter Coleman, Charlie Kimber, Paul McGarr, Phil Marshall, Judith Orr, Kevin Ovenden, John Rees, Sabby Sagall, Mike Simons, Mark Thomas and Dave Waller

CONTENTS

Tariq Ali was involved in the anti Vietnam War demonstrations in the 1960s. The demonstrations against war on Iraq surpassed these in size even before war was declared

INTRODUCTION
TARIQ ALI

Empires have existed in different forms for over 2,000 years, but imperialism is of more recent vintage. Its first and crudest manifestation was the Spanish conquest of South America, but the process soon became more refined. Capitalism used its European birthplace as a launching pad to expand to all corners of the globe. It was this process of expansion that became known as modern imperialism. It was European colonialism that was responsible for creating the inequalities between North and South that still disfigure our world.

The 20th century—an epoch of wars and revolutions—witnessed the first serious attempt to challenge imperialism and capitalism. Nationalism and Communism resisted the old colonial empires. Inter-imperialist conflicts—the First and Second World Wars—led to the collapse of several empires. In 1917-18 the Ottoman, Austro-Hungarian, and Russian empires collapsed in a heap, the consequence of war and revolution. The end of the Second World War marked the beginning of the death agony of the British, French and Dutch empires. It also saw the emergence of the United States as the undisputed leader of the capitalist world. The rest of the century was consumed by the Cold War, punctuated by revolutions in Cuba, China and Vietnam, but the incapacity of the ruling state bureaucracy of the Soviet Union to resist the military, social, economic and political offensive of the US led to the ignominious collapse of the regime. As both the Chinese and Russian states embraced the market, the triumph of global capitalism appeared to be complete.

The victory of the US was real, not imagined. It created a two-decade hiatus, during which many on the left made their peace with the victors while European social democracy (of which the wretched Blair is only the most extreme example) virtually abandoned its entire programme. Despair reigned supreme, until hope re-emerged with the eruption of a new anti-capitalist movement in Seattle. It would be foolish to pretend, and the movement did not, that they possessed all the answers to the problems of the world. What was important was that the search for an alternative had begun. The process has, in general, been a creative one, but in the desperation for something 'new' it has occasionally led some of the movement's thinkers to veil themselves from reality.

It became fashionable to accept that the dispersal of manufacturing industry meant that it was no longer possible to talk of a First World and a Third World. There was widespread euphoria that the Washington consensus would lead rapidly to the trickling down of wealth, and that every citizen in Africa, Latin America and Asia could only gain from such a process. These thoughts, often written in essays and books, were somewhat premature. History has not been kind to this type of thinking. Global inequalities have increased—86 percent of the total world income inequality is inter-country. The economies of sub-Saharan Africa and Latin America, the first laboratories for the neoliberal experiment, collapsed dramatically. In the case of Argentina the 'cure' killed the patient. Then the enforcers of the IMF and World Bank turned their attentions elsewhere. One result has been the eruption of giant anti-neoliberal movements in almost every Latin American country. The whole continent is now in revolt.

How could anyone have imagined that the triumph of capitalism would lead to global harmony and that military interventions would only be 'humanitarian' in intent? In the case of the Soviet Union, it was never thus before the revolution of 1917, and it was foolish to think that it would be any different after its collapse in 1989. In reality, the US was now posed with a slight problem. In a world without enemies, how could it enforce its hegemony over other major capitalist countries? The invention of a new enemy was helped by the events of 11 September, but few seriously believe that an organisation of 2,500 to 3,000 religious fundamentalists poses a serious threat in any form. Behind the scenes a different debate was taking place. In mid-1997 a gang of US neo-conservatives launched the Project for the New American Century, chaired by *Weekly Standard* editor William Kristol, a veteran of the Reagan and first Bush administrations. The aim was straightforward—the preservation of US global hegemony via a massive boost in defence expenditure. Also, frontal assaults on 'regimes hostile to our interests and values', active promotion of 'political and economic freedom abroad', and recognition of 'America's unique role in preserving and extending an international order friendly to our security, our prosperity, and our principles'. In short, imperialism.

These 'principles' were codified in a founding statement, and the signatories included many luminaries from the old Bush regime as well as those who are now the leading figures in the new son of Bush administration. These include vice-president Cheney, Lewis Libby (his chief of staff), Donald Rumsfeld (secretary of defence), Paul Wolfowitz (deputy secretary of defence), Elliott Abrams (senior director of the National Security Council's Office for the Near East, Southwest Asian and North African Affairs), Paula Dobriansky (Undersecretary of State for Global Affairs) and Zalmay Khalilzad (currently a gauleiter in Kabul, but also special envoy and ambassador at large for 'free Iraq'). With the planned war and occupation of Iraq, only the very ignorant doubt the existence of the US Empire and imperialism. This is something real. It rules. It dominates. It makes war. It punishes enemies. It threatens rivals. The notion of 'Empire' as a nebulous entity without a centre is flippant, dangerous and apolitical. Flippant because this is the only time in world history when we have a globe dominated by a single empire—the United States of America. Dangerous because it disarms any potential resistance. Apolitical because the idea is a reflection of the postmodern retreat from politics that has dominated cultural studies departments in Anglo-Saxon university campuses for the last two decades.

The notion, from similar quarters, of an existing US imperialism challenged by the cultural studies illusion of 'Empire' is completely ridiculous. When I read Michael Hardt in the *Guardian* (18 December 2002) saying that the resistance to the US will come from the multitudes that are 'composed of different kinds of powers, including the dominant nation-states, supranational organisations, such as the United Nations and the IMF, multinational corporations, NGOs, the media, and others', I want to scream. In fact I did scream. And when the same writer insists that the global elites could pose a real challenge to US imperialism, one has to wonder which world he is writing about.

The resistance to the real Empire will come not from the elites who drink the milk from its teats, but from those who suffer—the real multitudes, peasants in Latin America, workers in China and India, etc. And increasingly it is being understood that this struggle cannot be isolated from the anti-capitalist protests. The politicians who impose neoliberal solutions at home are the same men and women who wage wars abroad, and it is done for the same reasons. How could it be otherwise? It is these realities that make books like this both timely and necessary.

Tariq Ali is a writer, activist and film-maker. He is an editor of *New Left Review*, and has written many books on politics and history, including *The Clash of Fundamentalisms*

Socialist Worker
STOP THIS
BLOODY
WAR
Fight US/UK
imperialism

Picture: John Clarence

ISSUES

A Edwardian General takes tea with several Indian maharajahs. The US often uses the same system of indirect rule over regimes today. As Tony Benn says, 'All you have to do is prop them up and they hold their own people down'

THE NEW IMPERIALISM

TONY BENN

When people say to you, 'What is imperialism?' what do you say?

Imperialism has a long history. It is a product of economic and industrial power that is used for the benefit of the ruling classes of those countries that possess it in order to occupy and exploit the nations into which they move, for resources, for cheap labour, or for military and strategic advantage.

Looking back over the history of imperialism, how do you see the link between capitalism and the growth of the various empires?

Capitalism is a relatively modern development. In the ancient Chinese Empire the horse was the means of delivery and gunpowder was the warhead. Genghis Khan came across using the horse and gunpowder. The Roman Empire grew because they used the horse rather than the ox. The ox could only go a certain distance every day, so the towns in the countries in Asia that used the ox were small, whereas those in the Roman Empire where they used the horse were bigger. With that came the development of metalwork and spears, and so on.

Modern imperialism, by which I mean capitalist imperialism, was motivated by the drive for raw materials, for markets and for profit. Originally of course it was not just a trade in goods. It was a trade in people—the slave trade. The *Economist* in 1848 had a lead-ing article on the slave trade saying you cannot abolish the slave trade because there are all these blacks in Africa with nothing to do and they are needed in the plantations in America. The *Economist* thought you should regulate the slave trade—perhaps regulation would have been carried out by a body called Ofslave. It could have named and shamed slave ships that failed to meet sanitary require-ments. And as recently as 1936 there was in Rhodesia, now Zim-babwe, a law passed, the Industrial Conciliation Act, which made it illegal for an African to have a skilled trade. In Africa we occupied the countries, sold the land, and sold the people into slavery.

We called this 'the white man's burden', presenting it as a humanitarian gesture, just as is happening again today. When Bill Clinton bombed Sudan in 1998 I remembered that in 1898 we sent an army into Sudan, killed 11,000 Sudanese people, and the prime minister said the Africans will have grounds to thank us for what we have done. The domestic presentation has always been in humanitarian and moral terms.

Military glory has always been a part of this. The British Empire was based on the navy. The ships were powered first by sail and then by coal-fired steam engines. All the empires, like the French Empire, expanded by Napoleon into the whole of Europe, were for the expansion of the wealth and power of the ruling classes. Capitalism gave the greater base of industrial strength and in some cases more specific economic resources.

It is interesting what you say about the growth in industrial capacity being a key characteristic of capitalist imperialism. What do you have to say about the various phases in the development of capitalism? Obviously there was an absolutely critical phase of the world's history which was to do with direct colonial rule—the direct civil administration of the colonies by the major powers.
There have always been competing imperialisms—British, French, Portuguese and so on. And this led to conflicts like the wars in Africa about who controlled what. It was about power. And of course religious ideas were a part of this struggle as well as more

strictly economic questions. The 'fight against heathens' was a big propaganda argument.

Colonialism also made use of two other tools. Mercenaries, like the Gurkhas, saved your own troops, and you didn't have to pay them as much. And secondly there was indirect administration. The British in India used a system of direct colonial administration, but they also used a system of indirect rule through the maharajahs and rajahs. They were allowed to remain there as long as they did what the British told them. It's rather like the regimes in some parts of the world today that are allowed to remain there as long as they do what the Americans tell them to do. It's a system that saves a lot of military effort. All you have to do is prop them up and they hold their own people down. This was described as part of Queen Victoria's 'civilising mission'. People were told that the British were in India to prevent widows being thrown on the funeral pyres of their husbands, just as today we are told that the US and Britain went into Afghanistan to prevent women being forced to wear the burqa.

But for all this, colonialism was eventually overthrown. The British Empire reached its peak before the First World War. The two world wars weakened all the European empires, partly because they slaughtered each other in such large numbers. The second factor is the rise of anti-colonial leaders. These people were, in a certain sense, products of the empire. Gandhi was a barrister in London. Nehru was educated at Harrow. Nkrumah was at an American university. These and many others were able to draw from the imperial power ideas and education that helped them with their national struggle. But then it was a question of their own national movement and its allies in the imperialist nations. Annie Besant and Bradlaw worked with the Indian national movement. It was a combination of the progressive forces in the imperial country and the anti-colonial movements, most of whose leaders were put in jail. The lesson I draw from that is that the most important allies in undermining the American Empire are the people in America itself.

This anti-colonial movement went on even when the Cold War froze into pro-Moscow or pro-Washington positions. The non-aligned movement was very important in this respect. It represented the anti-colonial movement at a time when they

had not yet completed their victories. It also represented a
transformation of the United
Nations which, when it was set
up in 1945, was a recreation of
the League of Nations in that it
was white dominated. Nehru

**The victories of the
anti-colonial struggle
didn't see an end to
imperialism. The term
neo-colonialism began
to be used**

and others brought the anti-colonial agenda into the United
Nations. But since the end of the Cold War these countries have
had to come to terms with American dominance. This eroded
the non-aligned movement. The Indian government, for
instance, has been little use on any issue, although this was not
always the case.

But the victories of the anti-colonial struggle didn't see an
end to imperialism. The term neo-colonialism began to be used
almost as soon as national liberation was achieved. The economic
power of the dominant nations was reasserted after the political
power had gone. To a certain extent the colonial national leaders
who had fought so hard against colonialism became the maharajahs of the new world order. They were allowed to remain in
power so long as they did what they were told.

This is why the socialist argument reappeared as soon as the
national victory was achieved. This is a theme that the anti-
globalisation movement has now rediscovered. The United States
was the first country to break with the British Empire. George
Washington was a colonial leader—a terrorist of note. America
used this heritage as part of the anti-colonial movement to break
up the old empires, partly because it wanted to destroy the old
empires because they were too strong and partly because it
wanted to build up its own empire. The US role in the Suez crisis
was to break British power in the Middle East. When the US
installed the Shah in Iran its advisers used this advantage to try
and get the Anglo-Iranian oil company out so that US oil companies could go in. So the US has played an anti European colonial
role, but a pro American colonial role.

Now, as the only remaining superpower, the US is obviously
a formidable force. The doctrine of 'full spectrum dominance'

means that the US wants superior military power on sea, land, air, space, and in information. It used to attack Russia as an imperialist power. But now imperialism has disappeared from the category of bad things and reappeared in the category of good things. 'Regime change' is, of course, exactly what the British Empire used to do when it would remove sultans it thought troublesome.

But the American Empire also has its weaknesses. An empire cannot be run without body bags. The British Empire tried high level bombing in Iraq in the 1920s, but you can't run an empire without risk. The US policy seems to be that it does the bombing and then leaves the British or some other mercenaries to run it after the war is over. But this makes the empire vulnerable. And in the case of China the US faces an emerging imperial rival. Also, it can't keep people in ignorance in the way that it did before, now that the internet has made information available. The suicide bombers and the attack on the World Trade Centre prove that even big powers are not infallible. That's something we never had to face. I don't think there were many open terrorist attacks on Britain to get rid of imperialism, other than in respect to the Irish. I remember the 1930s, when they put bombs in letter boxes in London. You were told to be careful about it.

Now, compared to the earlier post-war years, the Americans are vulnerable in another sense. They are not as overwhelmingly economically superior as they were at that time. They talk about not being able to 'nation build', by which they mean spending money in Afghanistan or in the Balkans, whereas after the Second World War they could launch a Marshall Plan for Europe. So it is not so interesting why they keep winning the wars—that's obvious, they have the military power—as it is interesting why they have to keep fighting the wars. They have to keep fighting them because they can't stabilise the world economically in the way they did in the 1950s and 1960s. The Marshall Plan was actually designed to fight Communism in Europe. An ambassador who came to the House of Commons admitted that was the purpose of it—to buy off Communism. The whole plan at that time was a sort of colonial reconstruction of

Europe. Another fear for America is the growth of China. In terms of influence, there will be another superpower—there is already an embryonic superpower—not very far ahead in the future. Also, if you talk to the sort of Heathite European, they agree with Europe acting as a kind of counterbalance to US power. This is an imperial concept. They think that Europe threw away its colonies by fighting itself into two world wars, and that a united Europe will create a new European neo-colonialism. I don't think it will work, but it is in the minds of people in Europe.

After the end of the Cold War the Western allies are no longer bound together in the same way, and I do think the rift between Gerhard Schröder and the Americans over this planned war in Iraq is a significant sign of that.
Well, it's a combination of things. First of all, I think the French and maybe the Germans have got economic interests in Iraq. If General Franks were put in charge all the oil complex would go to the Americans. And secondly, the Europeans feel the Middle East is *their* back yard, in the way the Americans see Latin America as their back yard, and they don't want the Americans taking over. So there's that, but I don't think that is so much the European empire as just a conflict of economic interests between Europe and America vis-à-vis the Middle East. Mind you, the American back yard is not so very strong if you look at Argentina, Venezuela, and so on. The Americans have got a hell of a job to hold that together with Castro still there. So I don't think it will work out the way they hope it will. But it could be a very messy and bloody business in the meanwhile. The other thing, of course, is the cynicism of the Americans in using Islam to defeat Communism and then turning on Islam. Even Willy Claes, secretary general of Nato, who was removed for corruption, said that now Communism is gone, Islam is the enemy. The total transformation of interests—it isn't very credible. People see that. Also Islam is quite a powerful force in the world, and when Bush talked about the Crusades he forgot that during the Crusades the Brits went in and slaughtered the Jews and the Muslims. *They* remember it. We don't. The denial of history is a factor here. It is the privilege of the victors to abolish the history of

the vanquished. I spent a year in Zimbabwe, and Zimbabwe is named after the ancient Mazimbabwe ruins, beautiful buildings. The first function of every newly liberated colony is to rediscover its own history, and the rewriting of history is an integral part of the imperial strategy. You have to tell everybody that you are liberated and they are all primitive, etc. And the use of religion is a very, very dangerous force indeed, I think.

Unavoidably we've already discussed the Middle East in a number of ways. But it has a very long and central place, perhaps *the* central place, in terms of the preoccupations of the major powers.

Well it is, of course, the cradle of our civilisation. I think this is a thing that annoys a lot of people in the Middle East—that we treat them as Third World countries. When I went to see Saddam in 1990 somebody gave me a briefing on it, and so the first thing I said was, 'Mr President, it is a great honour to be in the country where, between the Tigris and the Euphrates, the three great religions of the world, Judaism, Christianity and Islam, were born.' Now, I think he was a bit surprised, because so many people go there who don't know, when actually it is a very old civilisation. So there's that. But it's the oil, and also the central role the Middle East has played in communication. It isn't by accident the Suez Canal was taken over, when it opened up the route to India. And the war in 1956 was over Nasser nationalising the Suez Canal. Using the Suez Canal was quicker than going round the Cape of Good Hope and whatever else. You don't have to go round Africa. And, of course, it is the linchpin between Europe and Asia .

Now, though, it's oil. It's interesting, I looked up Churchill's speech in 1914 when he nationalised the Anglo-Persian Oil Company. He paid £2 million to nationalise it. And the reason he gave was that Britain is being exploited by the oil trusts—he was then first supporting the Admiralty—the reason was that we were shifting from coal-fired ships to oil-fired ships, so we needed the oil. So he nationalised the company. It was the first national oil company. All the other national oil companies set up later. Britain was the first one to have a nationalised oil company, British Petroleum. So it was oil. And of course the religion, because the Crusades were about—I suppose it was about economic interests, enormous economic interests—but the theory was getting back to the holy places of Christianity. The pope introduced sanctions against Muslim countries during the Crusades, except for Venice—whose trade depended entirely on trade with Muslim states! They had a seminar on the Crusades in Cairo, and there was an old friend of mine who was a former foreign secretary in Algeria, and I said, 'We've had the seminar, what did you discover?' 'Well,' he said, 'during the Crusades the European arms manufacturers sold bows and arrows to both sides!' I think history is very important. I think that's why they dominate history. They know.

The media tells you what to believe today. There's a gap of about 25 years when you have got freedom to think—and the media have forgotten all those other issues—before the historians distort it. Reinterpreting the recent past is the one area we have open to us, and then the historians have to be careful. They are the backscratchers of history!

There is a huge constituency of people who are currently part of the anti-war movement, and in the past have been part of the anti-colonial movements. The vast majority are not socialists, but obviously socialists have something to say.

Well, I think with the new situation—first of all, there are a lot of people from other countries here. When I was born there were all boring whites who ate bangers and mash and went to the cinema. And now the impact of people from other countries here is quite formidable really. And I suppose in America the Afro-Americans are very big in cultural terms. You know, there are more Afro-Americans in prisons than there are in universities there. It is an astonishing thing. The liberation movement in America—the civil rights movement—was a colonial liberation movement. Paul Robeson, mind you, his father was a slave. It was not so very long ago. So there was the influence of that, and then, I suppose, the influence of socialist ideas—and remember, all the anti-colonial movements really were socialist, because they had realised that it was between imperialism of occupation and exploitation. That exploitation-focused element—the socialist element—diminished when they became independent, whereas they were victims of an international economic system.

But all these things are shifting now. And I suppose you learn your socialism by experience. If you say, 'Why did this happen? Who gave him the right to do that to me?' you begin to think about it and come to your own conclusions. I think people become Marxists less by reading *Das Kapital* and more by thinking about their own situation. After all, the anti-globalisation movement—there were big socialist elements in it, but whether there were people going to Genoa and Seattle because they are socialists I am not so sure. They go because of privatisation, unemployment—they feel exploited. And I think we should think of this not in terms of the education of the world through Marxism, but the discovery by the world that Marx had something very useful to say which helps them. And that is the way I look at it. I say that as a latecomer to *Das Kapital*. When I read it I realised what a fool I was to not to have realised that all these ideas I was beginning to form had already been covered years ago. And that is why you shouldn't be worried if there aren't lots of people busy spreading the message. And I also think socialism spread as a religion can be seen as a top-down movement instead of a popular one. It just helps people to understand, put the analysis at their disposal, and it clicks.

PR people say about blockbuster films that you can get a good first week by doing a massive advertising campaign, but the thing they all most value is word of mouth recommendation. That's what really produces a big blockbuster. I think that's like socialist ideas. If someone you know, in your family or someone you work with says something, you know they've got no axe to grind. They are saying it because they believe it, not because they are paid to say it. That and people's own experience is what is convincing.

Yes. What frightens the establishment about socialism is that it keeps reappearing. Just when you thought you'd put it out it pops up somewhere else—pops up in different forms in a way that can't be controlled. Of course, during the Algerian War French intelligence came up with this idea of hearts and minds, which the American CIA didn't understand—that somehow you could control people. It doesn't work. You can't control people. People are much better informed than they used to be and better educated than they used to be. A hundred or 200 years ago people couldn't even read. The media, with all their distortions, do get some people thinking. Did you see the *Panorama* programme last night about Iraq? It was just the most crude distortion you can imagine. It never mentioned that we armed Saddam. Just a war propaganda film. And I think that enough people now know that not to be persuaded fully.

There's a thing that Gramsci says, that people have two competing sets of ideas in their minds. They have 'common sense', which is what they get from the media—the day to day ideology of the bourgeoisie—and they have 'good sense', what they learn from labour traditions, the unions and so on.

This may sound too theological for you—this is another thing, this idea of conscience. I know somebody in the BBC the other day who said there's now no difference between the left and right. I won't argue about that, but there is still is a difference between right and wrong—when people do things they know are wrong, and people don't know why it's wrong but they do know it's wrong. There's still a small voice of conscience. It's a great recruiting agent for socialism in my opinion. After all, Marx in *Das Kapital* could have written a book about capitalism without criticising it. He could have just described it. It could be analytical and brilliant, but with no moral element. But he thought it was wrong. And that element is something, I think, that is an ally we ignore at our peril. I don't know if that makes sense to you. Our morals, the people's morals, against the imperialist morals. It's about responding with what you would call the 'good sense'. It's also something a bit deeper than that.

Tony Benn was first elected as an MP in 1950. He retired at the general election in 2001, saying that he wanted to 'devote more time to politics'. He has written many books, including *Free at Last! Diaries 1991-2001* and *Arguments for Socialism, Arguments for Democracy*

He was interviewed by John Rees

OIL AND IMPERIALISM

OIL: THE EARLY DAYS

Oil is a strange substance. Up until the middle of the 19th century it was virtually useless. There were no cars, lorries, planes or huge industrial enterprises and manufacturing monopolies that required vast quantities of the black, sticky substance. Yet today it is the world's most valuable commodity. The history of conflict in the Middle East is rooted in the imperialist scramble for its oil reserves—which are the largest in the world. Saudi Arabia is the country with the largest proven oil reserves in that region, and its borders were first drawn up by British imperialists. The stability of Saudi Arabia and the other Gulf states has therefore been a central concern for the imperial powers for over a century. This is why the Gulf War of 1991 was the first decisive episode of the new imperialism. The US, the biggest consumer of this important fuel, wants to have access to the world's oil supplies not only to fulfil the needs of its own industries. It also wants to control supply so that every other country has to buy through or from it. Essentially, whoever controls the global taps of oil gains political dominance over the rest of the world's economies.

Oil was first discovered in the United States. Many of the early explorers of America encountered petroleum deposits in some form. Oil slicks were seen off the coast of California in the

16th century. A form of oil, similar to kerosene, was distilled from shale even before the industrial revolution, and some of the early settlers used some oil as grease for wagons and tools. In 1859 Samuel Downer Jr, an early US entrepreneur, patented 'Kerosene' as a trade name for rock oil distilled from shale. It was used in cheap oil lamps. This gave the incentive for others to look for other sources of oil and other uses for it. On 27 August 1859 William Smith, an expert salt driller, struck oil at a depth of 69 feet near Titusville, Pennsylvania. So far as is known, this was the first time that oil was tapped at its source, using a drill.

Anthony Sampson writes:

> In its murky trail, from the hills of Pennsylvania to the flatlands of Texas to the oil compounds of Saudi Arabia, the black stuff has always seemed to be spurting up in the most impossible places, one moment in excessive quantities, the next moment threatening a terrifying shortage... It was like water in its bulk and its problems of storage, but unlike water it had to be carried across the world, to transform the economies of nations.[1]

Oil was discovered in Iran at the beginning of the 20th century. It quickly led to the realisation that a great deal more might be lying under the deserts of the Middle East. Today the oil multinationals and their subsidiaries dominate the globe. ExxonMobil, BP, Shell and Esso are the symbols that have become the focus of protest and anger from the anti-capitalist movement. So central are the production, distribution and sale of oil to the world economy that even the slightest interruption of supply or fluctuation in price can have devastating consequences. The history of oil is tied up with the development of capitalism and with the growth of industrial production. Yet, like the substance itself, it has a murky side—one of corruption and cartels, of bribery and bullying. The oil companies influence governments, direct policy and even bring down regimes. You only need to look at the experience of the Chavez government in Venezuela to see how threatening his presidency appears to international capital—he controls a country which is the fifth biggest oil producer in the world. In regard to the

Middle East, there has been an important shift in relations between the US and Saudi Arabia in recent years. Once the closest of allies, since the first Gulf War there has been a growing rift, initially fuelled by resentment caused by the presence of US military bases in Saudi Arabia. The US, and other Western powers, have had to start looking for more stable sources of oil outside the Middle East—which is becoming a cauldron of anti-imperialist feeling. More of the history of imperialism in this region and the way in which the discovery of oil has shaped its development is explored in other chapters. Although other regions in world are now being exploited for their oil resources, the significance of the Middle East remains central.

THE NEW SCRAMBLE FOR OIL: THE CASPIAN AND CENTRAL ASIA

Almost nothing was known about the issue of Caspian oil and gas resources outside the oil industry and some specialist publications when the Balkan War began in 1999. Now, just a few years on, there can be little doubt of the oil and gas reserves that lie in the Caspian and Central Asian region. For instance, Ahmed Rashid's authoritative account argues:

> The Caspian represented possibly the last unexplored and unexploited oil-bearing region in the world, and its opening up generated huge excitement amongst international oil companies. Western oil companies have shifted their interest first to Western Siberia in 1991-92, then to Kazakstan in 1993-94, Azerbaijan in 1995-97 and finally Turkmenistan in 1997-99.[2]

The US ruling class was well aware of the importance of the Balkan War to secure access to this oil. Only a year before the war US energy secretary Bill Richardson said:

> This is about America's energy security... It is also about preventing strategic inroads by those who don't share our values. We are trying to move these newly independent countries toward the West. We would like to see them reliant on Western commercial and political

interests rather than going another way. We've made a substantial political investment in the Caspian, and it's very important to us that the pipeline map and the politics come out right.

The US government was committed to finding a pipeline route that avoided both Russia and Iran. This point was first demonstrated in practice during the 1999 Balkan War, when plans were advanced for the pipeline from Baku to Ceyhan in Turkey, from where oil would be shipped westward through the southern Mediterranean and Aegean. The completion of the pipeline (from Baku to Suspa on the Black Sea, from where oil would move onward through the Bosphorus Straits) made the point a second time. And after the war the revival of plans for a Bulgarian-Balkan pipeline made the point a third and definitive time. No such project could have continued without a Nato victory in the Balkan War.

The whole debate about oil pipelines in the Caspian, the Balkans and Turkey is driven by the fact that the Western states and corporations do not want to export through either Iran or Russia—despite the fact that both are cheaper than the options now being developed. And the search for alternative oil and gas reserves and alternative pipelines—the 'multiple pipeline routes' strategy that is now official US policy—is driven by fear of dependence on the Middle East alone.

AFRICA

At the same time that all eyes are on events in Iraq, there is also a scramble for oil that is reshaping Western policy towards West Africa. It could also lay the basis for civil wars, tension between the US and European powers, and future military intervention.

For years the multinationals and powerful states have generally regarded Africa as a 'basket case', its suffering contemptuously ignored. Large parts of the continent were seen as not worth the risk of exploiting. But that is now changing. A conference at the end of 2002, involving US officials, oil executives and African politicians, met to organise a new carve-up of Africa's resources. It was organised by the Corporate Council on Africa (CCA), which was established in 1992 and brings together 160 US companies which control nearly 85 percent of total US private

Pressure for war on Iraq shows the US wants to dominate the Middle East. But it is also seeking alternative oil supplies

sector investments in Africa.

From Angola came the vice-minister of petroleum, the national petroleum director and various other top officials. Nigeria sent the presidential adviser on petroleum and energy. Cameroon supplied its minister of mines, water resources and energy, and Chad's delegation included the minister of petroleum. The conference programme announced, 'This event is sponsored by ExxonMobil and ChevronTexaco with support from Vanco Energy, Marathon Oil Company and PennWell.'

This meeting confirmed a trend that has been accelerating sharply. In September 2002 George W Bush held meetings with the presidents of 11 African states, all of them oil producers or allied closely to oil producers. The pressure for war on Iraq shows the US wants to dominate the Middle East. But it is also seeking alternative oil supplies. In recent years the country has imported more and more oil from sub-Saharan Africa. It is relatively easy to ship oil from West Africa to the US. The key state is Nigeria (whose output will rise to 4.4 million barrels a day by 2020).

As a sign of goodwill, US soldiers have been sent to train Nigerian forces. Bush's advisers would not only like to have Nigeria firmly in the US camp, but also plan for Nigeria to be a regional power that might discipline the whole of West Africa in US interests. The other prime target is Angola, which is at the centre of the oil boom. Its output has increased from 722,000 barrels a day in 2001 to 930,000 in 2002, and by 2020 it is expected to reach 3.28 million barrels a day. Elsewhere in the region it was recently announced that the Chad-Cameroon oil pipeline project would go ahead with World Bank support. The US companies ExxonMobil and ChevronTexaco are major partners in the scheme.

Such investments require military backup. The US government is moving to an agreement with São Tomé and Principe, the island-state off the west coast of Africa, to establish a naval base there. But the US is not going to have it all its own way. There is already competition with rivals, and battles for control.

Many of the countries that US firms are moving into are former French colonies, and French-based TotalFinaElf has strong (and incredibly corrupt) ties with governments in Congo and Gabon. TotalFinaElf also owns the huge Girassol field in block 17 off the waters of Angola. Royal Dutch/Shell and BP are pouring money into West Africa too.

George W Bush received financial backing from Pierre Falcone, one of the most notorious international arms dealers who boosted Angola's war. Falcone sold arms to Angola in breach of UN sanctions.

European countries are also strengthening their military intervention in West Africa. The British government has strong military links in Sierra Leone, and the French government has troops in several key African oil-producing countries.

Amid all the wheeling and dealing the vast majority of Africa's people have been entirely forgotten. The past crimes of the present US officials should certainly make Africans fear for their future. Defence secretary Donald Rumsfeld was one of the strongest lobbyists supporting Angola's murderous Unita movement in the 1970s. Dick Cheney was also a longtime supporter of Unita.

Such monsters have helped to create modern day Angola, a country of oil and diamonds where 1.5 million are starving, a third of the population have fled from their homes because of the civil war, and where there are nearly 100,000 disabled landmine victims. West Africa has become the place where oil and the US drive for global domination come together. For all the wrong reasons, it will no longer be a forgotten continent.

IRAQ

With the US making inroads into other parts of the world's oil supplies, why does it still feel it necessary to get hold of supplies in Iraq? Consider these simple facts.

Iraq has proven reserves of 112 billion barrels of oil. This represents just over 10 percent of the world's proven reserves. It is also of very high quality, and is easy and cheap to extract. On top of this is the fact that due to years of sanctions the true potential of Iraq's reserves has probably not been realised.

Given the amount of oil in the region, it is safe to assume that there is plenty more to discover.

US multinationals have not been able to get their hands on Iraq's oil. According to a recent US Department of Energy briefing, Iraq has signed over 30 deals with various companies offering generous rates of return. Some 300 Russian companies were doing business with Iraq at the end of 2002. According to the *New York Times* Russian companies had acquired the rights to sell roughly 40 percent of Iraq's oil on world markets.[3] According to a Deutsche Bank estimate, contracts to develop roughly 50 billion of the proven reserves of 112 billion barrels have already been parcelled out to mostly non-US foreign companies, representing an investment of more than $20 billion.

Bush and his friends in the White House are desperate to get their hands on some if not all of this. Already they have calculated that if they are able to achieve a quick and decisive victory in a war

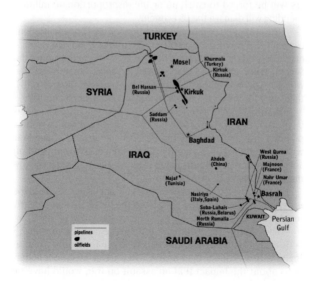

against Iraq then by 2005 production of oil could reach 3.5 billion barrels a day. This is 30 percent up on current production. It is estimated that production could then be doubled by 2010. According to a recent report in the French magazine *Petrostratégies*, if Iraq's oil was to be privatised following a US victory in the war, US companies would dominate the process, leaving 'consolation prizes to the Russians, a respectable portion to the British and, if possible, nothing else to European firms'.

PROBLEMS FOR THE US AHEAD

This is clearly a critical moment for US foreign policy. But the American Empire is not uncontested, as some may suggest. Imperialism is actually a product of competition. The reason why Western-driven globalisation needs a state as its armed wing is precisely because it faces challenges around the globe. And massive arms spending can't guarantee US ascendancy. Either other powers will be forced to catch up or the disproportionate military spending will damage the US economy.

The attraction of the military option for the US establishment conceals more immediate problems. The truth is that there is a mismatch between US military might and its economic muscle. After the Second World War the US accounted for approximately half the world's economic output. Although it has bounced back recently, that figure for the US still only stands at around 30 percent today.

Historically, US ascendancy in the West and elsewhere has been won with the carrot and the stick. The billions of US dollars pumped into a devastated Europe after the Second World War were crucial to the US's ability to rebuild markets and head off social unrest. Its meanness in post-war Afghanistan suggests how much things have changed.

A militarised foreign policy carries big political costs. With the exception of the ever loyal Tony Blair, the US's Nato allies clearly feel out in the cold.

They know they will have little stake in a war on Bush's 'axis of evil'. It is in their interests to argue for a policy of dialogue with so-called rogue states. They are also genuinely nervous about the impact that an assault on Iraq would have on regimes in the Middle East and beyond.

Despite the ten-year boom in the US, neoliberalism has been a negative experience for most, even in the capitalist heartlands. Real average income has failed to rise in the US over the last 15 years, despite a massive increase in working hours and job insecurity. The erosion of social security and healthcare provision has left millions without a safety net in society. Close ties between aggressive corporate capital and a compliant state are always in danger of spilling over into the public domain, as they did with the Enron scandal.

It is these experiences that gave birth to an anti-capitalist movement in both North and South. For all the wishful thinking of the ruling classes, 11 September has failed to derail that movement. In fact, the movement has become more passionately anti-imperialist in nature than it was before. Recession in the US and Europe, and economic stagnation in Japan, can only deepen discontent.

Against this background, the US turn towards a militarised foreign policy looks more risky. The US ruling class have neither the political confidence nor, more importantly, the economic strength they did when they attacked Vietnam 40 years ago. Whatever path Bush takes, it is fraught with danger. Yet, as we have seen, imperialism can be just as nasty and unstable today as it ever was.

NOTES

This chapter has been compiled with the assistance of Peter Morgan, John Rees, Chris Nineham and Charlie Kimber.

1 Anthony Sampson, *The Seven Sisters* (Coronet, 1976), p21.

2 Ahmed Rashid, *Taliban* (London, 2000), p144.

3 *New York Times*, 17 October 2002.

US intelligence image of Iraqi oilfields burning

OIL

According to British Petroleum the Middle East is the source of two thirds of the world's proven oil reserves.

Iraq is the only country in the Middle East that is capable of significantly increasing its oil production.

The borders of Saudi Arabia are a creation of British imperialism. The country has since been maintained by the US as an oil colony. Discontent among the

SAUDI ARABIA HAS `ONE QUARTER`
OF THE WORLD'S PROVEN OIL
RESERVES

IRAQ COMES SECOND, WITH
ALMOST `11 PERCENT`
OF GLOBAL OIL RESERVES

KUWAIT HAS `9 PERCENT`

IRAN HAS `8.6 PERCENT`

THE UNITED STATES HAS HEAVILY
INTERVENED IN THE RUNNING OF
ALL THESE COUNTRIES AT SOME
POINT

THE UNITED STATES BURNS
`ONE QUARTER` OF ALL THE OIL
CONSUMED BY HUMANITY

ROGUE STATES

JEREMY CORBYN

Historically, why have certain states been branded as 'rogue states'?

'Rogue states' is not really a new concept. Throughout history there have been times when particular states have been deemed to be harbingers of all kinds of bad things. For example, the Emperor Theodore of Ethiopia was seen as a great threat to Western interests in the region, and Sudan was treated in the same way. Throughout the 19th century, various Balkan states were initially treated as rogue states. The Ottoman Empire at one time was seen as the sick man of Europe that had to be eliminated. But more recently the West has sought to politically attack socialist systems or different systems, claiming them to be a threat to their neighbours and dangerously aggressive. The Soviet Union after 1917 was always treated as though it had expansionist aims. Indeed, throughout its existence the Soviet Union was treated in this way, even though there was no real threat of it invading any big Western power. In 1919 the White armies went in to try to destroy the Soviet Union. They were not successful, but nevertheless they made the effort.

More recently on the issue of rogue states, the United States had defined certain 'rogue states' as part of an 'axis of evil'. George W Bush delivered his speech in November 2001 where he talked about this 'axis of evil'. Iraq was declared part of the axis, and ever since then there has been preparation for war with Iraq.

None of us who are anti-war would be defenders of the Iraqi regime, considering the record of that regime. Nevertheless we will be the defenders of the right of the Iraqi people to live in peace within their own country. The US is clearly a threat to that. As in the past it has declared Iran to be a 'rogue state', it is increasingly suggesting North Korea to be a 'rogue state'.

Usually the declaration of rogue states is based on fear, based on anger, and based on a concocted, perceived danger to the big powers.

Another longer-running 'rogue state' is Cuba, which ever since 1960 has been subject to the US embargo. Quite clearly Cuba is not a threat of any sort to the US, unless one concludes it is a threat because it is an example of a country that can conquer illiteracy and provide healthcare for its people, which other Latin American countries have been unable to do.

In regard to the 'rogue states' rhetoric used by leaders today, how has the end of the Cold War affected how they seek to represent their enemies?
I think that the end of the Cold War was a defining moment in international political history, and in the relationship between the North and the South. Logically the end of the Cold War should have led to both the end of the Warsaw Pact and of Nato, and the development of the European Conference on Cooperation and Security. This had been a sort of Western European peaceful alternative to the Cold War. Instead Nato cast around for supposed enemies, and the enemy was Sudan, the enemy was Libya, the enemy was wherever else. There was a huge lobbying programme by Nato in order to create the illusion that there was a threat posed to Western interests by particular states, to justify the existence of Nato. Their first out of area activity was in the Balkans conflict, when the UN was deliberately underfunded and under-provided, particularly over Srebrenica, and therefore seen as incapable of controlling the situation. So Nato then came in. Nato was also used as a logistical back-up and not the main force during the Gulf War. In the current crisis over Iraq, Nato very

cleverly invoked Chapter Five after 11 September 2001, which allowed it to claim that the attacks on the Twin Towers and the Pentagon were equivalent to an external attack on a member state, and therefore all member states of Nato were under attack.

This intervention in the Balkans was followed by the formalisation of Nato expansion into Eastern Europe, with Poland, Hungary, the Czech Republic and so on joining Nato. Ukraine had been involved in Nato, and to some extent the Russian military were involved through the Rome treaty in the future of Nato. We now have Nato as, in effect, the only military alliance in the world. The United Nations is refused the ability to provide its own troops on any occasion by the power of the US, and particularly Britain. So Nato has become the world body, and it works essentially in the interests of the United States. Under the US constitution, American soldiers cannot serve other than under a US commander. Therefore Nato is the military arm of the United States.

Has the branding of a state as a 'rogue state' always been a pretext for actual military intervention in the region?

It has been a pretext for undermining the state concerned or for military intervention. North Korea has developed the capability to make nuclear weapons and probably develops actual nuclear weapons. Certainly that is wrong, and I would prefer it if every state disarmed completely, including North Korea. The declaration of North Korea as some kind of threat is, in a sense, a pretext for stepping up economic and military pressure on that country. The problem for the US is that the politics of the region has changed very fast, and South Korea is now no longer automatically an ally in the invasion of North Korea. Indeed, there is much evidence that the South Korean government has acted as a kind of moderating force on the US, which may wish to pursue military action against North Korea. I'm not saying that it is going to end there—I don't think it will. And I suspect this will be used as a way of helping to weaken, if not destroy, the North Korean economy in order to ultimately force some kind of integration between North and South Korea. Then we may see the spread of free market capitalism into North Korea.

Another example of what was termed a rogue state was Nicaragua from 1979 onwards, when the Sandinista government took over and the previous government disappeared. The Sandinistas posed no threat whatsoever of expanding beyond Nicaragua. But they were faced immediately by civil war by the Contra guerrillas, who were funded heavily by the US and wealthy Nicaraguan expatriates. All this completely undermined the social advancements that had been won by the Sandinista Revolution. The Sandinistas were then forced into an electoral situation where they were wrongly represented as a force that would lead only to the continuation of war. A vote for the opposition party was represented as a declaration of peace. Unsurprisingly the opposition party won. The social gains made by the Sandinista government were subsequently destroyed.

Nicaragua is no longer considered a rogue state, yet the drugs trade, the instability, the poverty and the violence are now worse in Nicaragua and El Salvador than at any time since the war.

Can you describe times in your own life when you campaigned against the mainstream government and media propaganda?

I was very involved in supporting the Grenadan Revolution from 1979 onwards. I visited Grenada in 1983, after the US invasion took place. I went with Bernie Grant and a group of others. It was a fascinating experience to see this massive US military presence in the country, and to talk to individual US soldiers. Most of them were slightly confused about why they were actually there. They were heavily loaded with arms, and very well trained as a fighting force, but would sit down reading comics that were fit for a five year old. I then visited the quarters where the Cuban construction workers were building a new airport, and had been housed, and found books there that they had been reading. So the contrast of the literate Cuban workers capable of reading books and the US soldiers reading comics was stark. The difference was that the Cubans had picks, shovels and drills, and the US soldiers had automatic weapons.

In the Grenadan Revolution the invasion was eminently

predictable in the sense that the US was building up a long time for it. The British government was complicit in this.

I was also involved in supporting Nicaragua and supporting the people of El Salvador during the civil wars there in the early 1980s. My first visit to Nicaragua was in 1983 and I subsequently visited on two other occasions, and then visited El Salvador. I went to El Salvador three times, and I saw both the FMLN-controlled areas and the capital. Some of it was very frightening, partly because there was a sense of fear that so many people had. But they also faced the situation with great bravery.

I went to a trade union conference which on one level was laughably disorganised, but I then found out there was a purpose to this. You were supposed to meet for 8am, whereas we actually met for half an hour at 10am. We adjourned for lunch at 10.30am, and the meeting resumed again at 2pm. I was told that the reason for all this was the workers knew that there were informers at the meeting, and that there would only have been a limited number of informers present. So it was possible to have quite useful bilateral discussions between different trade union groups, while the informers could only listen to one conversation at a time. And so the conference continued in this style for several days.

I went on a May Day march during that visit, and the group who had invited us had helpfully made us this enormous banner for us to carry, which read 'Sindicatos Britanicos in solidaridad con los trabajadores de Salvador'.

I said, 'Fine, but this is a bit over the top. It's not up to us to lead the May Day march. It's your May Day march—we are here in solidarity.' They said, 'No, we'll put you at the front because they are less likely to shoot you.'

So we marched through the centre of San Salvador carrying this banner with the rest of the march behind us, which was interesting!

On one occasion a group of us were staying in a hotel, and it was very obvious that we were under surveillance. We tested this out by putting strings of cotton round our bags, which were searched every day by hostile forces.

We had taken to having breakfast each morning in a small

cafe—more of a shack, really. We went there one morning and found it closed. So we asked a man what happened, and he said the workers were killed during the night by the militia forces. They were deemed to be part of the FMLN. The situation was often very frightening. When one night we came back from a very private meeting hosted by representatives of the FMLN, we were driving back to where we were staying in San Salvador and were stopped by a military roadblock. The soldiers said that the city had been taken over by the FMLN, and this guy sitting next to me, who was a Yorkshire miner, said, 'Thank Christ for that, but why are the soldiers still here?' I said I didn't know what was going on, and we had this long argument with the soldiers, who took the keys to the vehicle, our passports and the driving licence of the driver. None of it was true. There was no FMLN takeover of the city. This was actually just a bit of tax collecting by the army. We then negotiated a figure. They started off wanting $90, and we took them down to about $30 or $50.

These were the dangers of the situation, which were in fact quite minor for visiting delegations. Trade unionists and others trying to organise food co-ops, education or anything else like that in the shantytowns were getting killed in the process. This was after the defeat of the Sandinista Revolution in Nicaragua had descended into an awful lot of criminal activities, ultimately sowing the seeds of future social resistance and change over there. These things don't go away because a market economy has been imposed. It doesn't mean that there is peace or justice for the people.

What difference do you think protests and campaigning have made in this context?

An enormous difference. If we go back to the experience of Nicaragua and El Salvador, and the practical support that we were able to give the different co-operatives and so on, the sense of international solidarity made it much harder for the US to push through every piece of funding for the Contras. I don't say it changed the situation in the end, but it did give some political space and some political support to people within Nicaragua.

Likewise, I think the solidarity movements around the world against the US blockade against Cuba have had a very good effect. They have isolated the US, and meant that Cuba has been able to trade with many other countries in the world. They meant that Cuba survived despite the blockade and the fall of the Soviet Union in the early 1990s. At the time of the Soviet Union collapsing and the likes of Comecon, the Cuban economy virtually collapsed with it. Yet it survived largely through solidarity actions. This has been important.

It is also important to give a sense of hope to people. One thinks back to the struggles of the apartheid years. People in the ANC and other groups told me that solidarity from the West played a crucial part in the abolition of apartheid. They felt that people were arguing and fighting for them. When they heard about support from the West in the news, this emboldened them still further in their struggle.

Solidarity is absolutely crucial. But the best solidarity we can always give is political change in one's own society. If we want to help the people in the Middle East to be able to live in peace and justice, the best way surely is to keep the British and American forces out of the Middle East.

In anti-war campaigning against war on a 'rogue state', can you talk about how activists can win the political debate, and have won it in the past?

I've been in parliament since 1983, and I have been very involved in the peace movement, the anti-nuclear campaign, the campaign against the Gulf War, the Afghan War, and now war on Iraq. I wasn't in parliament during the Falklands War, but I did take part in demonstrations. We were part of a minority who opposed war in the case of the Falklands. We said that it was a war between a bankrupt government (Thatcher's Conservative government) and a bankrupt general (Galtieri). The Falklands were, and still are, very rich in oil and fish. Once you take this into account, one begins to see what the wider agenda always was. It was about resources. Then, more recently, came the revelation that Thatcher eventually confirmed and which we alleged at the time—that Pinochet, the Chilean dictator, was crucial in ensuring the British victory.

Saying all this now doesn't arouse any hostility, and people listen to you with some respect. The members of parliament Tony Benn and Tam Dalyell were opposed to the war at the time, and were vilified for it, but they are now seen with greater respect because of the consistency of their position.

When we opposed the Gulf War in 1991 we did not support the regime in Iraq. Indeed, we had always opposed arms sales to Iraq, and supported the opposition movements in Iraq and in the West. You saw the hypocrisy of the West, in particular of the US embassy in the region, which in effect approved of the invasion of Kuwait to start with and then decided against it. They used their new position on the invasion as a pretext to further war with Iraq. This resulted in the deaths of American and British soldiers, yes, but many, many, more Iraqi soldiers and Iraqi civilians through the use of depleted uranium weapons, and through the sanctions policy against the civilian population. Our anti-war movement, our solidarity movement with ordinary Iraqis, possibly helped to reduce the longevity of the war to some extent, and gave a voice to those who opposed war. It also gave hope to people in Arab countries who were also against the war.

I think that a more significant shift has occurred since 11 September 2001. Few would have seriously supported the kind of action that killed so many civilians in the World Trade Centre, or anywhere else. But what has happened since then has been the deaths of at least 8,000 civilians in Afghanistan and the reimposition of warlord rule there, when the leaders said that democracy was going to return to Afghanistan. Now there are also preparations for war on Iraq.

What 11 September has done is to politicise a whole new generation who want to live in a world where there is peace and justice. They understand that the two things are indissoluble. They have become more interested in world affairs and the way in which global corporations and powers exploit the Third World. I think the size of the anti-war movement, particularly in Britain, has been born of frustration with the mainstream political situation. They are also frustrated at a wealthy, free market, consumerist West deliberately reducing the living standards of some of the poorest countries in the world. This new generation has been further politicised over the planned invasion of Iraq, and they are not going to disappear. They are the equivalent of the Vietnam generation that I grew up as part of. My first political actions were in War On Want and the Vietnam Solidarity Campaign in the 1960s. I was growing up in Shropshire, where it wasn't a popular thing to do!

How do you think the movement now compares with the movement against the Vietnam War?

It is difficult to compare different periods. Communication is now much easier and arguments easier to convey in the form of mobile phones, e-mail, and a plethora of different TV channels. What is different is the general depth of the politicisation of the movement, its size at the moment, and above all the political unity surrounding the movement. The Stop the War Coalition has succeeded in uniting a wide diversity of opinion in Britain who agree on a minimal common denominator. This has been more effective than different small groups pursuing their own separate political lines, who would have been unable to put over 1 million people on the streets demonstrating against war on Iraq. We have changed the politics of this country.

Jeremy Corbyn has been an anti-imperialist campaigner for a number of years, and a Labour MP since 1983

He was interviewed by Farah Reza

FEDERAL RESERVE NOTE

CAPITALISM MEANS WAR

ONE DOLLAR

THE BLOODY
HISTORY OF
US IMPERIALISM

1898-1910: PHILIPPINES, seized from Spain, 600,000 Filipinos killed
1898: PUERTO RICO, seized from Spain
1901-14: PANAMA, separated from Colombia and canal zone annexed
1903: HONDURAS, marines intervene against revolution
1912-33: NICARAGUA, 20-year occupation and war against guerrillas
1914-34: HAITI, occupation
1916-24: DOMINICAN REPUBLIC, occupation
1917-33: CUBA, military occupation, made into economic protectorate
1917-22: RUSSIA, five landings of troops to try to overthrow revolution
1919: YUGOSLAVIA, marines intervene against Serbs
1925: PANAMA, marines suppress general strike
1927-34: CHINA, marines stationed throughout country
1932: EL SALVADOR, warships sent during revolt
1945: JAPAN, Tokyo and other cities firebombed, atomic bombs
        dropped on Hiroshima and Nagasaki
1950: PUERTO RICO, independence rebellion crushed
1950-53: KOREA, US and South Korea fight China and North Korea to
        stalemate. US threatens to use nuclear bombs. At least 2
        million Korean civilians killed or wounded
1953: IRAN, CIA overthrows democracy
1954: GUATEMALA, CIA directs invasion after government nationalises
        land belonging to US United Fruit company
1958: LEBANON, US troops land
1960-75: VIETNAM, 2 million Vietnamese killed in longest US war
1965: INDONESIA, 1 million killed in CIA-assisted coup
1966: GUATEMALA, troops intervene
1969-75: CAMBODIA, US carpet-bombs, 2 million killed by years of
        bombing and starvation
1973: CHILE, CIA-backed coup overthrows democratically
        elected government
1976-92: ANGOLA, CIA assists South African backed rebels
1981: LIBYA, two Libyan jets shot down
1981-92: EL SALVADOR, troops and air power assist death squads,
        75,000 killed
1981-90: NICARAGUA, CIA directs Contra invasions
1982-84: LEBANON, US forces intervene, navy shells Beirut
1983-89: HONDURAS, US troops build bases for death squads
1983: GRENADA, US invasion
1983: LIBYA, capital Tripoli bombed in effort to kill President Gadaffi
1987: IRAN, Iranian passenger jets shot down over Persian Gulf
1989-90: PANAMA, invasion, thousands of civilians killed
1990-91: GULF WAR, US-led coalition kills 100,000 Iraqis
1992-94: SOMALIA, US-led United Nations occupation
1995: FORMER YUGOSLAVIA, Serbs bombed and ethnic cleansing assisted
1998: SUDAN, pharmaceutical factory bombed
1998: IRAQ, four days of air strikes
1999: SERBIA, 78 days of Nato air strikes
2001-02: AFGHANISTAN, US-led war kills thousands
2003: IRAQ...

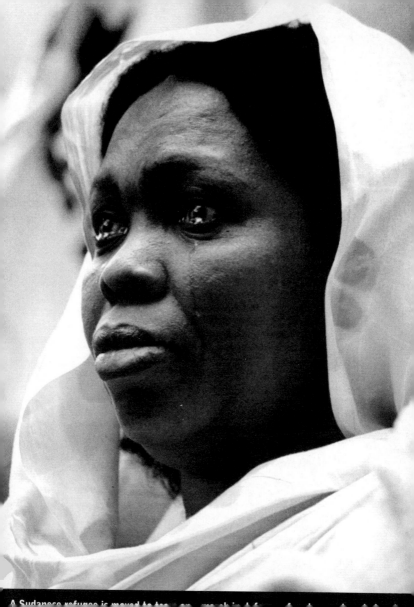

A Sudanese refugee is moved to tea... so much in t f...

RACISM
HASSAN MAHAMDALLIE

'**S**and-niggers'. This is one of the descriptions favoured by racists in the United States for anyone who 'looks' remotely Muslim. The insult synthesises the rooted racism towards African-Americans with a new target.[1]

We should not be surprised at this. Racism has historically taken many forms according to the needs of the system.

This oppression, the systematic discrimination against those deemed inferior by their 'race', has its origins at the start of capitalism with the biggest forced mass migration in history—the transatlantic slave trade. To justify the enslavement of fellow human beings, those who profited from the trade denied the humanity of the Africans.

Racism in the colonial period took the guise of paternalism—that the Africans and Asians were children who did not have the means to 'progress' themselves into modernity. 'We' would give them 'civilisation' (at the point of a gun). 'Their' part of the deal was to have countries occupied and their wealth stolen. This was the so-called 'white man's burden'.

Modern racism has been used to scapegoat incoming black and Asian migrants pulled into the Western economies, and to divide them from white workers. Today we can see the development of other variants of racism stemming from this era of globalisation and imperialism.

Firstly, there has been an increase in systematic hostility against asylum seekers across Europe, stoked by established parties and governments of both the traditional left and the right. That has in turn encouraged the re-emergence of fascist and xenophobic parties. Racism against asylum seekers is rapidly becoming an acceptable currency—especially on the front pages of newspapers such as the *Daily Mail* and *Express*. Their targets are not necessarily black or brown—migrants from Eastern Europe suffer racism as well.

The destruction of whole societies by neoliberal economics and the policies of the IMF and World Bank has uprooted many people in the poorer countries. The response of the Western governments has been the erection of savage border controls and a 'Fortress Europe'. Vast amounts of money are spent on keeping out the poor and the oppressed, from gunboat patrols in the waters separating Africa from southern Europe and the utilisation of the latest technology to X-ray trucks entering Britain's ports or scan the irises of people's eyes, to the incarceration of whole families in Stalag-like detention centres, the setting up of a Kafkaesque parallel social security system (the National Asylum Support Service) to deal with, disperse and punish asylum seekers, and the staging (sometimes for the cameras) of mass deportations.

How dare our rulers preach the superiority of Western 'civilisation' and 'values' at the same time as they enforce such cruelties in our midst?

We are forever being told that 'bogus' asylum seekers and 'illegals' are laying siege to our economies. The terms used against asylum seekers and migrants—'sewage', 'scum', 'floods'—defines them as a plague infecting an otherwise healthy national body, instead of what really they are—*people* who are victims of unimaginable oppressions, and the poor forced to follow the wealth flowing out of their countries into the West.

Home Office figures from July to September 2002 show that the 'top three' countries from which asylum seekers came were Iraq, Zimbabwe and Somalia. These countries made up four out of ten of all cases. Are we saying that people fleeing these countries are 'bogus' (especially those from Iraq, given that the government has

FBI figures show that reported hate crimes against Muslims have soared by 1,600 percent in the year since the attack on the Twin Towers

characterised it as an 'evil' regime as part of its drive to war)?[2]

Secondly, there has been a huge onslaught against Muslims as a consequence of the 'war on terror'. When, in the aftermath of 11 September, George W Bush declared, 'You are either with us or you are with the terrorists,' he did not just mean for or against war—he also meant for or against what he termed 'Western values'. The Muslim world was recast as the new 'evil empire' and those Muslims living inside the West as a dangerous fifth column.

In an accurate reflection of what is happening on the world stage, to be barbarous is to defend 'civilisation'. So when Balbir Singh Sodhi (a Sikh living in the US) was murdered in supposed revenge for 11 September, his racist killer told police, 'I stand for America all the way'.[3] Official FBI figures show that reported hate crimes against Muslims soared by 1,600 percent in the year after the attack on the Twin Towers.[4]

The right often claim that they are not being racist when they attack Muslims because they are attacking a religion, not a race. But Muslims have been given a racial 'type'—fanatical, barbarous, devoid of civilisation and out to kill all 'freedom loving' people. Their features are stereotyped in cartoons in much the same way as Jews have been in the past. Islam has become demonised as the religion of terror (even as Bush and Blair ride to a bloody series of wars against a rendition of 'Onward Christian Soldiers').

Far right parties in Europe have based their entire electoral appeal on anti-Muslim racism and opposition to a multi-ethnic society. For them all Muslims are equally guilty. Take the Danish People's Party—its MEP Mogens Camre recently said of Muslims, 'There is a straight line from the most despicable racist to he who circumcises his daughter, forces his wife to wear the headscarf, and to he who in religious fanaticism takes a passenger plane into the World Trade Centre'.[5] (Camre became notorious in 1998 when, as a Social Democrat politician, he advocated curbs on Muslim immigration to Denmark, declaring, 'There is an enormous pressure being put on European culture. On average a woman in Palestine gives birth to 8.7 children, while here in Denmark the average is 1.2... Muslims and their overweight wives drive around in Mercedes while Danes drive Skodas. When I see immigrants driving around in fancy cars it makes me wonder where they got their money'.[6])

The stormtrooper of the anti-Islamic fanatics is without doubt veteran Italian journalist Oriana Fallaci. In the aftermath of 11 September the New York based Fallaci wrote an anti-Islam rant, *The Rage and the Pride.*

I quote it at length to show the depths of anti-Muslim racism.[7] In an extreme (but wholly representative) passage she writes:

As blinded as you are by the myopia and stupidity of the politically correct, you don't realise or don't want to realise that a war of religion is being carried out. A war they call Jihad. A war that does not aim at the conquest of our territory maybe (maybe?) but certainly aims at the conquest of our souls and at the disappearance of our freedom. A war which is conducted to destroy our civilisation, our way of living and dying, of praying or not praying, of eating and drinking and dressing and studying and enjoying life... By god! Don't you see that all these Osama Bin Ladens consider themselves authorised to kill you and your children because you drink alcohol, because you don't grow a long beard and refuse the chador or the burqa... I have no intention of being punished for this by retrograde bigots who, instead of contributing to the improvement of humanity, salaam and squawk prayers five times a day.[8]

We collapse in every way, my dears. Because our civilisation dies out and we end up with the minarets in place of the belltowers, with the burqa in place of the miniskirt, with the camel milk in place of our little drink... Can't you understand it, dammit? Blair did.[9]

Fallaci turns her attention to those who she considers 'the enemy within' in her former native country:

The mosques of Milan and Turin and Rome simply overflow with terrorists or candidate terrorists who dream of blowing up our belltowers, our domes.[10]

They [Muslims] stay in our countries, in our cities, our universities, our business companies... They nest in the ganglia of our technology.[11]

Fallaci pours scorn upon Muslim women:

If in the Muslim countries women are so stupid as to wear the chador or the burqa, if they are so silly as to accept the fact of counting less than a camel, if they are so foolish as to marry a dissolute who wants four wives, all the worse for them.[12]

Fallaci sneers at Somali (Muslim) refugees protesting against Italy's anti-asylum laws, and they are characterised by her as animals fouling the streets of her beloved Italy. According to Fallaci, because of Muslim immigration the city of Turin now 'does not even look like an Italian city—it looks like an African one'.[13]

Fallaci ends by attacking the 'soft' Italian people for indulging Muslim immigration and a multicultural society. As with other anti-Islam commentators she explicitly links an argument against Third World immigration with hatred of Muslims, attacking 'the Albanians, the Egyptians, the Algerians, the Pakistanis, the Nigerians who fervidly contribute to the commerce of drugs (apparently a sin not condemned by the Koran)'.[14]

Promoting *The Rage and the Pride* at a lecture at the American Enterprise Institute in October 2002, Fallaci went even further (if that can be possible), describing herself as a soldier against Islam, and characterising Islamists as 'the protozoa of a cell which splits...to infinity'. For her the only difference between adherents to 'moderate' and 'radical' Islam is 'the length of their beards'.[15]

Using a tactic also employed by home secretary David Blunkett, Fallaci defends her anti-Muslim racism as a defiance of 'political correctness'. She claims that no one is allowed to criticise Islam, despite the fact that she has spent the past year profitably doing exactly that with total freedom.

Fallaci's book has so far sold 1 million copies in Italy, and hundreds of thousands in Germany and France. Fallaci's French soulmate is the novelist Michel Houellebecq, who was

The right wing press needed no encouragement to argue that all asylum seekers were terrorists

unsuccessfully prosecuted in 2002 for incitement to racial hatred, having described Islam as 'the dumbest religion'.

The evident logic of Fallaci and her cronies' argument is that all Muslims in the West should be rounded up and expelled, without any regard to their rights. So much for 'civilisation'.

As Bush and Blair have intensified the drumbeats of war we have seen a new development—the fusing of different manifestations of racism. Tony Blair immediately seized on the killing of Manchester policeman Stephen Oake during a bungled raid to pick up an asylum seeker as 'proof' that deadly Islamic terror was stalking Britain. The right wing press needed no encouragement to argue that all asylum seekers were terrorists. 'Britain is now a Trojan horse for terrorism,' as the *Sun* put it, launching a campaign to 'End Asylum Madness'. Tory ex-minister Norman Tebbit wrote in the *Sunday Express*, 'As things stand, Saddam's army could arrive at Dover, claim political asylum and be admitted while their applications were considered'.[16]

As the Russian revolutionary V I Lenin wrote 90 years ago:

> The civilised people have driven themselves into the position of barbarians. Capitalism has brought it about that in order to hoodwink the workers the bourgeoisie is compelled to frighten the people in England with idiotic fables about 'invasion'... Capitalist barbarism is stronger than civilisation.[17]

The ideological link between the new imperialism and the resurgence of anti-Muslim racism can be found in the 'bible' of today's warmongers—Samuel P Huntingdon's influential book *The Clash of Civilisations and the Remaking of World Order*, which was first published in a US foreign policy journal, *Foreign Affairs*, in 1993. It became a phenomenally successful book whose core arguments have their echoes in the speeches and actions of those conducting the 'war on terror'.

Huntingdon is a faithful friend of the US ruling class. During the Vietnam War Huntingdon advocated the saturation bombing of villages. In *The Clash of Civilisations* he assesses the threats to US power after the end of the Cold War, deciding that Islam and then China pose the greatest threats to American 'civilisation'.[18]

Huntingdon states that 'Islam's borders are bloody and so are its innards', and that there is a 'Muslim propensity towards violent conflict' shown by 'the degree to which Muslim societies are militarised'.[19] Laying to one side whether or not the US is 'civilised' (as I write this the state of Mississippi is fighting to assert its 'right' to execute juveniles[20]), the clear inference is that the Islamic world is 'uncivilised' and thus inferior to the West.

There is a clear line between this attitude and the one that permeated the British Empire during its imperial heyday. The claim that Islam has cornered the market on violent conflict is extraordinary coming from a member of a ruling class that resorts to mass destruction as a way of protecting and furthering its economic and geopolitical interests. And if the US is not a militarised society, with a weapons budget this year of $396 billion, what society is?

Huntingdon's view of Islam is similar to Fallaci's—he considers Islam per se as a threat: 'The underlying problem for the West is not Islamic fundamentalism. It is Islam, a different civilisation'.[21]

This logic means that Muslims in the West represent 'the enemy within'. In a classic racist construction Huntingdon talks of 'civilisational differences and of the need to protect what distinguishes "us" from "them".'[22] For him a great danger to the West is migrants from the Third World, especially Muslim ones—those who even acknowledge that the US is made up of different peoples are guilty of undermining Western civilisation. This ideology suits the US's imperial ambitions by dividing up the 'civilised' West and 'uncivilised' Islam.

This worldview is also promoted by the Christian fundamentalists who surround the White House. Most prominent among these is Jerry Falwell, who theologian Karen Armstrong, in her useful book *The Battle for God: Fundamentalism in Judaism, Christianity and*

Islam,[23] characterises as attempting to create through his churches and religious colleges 'an alternative society to undercut secular humanism'. Armstrong writes that Falwell's stated aim is to create 'a spiritual army of young people who are pro-life, pro-moral and pro-America', with the watchword that neoliberal capitalism is the only 'godly' way of life permitted.[24]

It was Falwell who last year pronounced that 'Mohammed was a terrorist'.[25] These Protestant fundamentalists are giving unconditional support for the Israeli state in its oppression of the Palestinians, despite their ultimate belief that the Jews need conversion to Christianity. Armstrong describes the fundamentalist's political programme thus:

> When the Kingdom comes, there will be no more separation of church and state; the modern heresy of democracy will be abolished, and society reorganised on strictly biblical lines. This means that every single law of the Bible must be put literally into practice. Slavery will be reintroduced; there will be no more birth control (since believers must 'increase and multiply'); adulterers, homosexuals, blasphemers, astrologers and witches will all be put to death. Children who are persistently disobedient must also be stoned, as the Bible enjoins. A strictly capitalist economy must be enforced; socialists and those who incline to the left are sinful. God is not on the side of the poor. Indeed as [Oliver] North explains, there is a 'tight relationship between wickedness and poverty'. Taxes should not be used in welfare programmes, since 'subsidising sluggards is the same as subsidising evil'. The same goes for the Third World, which has brought its own economic problems on its own head because of its addiction to moral perversity, paganism and demonology. Foreign aid is forbidden by the Bible.[26]

These are the most powerful fundamentalists on earth, and in Bush they see their man. As one US newspaper commented, 'For the first time since religious conservatives became a modern political movement, the president of the United States has become the movement's de facto leader... A procession of religious leaders who have met with him testify to his faith, while websites encourage

The new imperialism is eroding human rights worldwide

people to fast and pray for the president'.[7]

These people clearly believe that the war against Islam is some kind of crusade. However, we should not be seduced into believing that their attitudes are the root cause of anti-Muslim racism. Their crazy notions provide an ideological cover for the 'war on terror', but the roots lie much deeper in the workings of modern capitalism.

Racism has always been the product of primary forces in society. This is not a religious war that Bush and Blair have embarked on. There are Muslim states that Bush and Blair are happy to back—for example Saudi Arabia and Pakistan. Blair was happy to use the plight of the Kosovan Albanian Muslims to launch a war on Serbia. The Americans built Bin Laden up to use against Russia in Afghanistan and want to use Turkey as a launchpad for US bombers.

The racism against Muslims is tied up with the drive to war and control over a key region in the world for US capitalism—the oil-rich Middle East. For Bush and Blair this region must be brought under Western control. To fight an enemy you have first to demonise and dehumanise it. That is what is happening, both internationally and nationally. Just as in the days of old empires, to occupy and subdue a population for your own political and economic ends it is useful to argue that the conquered are 'uncivilised' and inherently inferior.

According to this outlook there are different values put on human life. Those killed in the World Trade Centre are remembered one by one, but where are the memorials proposed to the innocent victims of US bombs in Afghanistan or those who have died through sanctions in Iraq?

The new imperialism is eroding human rights worldwide. Witness the continued and indefinite incarceration in Guantanamo Bay of men captured in Afghanistan. Their recategorisation by the US administration from prisoners of war to a legal no man's land of 'unlawful combatants' allows the US to deny them any prospect of a fair trial (or even a trial at all), in defiance of the Geneva Convention. Other prisoners of the US have been tortured by the CIA

AN ASYLUM SEEKER'S STORY

'Living at home with my family in Somalia I didn't even know the word "refugee". Then my husband was thrown in jail. The rest of my family were killed. Everything I had has been taken from me.'

Before their lives were devastated by civil war, Amina and her son Mustafa lived in a villa in Mogadishu. Her family owned property and several successful businesses. In April 2002 Amina and Mustafa, now five, were forced to flee persecution from ruling militia. They now live in a hostel in Bristol.

'Men and women live together in the hostel,' says Amina.
'I have no privacy and I do not feel safe. The keys can open any room and the men tend to open the doors. I keep my son with me 24 hours a day, even when I go to the bathroom.'

When she steps outside of the hostel, Amina feels lost. 'I feel isolated. I can't say whether British people are friendly or not because we don't intermingle. Mustafa needs to learn English and mix with other boys.'

Amina was very ill when she arrived in Bristol, but finding medical attention for herself and her son was a struggle. She was sent away from a local surgery several times because there was no interpreter available.

'I went to the GP about problems with my eyesight. He said, "We don't treat eyes here." He was very rude. He could have sent me to someone who could help me. In the end I went to a supermarket. I don't speak English so I just pointed at my eyes. They told me where to get help.'

'One night my baby woke up screaming. A discharge was coming out of his ears. I went to the GP and the receptionist said, "Who sent you here?" She said I needed documents from the Home Office. After an hour the doctor said, "We can't do anything for you." He gave me antibiotics and sent me away.'

Amina's application for asylum has been rejected by the Home Office. She is appealing against the decision.

REFUGEE ACTION www.refugee-action.org

The destruction of the human rights of minorities paves the way for the destruction of the rights of the majority

before being handed over to other friendly secret services to finish the job. Such is the terror being unleashed by this 'war on terror'.

In the US, in the aftermath of 11 September, thousands of Arab-Americans were rounded up and interned without charge. The same has happened in Britain, with a section of the top security prison Belmarsh set aside for the incarcerations. They are not allowed to hear the evidence against them, what they are suspected of, or whether they will ever 'have their day in court'. Those who human rights lawyers have so far managed to get into court in Britain have been freed after the state has failed to produce any evidence against them.[28]

In the US a law was rushed through ordering all men aged 16 or over from mostly Muslim countries to register with the immigration authorities on threat of jail or deportation. They must all tell the authorities where they live, where they work and when they travel abroad. When Arab-American men turned up to register in southern California just before Christmas 2002, 700 were snatched by the authorities, shackled and dumped in prison cells. As one protester against the detentions wrote on a placard, 'What's next? Concentration camps?'[29]

This barbarism has first been honed on asylum seekers by governments across Europe and Western countries—most notoriously Australia, with its desert barbed-wire camps. And if you are an asylum seeker and Muslim, so much the worse. The treatment of the Afghan Ahmadi family reveals the racist depths to which the British state plunges—smashing down the door of a Birmingham mosque to snatch them and detaining the entire family, including children, capped by their illegal deportation to Germany.

The destruction of the human rights of minorities paves the way for the destruction of the rights of the majority. No jury trials for terrorists will be followed, if we allow it, by no jury trials for the rest of us. Identity cards for asylum seekers slip seamlessly into identity cards (or entitlement cards, as Blair-speak would have it) for all of us. Cutting benefits to asylum seekers paves the way for cutting benefits to all those in poverty.

The new racism skips from the international to the national at an alarming speed. Bush and Blair have provided a lightning rod for every racist to work their poison. It has been a very short step from the 'war on terror' to a domestic racist war against Asians conducted by the British National Party. Anti-Muslim prejudices spouted by those in power has been reprinted on the Nazis' odious leaflets and pushed through doors in Burnley, Oldham, Blackburn and elsewhere. This has resulted in Pakistani families who have lived in the run-down terraced houses for generations becoming 'foreigners' overnight, thanks to politicians such as David Blunkett. We are seeing a return to the racist 'Paki bashing' of the 1970s.

On the eve of reports into the 2001 uprisings in the north of England by young Asians against the Nazis and the police, home secretary Blunkett chose not to outlaw fascism but to attack its victims. In a newspaper interview he demanded that immigrants (code for Muslims) should accept British 'norms of acceptability' and demonstrate their 'Englishness'. He insisted that (poor) immigrants should do something that no other civilian in Britain has to do—sign an oath of allegiance to the crown and demonstrate their 'clear primary loyalty to this nation'.[30]

The BNP (the cause of the riots) grabbed gleefully at Blunkett's offering: 'Blunkett's attempt to steal the BNP's clothes will help us win seats! So keep it up Mr Blunkett...you're our favourite British politician at the moment.' Blunkett had given the Nazis a leg-up, and they went on to win three council seats in Burnley in the May 2002 elections, followed by another in Jack Straw's Blackburn constituency, and one in Halifax in January 2003.

Those who fought back against racist terror have found the apparatus of the state keen to punish them. In the aftermath of the riots relatives turned their sons and husbands over to the police, believing that 'British justice' would take account of the provocation they had faced. They learnt a hard lesson in the nature of institutional racism. The riot trial judge in Bradford, Stephen Gullick, was quite open that he was meting out a

The new imperialism pursued by Bush, Blair and their cohorts has spawned a new racism collective punishment to the Asian community, telling two men he jailed, 'The charge includes not only the actions of individual defendants such as yourselves, but also the unlawful conduct of all those around you as well.' The punishments handed out have been savage: Istifar Iqbal—11 months for picking up two stones; Asam Latif—four years nine months for lobbing six stones; Mohammed Akram—five years for throwing missiles; Mohammed Munir—four years nine months for throwing two stones. Blunkett, attacking the relatives' campaign for justice, branded the Muslim defendants 'maniacs' who had burned down their own areas—with no mention of the cause of the riots or condemnation of the BNP.[31]

Muslims, in the wake of the riots, have been accused of 'self-segregation'—of having an inherent desire 'to live with their own kind', and of refusing to learn English. Yet all studies show that Asians wish to integrate into society—the one thing that stops them is hostility towards them.[32] An in-depth study into housing patterns found that, on the part of Asians, 'we found little evidence of an unwillingness to mix with others... [We] found that most Indians, Pakistanis and Bangladeshis would be happy to live in areas where both Asian and white families live, although many have reservations about living in all-white neighbourhoods because of fears about racism'.[33]

So the new imperialism pursued by Bush, Blair and their cohorts has spawned a new racism. At the same time it has bolstered existing racism towards blacks and Asians. Afro-Caribbeans and Africans in Britain still face massive discrimination in employment, housing, health, education and the criminal justice system. New studies show that black people are six times more likely to be sent to prison than their white counterparts, and up to seven times more likely to suffer police stop and searches—a figure that is rising. (When a Home Office spokesperson was asked the reason for this disproportionality she replied, 'The reasons for this may be complex and are still being investigated'![34])

However, this intensification of racism, fear, violence and

hatreds has not gone unchallenged. Indeed, at every point of resistance to imperialism we can see glimpses of an entirely different world.

Against the national chauvinism of our leaders we are seeing a new internationalism. The anti-war movement is worldwide, with those in the Middle East able to witness on their TVs the huge demonstrations in the West against the war. The demonstrations themselves have proved to be an embryo of a world without racism, combining those with no affiliations with the left, anti-capitalists, and Muslim, trade union and peace organisations together in a common purpose.

Inside Western countries there are large and growing sections of the population who are sickened by the 'values' of their own rulers.

One product of a strong anti-war movement in Britain has been a generalised refusal to bend to the idea that we can't live together. One poll in November 2002 found that 84 percent of people in Britain agree with the statement, 'It IS possible for Britain's Muslims and people of other faiths to live peacefully together at close quarters,' with only 10 percent saying it was not possible. The same poll showed that, despite all the propaganda to the contrary, seven out of ten people agreed that 'Islam is mainly a peaceful religion; terrorists comprise only a tiny minority'. Seventy three percent of people polled also agreed that 'Britain's non-Muslims should do more to build good relations and mix with Britain's Muslims'. (On the other side 82 percent agreed that 'Britain's Muslim minority often keep too much to themselves'). As the pollster commented, the study revealed 'a massive appetite for tolerant, harmonious relations'.[35]

In another poll a full 86 percent of the British public disagreed that 'to be truly British you had to be white' (with 9 percent agreeing), and 78 percent of people agreed that 'it is important to respect the rights of minority groups (again with 9 percent saying the opposite). It is clear that the majority of people are comfortable with Britain being a mixed, diverse society.[36]

There are many, sometimes unexpected, points of resistance to racism. There was a satisfying rebuff to David Blunkett's calculated slur that refugee children were 'swamping' our schools when his own government hailed Fulham Primary School as the second most improved primary school in the country and the most improved in London. Fulham Primary has pupils speaking 34 different languages, and a third of them are asylum seekers. As the marvellous headteacher told a newspaper, the school's achievement was 'not in spite of, but in large part because of, the presence of so many children from the most war-torn corners of the globe'.[37]

We are now living through a racist 'blowback' from globalisation and the new imperialism. Fear of the outsider, whether that is poor migrants knocking at Europe's gate, asylum seekers fleeing war, Muslims settled in the West or the bogey of international 'Islamic terror', is increasingly used by our rulers in a way which dominates our lives, stoking racism and providing a convenient cover for the stealing of our hard-won civil liberties.

That is why the war against the war must go hand in hand with an unremitting war against racism, and ultimately a fundamental challenge to a world system that maintains itself through conflict and hatred.

Hassan Mahamdallie is an arts-in-education worker. He has written widely on issues of race and black history
hassm80@hotmail.com

NOTES
1   See Vijay Prasad, 'Shrouded by Flags', 19 September 2001, www.zmag.org/shrouded_by_flags.htm
2   Home Office published figures July-September 2002. Latest figures at www.homeoffice.gov.uk/rds
3   See Vijay Prasad, 'Shrouded by Flags'.
4   'Hate Crimes Against Arabs Soar, FBI Finds', *Washington Post*, 26 November 2002.
5   Mogens Camre speaking at the 2001 Danish People's Party (Dansk Folkparti) conference, quoted in European

Monitoring Centre on Racism and
Xenophobia, 'Islamophobia in the EU
After 11 September 2001',
http://eumc.eu.int/

6   Mogens Camre quoted in *Copenhagen
Post*, 17 September 1998.

7   All quotes from Oriana Fallaci, *The Rage
and the Pride* (New York, 2002), from the
essay 'La Rabbia e l'Orgoglio', originally
published by *Corriere Della Serra* on 29
September 2001. The essay is even more
rabid than the book—a translation can be
found at www.borg.com/~paperina/fallaci/
fallaci_main.html

8   Oriana Fallaci, *The Rage and the Pride*,
p84.

9   Oriana Fallaci, *The Rage and the Pride*,
pp87-88.

10 Oriana Fallaci, *The Rage and the Pride*,
p89.

11 Oriana Fallaci, *The Rage and the Pride*,
p97.

12 Oriana Fallaci, *The Rage and the Pride*,
pp95-96.

13 Oriana Fallaci, *The Rage and the Pride*,
p134.

14 Oriana Fallaci, *The Rage and the Pride*,
p132.

15 Quoted in 'How the West Was Won and
How it Will be Lost' in *Enterprise Online*,
October 2002, www.theamericanenterprise.
org

16 Quoted in Stephen Morris, 'Press Whips
Up Asylum Hysteria', *Guardian*, 24
January 2003.

17 V I Lenin, 'Civilised Barbarism and
Progress' (September 1913), in V I Lenin,
*Selected Works: Labour and British
Imperialism*, p39 (Lawrence and Wishart,
1969). Lenin was commenting on a row
that had broken out in Britain as to whether
or not there should be a Channel Tunnel!

18 Samuel P Huntingdon, *The Clash of
Civilisations and the Remaking of World
Order* (Free Press, 2002), p28.

19 Samuel P Huntingdon, *The Clash of
Civilisations*, p28.

20 Julian Borger, 'Mississippi Plan to Execute Juveniles Fuels Legal Debate', *Guardian*, 6 January 2003 (the article says that the only other country to execute those under 18 is Iran).

21 Samuel P Huntingdon, *The Clash of Civilisations*, p217.

22 Samuel P Huntingdon, *The Clash of Civilisations*, p129.

23 Karen Armstrong, *The Battle for God: Fundamentalism in Judaism, Christianity and Islam* (HarperCollins, 2001).

24 Karen Armstrong, *The Battle for God*, p275.

25 Jerry Falwell reported at CBS.com, 6 October 2002.

26 Karen Armstrong, *The Battle for God*, p361.

27 Dana Milbank, 'Religious Right Finds Its Center In Oval Office', *Washington Post*, 24 December 2001, quoted in Gilbert Achcar, *The Clash of Barbarisms—September 11 and the Making of the New World Disorder*, translated by Peter Drucker (Monthly Review Press, 2002)

28 See Islamic Human Rights Commission, 'The Hidden Victims of September 11: Prisoners of UK Law', September 2002, www.ihrc.org

29 Owen Boycott, 'America Arrests 700 Muslim Immigrants', *Guardian*, 20 December 2002. See also *Left Turn*, May/June 2002, www.leftturn.org

30 See Hassan Mahamdallie, 'Black and White Lies', *Socialist Review*, January 2002.

31 See Institute for Race Relations press release, 'IRR Expresses Concern Over Excessive Sentencing of Bradford Rioters', 5 July 2002, http://www.irr.org.uk/2002/july/ak000003.html

32 For a detailed rebuttal of anti-Muslim myths see Hassan Mahamdallie, 'Racism: Myths and Realities', *International Socialism* 95 (Summer 2002).

33 Dr Deborah Phillips and Dr Peter Radcliffe, 'Asian Mobility in Leeds and

Bradford' (unpublished paper, 2002).
Thanks to the authors.

34 Shahid Osman and Paul Harris, 'Black People Six Times More Likely To Be Jailed Than Whites', *Observer*, 29 December 2002.

35 Islamic Society of Britain, 'Attitudes Towards British Muslims: A Survey Commissioned for Islam Awareness Week 2002', http://www.isb.org.uk. Survey conducted by YouGov.

36 Commission for Racial Equality, 'The Voice of Britain: A Research Study Conducted for the CRE', April-May 2002, www.cre.gov.uk. Survey conducted by Mori.

37 'My World Class Pupils', *Evening Standard*, 5 December 2002.

Black
and
white
unite

Anti Nazi League

The Love Music Hate Racism carnival in Manchester in 2002 celebrated the strength of

ENGLAND EXECUTE PRISONERS OF WA

British imperialism used military repression to try and crush the national liberation

NATIONAL LIBERATION

CHRIS HARMAN

A century ago virtually the whole world was divided up politically between a handful of Western states. They were not
just dominant economically. They also directly ran the rest of
the world politically, through colonial administrations obedient
to ministers and monarchs in Western capitals.

Britain's government ruled an empire from London, encom-
passing a quarter of the globe, on which 'the sun never set'—and,
as critics noted, 'the blood never dried'. France ran nearly half of
Africa. Holland ruled the huge East Indies archipelago (present
day Indonesia). Belgium's King Leopold owned Congo as a personal possession. The United States had seized the Philippines
and Puerto Rico as colonies, and used repeated military intervention to dictate to supposedly independent governments in
Central America and Cuba. Monarchies based in Vienna, St
Petersburg and Constantinople ruled over much of eastern and
south eastern Europe—and in the Russian case across a vast
swathe of Central Asia reaching to the Indian and Chinese borders. China remained a supposedly independent country. But
over the previous 60 years the Western powers and Japan had
grabbed many of its key cities as 'concessions'—extraterritorial
enclaves of direct colonial rule.

The imposition of colonial rule usually led to the impover-
ishment of the mass of the local peasantry, with horrendous

famines in India in the late 1760s (10 million deaths), the 1860s (1 million deaths), the 1870s (half a million deaths), the 1890s (10 million deaths) and the early 1940s (3 million deaths), and in Ireland in the 1840s (around 1 million deaths).

A notorious sign in a Shanghai park summed it up: 'No dogs or Chinese allowed'

But it also created bitterness among sections of the old ruling class that had been displaced by the British. For colonial rule meant they were excluded from power and often subject to humiliating racist abuse. A notorious sign in a Shanghai park summed it up: 'No dogs or Chinese allowed'. 'Chinese' meant not just the peasants or the poor labourers, but also the mandarins and rich merchants.

Important Indian merchant and landed interests had welcomed the British conquest of Bengal from the late 1750s onwards. But the welcome turned to bitterness after decades of pillaging by British East India Company officials and growing racist treatment at the hands of white colonists who despised all Indians as 'niggers'. The great uprising against Britain, the 'mutiny' of 1857, was led by members of the traditional ruling elite. In much the same way, sections of the traditional Egyptian ruling class conspired against British rule in the 1880s and 1890s, and some of China's rulers sympathised with the 'Boxer' rebellion against Western domination at the turn of the century.

Colonial rule itself created a new social layer which increasingly resented its own inferior position. The colonial administrators could not run massive empires without recruiting local people to provide the bulk of the private soldiers and NCOs in their armies or do routine office jobs in the government bureaucracy. The Western firms which controlled the most lucrative sections of the economy required local clerks and overseers, and contacts with local groups of traders. In general, the bigger any imperial possession, the bigger the 'native' middle class within it. This middle class rubbed shoulders with the colonial elite, was educated to accept its ideas, and often came to speak its language as its first language. But it could not avoid a degree of resentment at its inferiority. Sections began to frame a programme of their own for fighting back. They formed the core of the Indian Congress, the Egyptian Wafd, the Chinese Guomindang, the Irish Sinn Fein. Central to all of these organisations was the affirmation that the oppressed of the colony were a 'nation', who had to fight for a state of their own, a governmental administration and army of their own and, usually, a language of their own. They set out to mobilise the mass of the population behind this demand for 'national liberation', encouraging protests, demonstrations, tax boycotts and, sometimes, strikes and armed risings.

Today the notion of 'nationality' is so ingrained in us all that we imagine it to be an unchanging fact of human life. But it is actually a quite recent historical development. The class societies that existed before the rise of capitalism in parts of Western Europe a few hundred years ago—and elsewhere more recently— were organised as states run by monarchs or aristocrats. But the mass of people had few organic links to the states which taxed and exercised violence over them. So whether you talk of 12th century England or 17th century Mogul India, the language of the monarchy (Norman French in England, Persian in India) was quite distinct from the disparate and often mutually incomprehensible dialects spoken by the mass of the population. People might identify with their local village or occupational groups, they might defer to the local priest, they might identify in a loose way with a religion or culture that cut across state boundaries ('Christendom' or Islam, for example), and they might even feel some loyalty to a particular ruler. But they had no sense of belonging to something called the 'nation'.

This began to change with the rise of capitalism in parts of Western Europe. As local capitalists carved out markets for themselves and came to exercise a decisive influence over a state, they also established one dialect as the uniform 'national language' of that state and sought to inculcate a sense of 'national belonging' within the population as a whole. So it was that by the 1780s the people of England, Wales and Scotland were being told they were all 'Britons', and the leaders of the

French Revolution of 1789-93 spoke of 'France united and inviolable'.

The rise of these capitalist states encouraged middle class people elsewhere to want to emulate them. But they were held down either by the absolute monarchies that still dominated much of Europe, or, in the cases of the British colonies in North America and Ireland, by the most successful of the rising capitalisms. They could only achieve their hopes by seeking to create nations of their own, in opposition to the existing order. In the mid-1770s the middle class of North America organised itself as a nation against British rule, and succeeded. In the 1790s sections of the Irish middle class sought to do the same, and were mercilessly crushed. In the 1810s and 1820s the American and French examples were copied, with more success, by the Spanish-speaking middle classes of Mexico, Chile, Argentina, Venezuela, Colombia, Bolivia and Peru. By the late 1840s movements fighting for unity and independence for Germany, Hungary and Italy shook all of Europe—and in the first two cases achieved their national goals by 1870. This in turn encouraged a plethora of other movements—among the Czechs and southern Slavs under Austrian rule, among the Bulgarians and Romanians under Turkish rule, among the Ukrainians and Finns under Russian rule.

In almost every case the national movements begun by sections of the middle class had one central effect. They weakened despotic states, making it easier for all their peoples to fight back, including those who shared the language of the ruling class. So revolts in Austrian-ruled Milan and Venice spurred German speakers in Vienna to rise up themselves, and revolts in Warsaw were an aid to those trying to overthrow Tsarism in Moscow and St Petersburg.

For this reason, those like Marx and Engels who were fighting against all forms of oppression and exploitation welcomed national risings in Hungary, Poland, Italy and Ireland as aiding the working class struggle for socialism. As Marx wrote:

> The English working class can never do anything decisive here in England until it separates its policy with regard to Ireland most definitely from the policy of the ruling classes, until it not only makes common cause with the Irish but even takes the initiative in dissolving the Union established in 1801 and replacing it by a free federal relationship. And this must be done not as a matter of sympathy with Ireland but as a demand made in the interests of the English proletariat. If not, the English people will remain tied to the leading strings of the ruling classes, because it will have to join with them in a common front against Ireland.[1]

As he put it elsewhere, 'A nation which oppresses another cannot itself be free.'

This tradition of hostility to colonialism was maintained after Marx's death by people like his daughter Eleanor Marx, the English revolutionary William Morris and the Polish-German revolutionary Rosa Luxemburg. But as the socialist movement expanded rapidly, one wing of it moved in a different direction. It began to believe it could change society by using the existing state to bring about reform. And this led people like the Fabians in Britain and the German reform socialist Eduard Bernstein to hold that their state could play a progressive role by colonising other parts of the world. At the international socialist congress in 1907 a minority of delegates argued in favour of the colonisation of Africa and Asia.

They did so just as colonial troops were crushing new movements of resistance in India, Egypt and elsewhere. For them there could be national liberation in parts of Europe, but not worldwide.

In 1914 the great empires threw themselves into a war against each other—the British, French, Belgian and Russian empires on one side, the German, Austrian and Turkish Ottoman empires on the other. One by-product was an astonishing display of hypocrisy from the rulers of every empire, a form of hypocrisy which we still encounter today. Each denounced at length the denial of freedom for Europe's oppressed peoples—provided they were oppressed by the rival side. So Germany denounced the oppression of Ireland and Poland, while Britain and France denounced the repression of the southern Slavs by Austria and of the Arabs by Turkey. The high point of hypocrisy was reached at the end of the war, when US president Woodrow Wilson called for 'self-determination everywhere'—except of course in US-controlled Philippines and Puerto Rico, or when US troops landed in Haiti, Cuba or Nicaragua.

But the war gave a boost to genuine movements for liberation from all forms of imperialism. In 1916 there was an uprising in Britain's oldest colony, Ireland, and guerrilla war raged there from 1919 to 1921. Massive, near-revolutionary movements arose in India and Egypt. There were mass protests against Dutch rule in the East Indies. Student demonstrations in China gave birth to a movement that fought for the next ten years to try to end the 'concession' system and unify the country.

The war and its aftermath gave the reform socialists their first chance to join existing governments, which they did in Britain and France and then, in the last weeks of the war, in Germany. Their talk of the 'civilising mission' of colonialism now turned into physical repression of national liberation movements. A leader of the British Labour Party, Arthur Henderson, was a member of the wartime government which executed the Irish socialist James Connolly for his part in the Dublin rising.

The war also produced the clearest argument yet about national liberation from the other, revolutionary, wing of the socialist movement. In a series of articles and speeches, the Russian revolutionary Lenin spelt out that the national movements of oppressed peoples could be the allies of the workers' movement in the oppressing country. Even though they were led by the middle class who only aimed to establish new capitalist states, they served to weaken the biggest, imperialist capitalist states and make it more difficult for them to hold down their own workers. The movement could also waken into political activity many millions of peasants and workers who would then begin to demand more than just a change of government. For these reasons, the workers' movement in the West had to support wholeheartedly the liberation movements in the colonies.

Chinese capitalists were keen to agitate against foreign domination and the Guomindang went so far as to help finance a long strike against British firms in Hong Kong

This meant unconditionally defending the right to self-determination, including independence if that is what an oppressed people wanted. Lenin argued strongly against those who said this encouraged the fragmentation of the workers' movement into opposed nationalities. People from an oppressed nation would only really feel part of the same movement as people from an oppressing nation if the latter defended the oppressed nation's right to determine its own future.

But this did not mean putting unlimited faith in the middle class leaders of the national liberation movements, or 'painting them red', in Lenin's words. If such leaders succeeded in creating a new national capitalist state, then they would soon direct it against the workers' movement. And even before that, they would hold back from agitating too strongly against imperialism for fear of workers and peasants taking action not just against foreign capitalists and landowners, but against the local capitalists who wanted to replace them.

Leon Trotsky spelt out this last point more fully in the 1920s as he observed what was happening in China. In the early 1920s some Chinese capitalists were keen to agitate against foreign domination, and the Guomindang went so far as to help finance a long strike against British firms in Hong Kong. But as the national movement roused more and more people to action, they no longer restricted themselves simply to fighting foreign exploitation and oppression. Workers and peasants began to confront Chinese capitalists and landowners as well. At this point the Chinese capitalists and the Guomindang did an about-turn, made deals with the Western colonialists, and butchered the workers of Shanghai and Canton. They preferred to abandon their national goals rather than risk a challenge to their class position.

Trotsky drew the conclusion that the only way to stop the sabotage of the movement which the middle class leaders had initiated was through the development of working class action independent of these leaders—a process he called 'permanent revolution'.

The Western powers succeeded in beating back most of the anti-colonial movements in the 1920s. The British government was forced to abandon control of three quarters of Ireland. But even there the middle class leaders of the liberation movement agreed to Britain retaining control of the richest part of the island, the six north eastern counties. The number of possessions held by France and Britain in Asia and Africa grew as they took over lands formerly run by Germany and Turkey.

The demand for national liberation could not be denied for all time. By the time the Second World War occurred, there were growing movements for national liberation not only in India, Egypt and the East Indies, but in Palestine, Syria, Iraq, Vietnam and the West Indies, while Africans in London and Paris were beginning to dream of freedom for their countries and linking up with activists from the Caribbean in a Pan-African movement.

Those who ran the European empires were determined not to abandon control over them. 'I have not become the queen's first minister,' insisted Britain's Winston Churchill, faced in 1942 with the biggest anti-colonial movement yet in India, 'to preside over the liquidation of the British Empire.' Yet after the Indian navy mutinied in February 1946 his successor, Clement Attlee, saw he had little choice. If he did not concede independence to India peacefully, it would be seized by force. In 1947 Britain withdrew from the subcontinent after 190 years. Two years later the former guerrillas of the Chinese Liberation Army entered Beijing and finally ended the Western carve-up of the country.

The end of the empire in India was not meant to begin winding up the British Empire as such. British troops bombed, burnt and maimed for another dozen years in attempts to hang on to Kenya, Malaysia, Cyprus and the mineral-rich areas of Central Africa. France waged a full-scale nine-year war in Vietnam, followed by a full-scale seven-year war in Algeria. Portugal was still trying to crush independence movements in its African colonies of Angola,

Mozambique and Guinea-Bissau at the beginning of 1974.

But by the early 1960s the main European powers were admitting to themselves that they simply could not afford the cost of maintaining direct colonial control in the face of a hostile local middle class able to rouse the mass of the population in revolt. It was much easier to hand over power to local capitalist interests— or to middle class politicians who aspired to develop local capitalism. Then the sheer economic power of the great Western corporations could be brought to bear to ensure that these new capitalists (or state capitalists) cut profitable deals.

Forty years later almost all the old-style colonies had disappeared. In southern Africa white colonists in Zimbabwe, Namibia and South Africa had finally accepted black majority rule. Hong Kong had been handed back to China. Even in Ireland, British governments began negotiating with the IRA in a desperate attempt to unscramble the mayhem colonialism had caused.

But the question of national liberation has clearly not gone away. First, it exists in one small but very important part of the Middle East. In order to protect its oil supplies and its route to India, the British government, which took over most of the region at the end of the First World War, promised Jewish colonists from Europe that they could establish their own 'homeland' in territory inhabited by Palestinian Arabs. When Britain abandoned this bit of its empire in 1948 the colonists, armed by the US and Russia, seized 78 percent of Palestine for themselves—and then after a war in 1967 occupied the rest, displacing Palestinians once again to make room for new settlements.

This has suited the US, which sees Israel as a reliable watchdog prepared to take action against any state or movement that threatens US domination of the world's biggest oil reserves.

Second, many of the national states created over the last two centuries contain their own national minorities who are oppressed. This is true even of old states, like Spain, where many Catalans and Basques resent being ruled by Castilians, and do not see why they should not be allowed a national state of their own. It is true through much of Asia and Africa that the states which achieved independent nationhood in the decades after the Second

World War kept the quite arbitrary boundary lines drawn up to separate the colonies of one Western country from those of another. In many cases the middle class or capitalist grouping which took control of the new independent national governments came from one ethnic group, and tried to impose its language and, sometimes, its religion on others. In countries like Sudan, Iraq, Turkey, India, Pakistan, Sri Lanka and Indonesia new national movements arose among minorities in opposition to the dominant nationalism of the state.

This was also true of the collapse of the last great multinational empire, the USSR. In the 1920s Joseph Stalin had buried the revolutionary ideal of a confederation of equal nationalities, each free to leave the USSR if it so desired, and had imposed central rule and Russian domination from Moscow. In effect he had produced a reborn Russian Empire. Groups like the Chechens, who had suffered most at the hands of conquering Tsarist armies, now suffered even more grievously as they were deported thousands of miles from their homelands. As the USSR stumbled from crisis to crisis in the late 1980s and early 1990s, national movements emerged in an arc from the Baltic through Byelorussia and Ukraine round into Central Asia. They demanded an end to oppression. They were met with further oppression until finally getting their independence (often under the local members of the old all-Soviet Politburo!) when the USSR collapsed in 1991. But these new states usually contained their own minorities who still suffered oppression. The Chechens were not allowed to escape from oppression by the Russian Republic, in which they were compelled to remain.

Meanwhile the great capitalist powers have developed a great expertise in tailoring the language of 'national self-determination' to their own ends. Britain used this to justify hanging on to north eastern Ireland in the 1920s, claiming that their religion made the Protestant Irish of the region into an 'Ulster British' nation entitled to their own little state that discriminated against the Catholic third of the population.

In much the same way, Britain encouraged the idea in the late 1930s and early 1940s that the diverse groups of people practising different forms of Islam across the Indian subcontinent were a separate 'nation' which would be oppressed by Hindus and Sikhs in a united independent India. They turned the language of self-determination into an excuse to protect empire through divide and rule.

The same language was used by Israeli settlers in 1948 to justify seizing 78 percent of Palestine.

The British government of Margaret Thatcher fought a war against Argentina over the Falkland Islands/Malvinas, supposedly in support of the 'self-determination' of a 2,000-strong population, while at the same time countenancing the eviction of the 2,000-strong population of the Indian Ocean island of Diego Garcia in order to provide the US with an air base.

In the early 1990s, as the Yugoslav state went into crisis, Austria sought to increase its own influence by suddenly discovering the right to national independence of neighbouring Slovenia. It was followed by Germany, which saw great gains in Croatian independence. And then the US intervened, proclaiming the Muslim section of the Bosnian population as an oppressed minority.

When the Iraqi state was allied to the West in the 1980s, the plight of its Kurdish population was ignored as Saddam Hussein used poison gas against them. But when the West fell out with him, the American CIA suddenly started financing the Kurds, backing their demand. Meanwhile the main political party of those Kurds who are just across the border in Turkey, the PKK, is on the US list of 'terrorist organisations'.

While the great imperialist powers misuse the language of national liberation in this way, so do many of the regimes that have emerged elsewhere in the world. Local capitalist classes that collaborate with the multinationals and the Western powers will wave the national flag in order to denounce as 'anti-national' workers who strike, peasants who seize land or oppressed minorities who fight for their own rights. They will do their utmost to stir up mistrust among workers and peasants against those in other countries. And they will claim to be 'anti-imperialist' in foreign conflicts which are only really about fighting for their own interests against those of capitalist governments in neighbouring states. Even when they clash with the great capitalist powers, it is usually only part of hard bargaining over improving the terms on which they collaborate with them. Their nationalist, anti-imperialist language is used as an opiate, designed to make local workers and peasants put up with greater exploitation from local capitalists.

A group which has itself been oppressed in the past may then decide to use the language of liberation in order to justify oppressing some other group

This means that sometimes you have to look at talk of 'national liberation' with some care. It can be just an excuse to maintain a wider system of oppression. Even when a group of people are genuinely oppressed, the very weakness of their forces can lead them to align with a state whose global goal is greater oppression of much wider numbers of people. A group which has itself been oppressed in the past may then decide to use the language of liberation in order to justify oppressing some other group.

The core insights of Marx when writing on the Irish question remain true. A nation which oppresses another nation cannot itself be free. The powers which rulers use to crush national minorities at home or peoples abroad will also be used to crush opposition from the mass of non-minority people at home. You cannot fight against what your ruling class does to you unless you fight against the harm it does to others.

This means making a clear distinction between the nationalism of oppressor states and the nationalism of the oppressed. The first seeks to bind its own people to it by giving them a false sense of superiority over other peoples. The second mobilises people against humiliating and damaging forms of oppression, whether on the basis of language, religion or skin colour.

Equally relevant are the core insights of Lenin. We live in a world in which the rulers of the more powerful states repeatedly seek to coerce the rulers of much weaker states. That coercion arouses feelings of anger and resentment among wider layers of people who have memories of direct colonial rule. In that situation, anti-capitalists in the West cannot simply sit back and say all rulers are equally bad. We have to throw our main efforts into seeking to thwart the imperialist ambitions of the already powerful.

Finally, we must also remember Trotsky's point. Those who rule over the weaker states today are much more fully integrated into the world capitalist system even than the capitalist and middle groups he wrote about in the 1920s. They may make occasional gestures against the great imperialisms, if only in order to try to buy some domestic popularity. But they are much more likely to join with the multinationals, the IMF, the World Bank and so on than to keep fighting them. The ruler who talks about the national fight against imperialism today is likely to become involved in oppressing other people tomorrow. True liberation, national and otherwise, will only come when people take things into their own hands from below and stop putting their faith in such rulers.

Chris Harman is the editor of *Socialist Worker* (www.socialistworker.co.uk) **and has written a number of books including** *A People's History of the World* **and** *Economics of the Madhouse*

NOTES

1 Letter from Karl Marx to Kugelmann, in Karl Marx and Frederick Engels, *Selected Correspondence* (Progress Publishers, 1975), available on www.marxists.de/archive/marx/works/1869/letters/69_11_29-abs.htm

Nuclear explosion on Christmas Island in the 1950s. Bush wants to restart nuclear test

NUCLEAR WEAPONS

RAE STREET

By the day it seems the people of the world grow more and more divided. There is the fearful gap between the rich and those who live in absolute poverty. There is also a divide between the small, enclosed world of the governments tied in with the multinational corporations and the space where the vast majority of the people on earth live. From the rich world there is one dominating voice, and that is President Bush of the US and his surrounding henchmen who represent the multinational corporations. Let us take one clear example. When the dominators, the politicians and their interpreters and supporters in the press, talk about security they mean 'military security'. When those living in abject poverty think of security they think of a distant dream existence where they might have adequate food and shelter, basic healthcare, a job which pays a living wage—or even possibly education for their children. These are two different worlds.

To cajole people into giving their taxes to the military, governments sell the military, just like any other commodity. In the last century the skills and resources of the capitalist world were applied to working out how you marketed and sold products. University departments were formed, and scores of books were written on the subject. The principles, the public relations, worked out are now applied. To start with, governments must convince people that they are in dire need of a certain product—in this case, military products.

They have to convince people that there is a threat to their lives that needs to be deflected. Bush has now said that Iraq is an immediate threat, in a reference to Iraq in the National Security Strategy, where it was written that we have to act against a 'terrorist enemy whose avowed tactics are wanton destruction and the targeting of innocents'.

Then the administration, the military planners and the defence contractors will show that their products—the vast arsenals, the armed services, the command and control systems—are the answer to the threat. The only answer in the current case of the US versus the world is military might. But it is a military might that is packaged and presented as being benevolent.

Here the use of language is key. Euphemisms abound. No one speaks of bombing anymore—just 'air operations'. Or maybe there are 'air strikes'—'strikes' of course gives the impression that modern bombs are clean and targeted. Indeed, with high flying planes, the US is unlikely to lose any of its military. War can be presented to those back home as a computer game. As long as the enemy has been demonised, the bombing is never questioned. The US administration will overlook and not talk about the deaths of innocent civilians in US wars. In the war on Afghanistan, even by December 2001, it had been shown that over 4,000 civilians had been killed in the bombing raids. Now the figure has been worked out as nearer 10,000. It is ugly to make comparisons, but when we are constantly bombarded with the arguments stressing the dangers to the people of the US it is important to remember that far more civilians have been killed and wounded and their lives devastated in Afghanistan than the people killed in the attacks on the US.

The same soft, bland language is used by the military manufacturers. In an advertisement which appeared in October 2002 BAE Systems (Britain's prime military manufacturer, but note the bland name) described their role as being innovators in the 'world's latest peacekeeping technology and equipment'.[1]

In selling and image-creating, no body is more skilled than Nato, which likes to be known as an 'alliance'—missing out the preceding word 'military'. If you look at any page of the *Nato Review*, you will find the words 'peace', 'defence' and 'security'. Then there are the images of soldiers helping poor women and children to safety, not revealing that that they bombed the same community. In one memorable cover to *Nato Review*,[2] the issue entitled 'A More Capable and Balanced Alliance', there is an image of a dark green world, where the Nato areas of North America and Europe are highlighted in glowing yellow (supposedly bringing light to the world?). In the introductory leader of the same issue, by Lord George Robertson, the word 'security' occurs no fewer than six times, including phrases that depict Nato as preserving 'peace and security', and 'providing security for generations to come'.

If you give people on the street a clear choice between money for weapons and money to help poor children, there is rarely any hesitation in their reply. They want the money to go to the children. Yet governments persuade people year after year to vote for leaders who not only spend vast sums of taxpayers' money on the military, but increase spending on the development of more horrendous bombs and ways of killing people. They already have the means to destroy the planet many times over.

Governments and defence contractors need to have an enemy at which they can target their weapons. In the Cold War this led to the arms race and the 'mad' development of nuclear weapons. Today the Bush administration has its 'rogue states' and, in the case of Saddam Hussein, 'the evil empire'. This is then extended by governments to other wars, even to wars on drugs. The latter can be seen in South America, where, under the guise of a 'war on drugs', the US supplies arms and military aid to the Colombian authorities, who use the dollars in their barbarous regime against the poor, and against everyone, including trade unionists, who stands up for human rights. Of course after 11 September the 'enemy' is everywhere. It is 'terrorism', as defined by the Bush administration.

Whether we like it or not, most people in the Western world have seared on their minds the date of 11 September 2001. Naturally our sincere sympathies go out to the families and friends of all those who were killed or suffered as a result of the attacks on the US on that date. But many of us will equally remember other dates when innocent people were killed and maimed in bombing attacks, from those Japanese civilians bombed by the US on 6 and 9 August 1945 to the thousands of Afghans post 6 October 2001. Or some will choose to remember other dates where horrendous death and illness have been caused by man-made disaster, and where the innocent victims have received little or no help from the originator of the disaster. I am thinking here of 3 December 1984, when the chemical plant at Bhopal blew up and 18 years later the owner of the firm, Union Carbide, has not paid out any significant compensation or been held accountable. The victims were impoverished Indians. Union Carbide shares on the US stock exchange flourish, while children are still being born with disabilities in Bhopal as a result of the disaster.

There can hardly be anybody in Britain now who has not heard of the 'threat of weapons of mass destruction'. But of course what they have heard of is the 'threat', with no hard evidence of what Saddam Hussein might do. But what would be in the interests of people both here in Britain and across the world would be to hear about the threat of existing, and developing, nuclear arsenals. These are overwhelmingly owned by the US, closely followed by Britain, and the other nuclear weapons states including Israel.

Colombia is the third largest recipient of military aid from the US (after Israel and Egypt). 'Plan Colombia' has basically been the Pentagon's plan to force IMF austerity policies on impoverished Colombian people. This means that US banks can continue to make profits out of the country. colombia.indymedia.org

Any discussion on nuclear arms needs to take into account Nato, the ever-expanding military alliance that not only retains a nuclear so-called 'deterrent' policy but has not given up its policy of 'first use'.

When considering the build-up of nuclear weapons, particularly by the US, after 11 September, we cannot leave out the role of the defence contractors, again mainly US ones. Most of Bush's close advisers, including Donald Rumsfeld and Dick Cheney, have close connections with the defence contracting industry. It is in the Bush administration's best interests to continue to push for more and more money to be spent on military hardware, and the accompanying command and control structures. War will always be good business for some. The US multinational defence corporations—Lockheed Martin, Boeing, Brown and Roots, Smith Industries—are involved in all our economies. In turn these companies with their funds are able to heavily influence the direction of research in science institutes and universities. Hundreds of examples could be given, but I will cite just one. In Britain the Boeing corporation, which will be the largest recipient of money from the Ballistic Missile Defence (Son of Star Wars) programmes, has funded a research institute at the University of Sheffield (where the BMD bases are situated) to the tune of £15 million, which includes military and defence work in its brief.

Let us turn to the question of the relevance of nuclear weapons to our security. For years—and this is when the date of 11 September does become significant—we who oppose nuclear weapons have been told we need nuclear arms to keep the peace. Thus during the Cold War there occurred the largest and most deadly arms race in history between the US and the USSR, each striving to achieve superiority and devising deadlier ways of killing populations. At the same time others registered in the 'nuclear club'—Britain, France and China, and later Israel. Then came the collapse of totalitarian Communism and the end of the Cold War. But the addiction of the nuclear weapons states to nuclear weapons was not curbed, and in the US in particular the drive for world domination and power over resources kept it developing and expanding its nuclear weapons. The US was aided and abetted in its policies by its allies in Europe—Britain and France. Both the latter and all of the now 19 members of Nato subscribe to a doctrine of the requirement for a 'minimum nuclear deterrent'. India and Pakistan joined the 'nuclear club' with full capabilities in the late 1990s.

But were there changes in nuclear weapons policies after the attacks on 11 September? These were attacks which were not carried out with what had been previously described as 'weapons of mass destruction', such as nuclear weapons, but passenger aeroplanes, penknives and the minds of the planners. Anyone observing the devastation on 11 September could see that the country with the largest nuclear arsenal, not to mention the widest network of 'intelligence' gathering forces and military communications systems in the world, had been unable to 'deter' the attack. For years those opposed to weapons of mass destruction had been pointing to the fact

For years those opposed to weapons of mass destruction had been pointing to the fact that the weapons do not deter conflict or war, and do not bring security

that the weapons do not deter conflict or war, and do not bring security. In the extended analysis, they are responsible for endangering the whole of global stability. There is no doubt that the vast majority of the citizens in the US were shaken by this breach of the military cordon. They had thought themselves 'secure'. Nuclear deterrence did not work. US leaders began to voice what had never been admitted. Donald Rumsfeld told an audience at the National Defence University in January 2002 that the 'terrorists who struck us on 11 September were clearly not deterred from doing so by the massive US nuclear arsenal'. Later, Under-Secretary of State John R Bolton said that the 'idea that fine theories of deterrence work against everybody has just been disproven by 11 September'. As President Bush said in his new US foreign policy, 'Traditional concepts of deterrence will not work against a terrorist enemy'.[3]

So what did the US government and the decision makers decide? Did they begin to look at the root causes of the widespread hatred of the US and its institutions? Did they begin to look at redressing at least some of the world's inequalities—economic, environmental, human rights? No. Did they begin to question the relationship between the military and genuine security? No. Of course many commentators both within the US and across the world did, but not the US government and its advisers. They turned their minds to an even larger military budget of, in this fiscal year, $379 billion.

The US Natural Resources Defence Council (NRDC) has studied the Nuclear Posture Review (NPR) published in April 2002 and concluded that 'not since the resurgence of the Cold War in Ronald Reagan's first term has there been such an emphasis on nuclear weapons in US defence strategy'. They continue, 'The Pentagon is preparing to honour Start II by reducing the number of operationally deployed nuclear forces from today's 8,000 warheads to 3,800 by 2007, and it will reduce the number of operationally deployed weapons to about 2,000 by 2012.' But behind these illusory numbers lie another 12,770 nuclear warheads that can be redeployed and used to attack nations from Iraq to Indonesia, Korea to Colombia.

There are:
▸ 240 Trident submarine warheads being overhauled.
▸ 1,350 strategic missile and bomber warheads in the responsive force reserves.
▸ 800 non-strategic nuclear weapons deployed on US/Nato dual capable aircraft.
▸ 320 non-strategic sea-launched cruise missile warheads in the reserve force.
▸ 160 'spare' strategic and non-strategic warheads.
▸ 4,900 intact warheads in the 'inactive' stockpile.
▸ 5,000 stored primary and secondary components for reassembly.

As the NRDC reports, 'The Bush administration is actually planning to retain the potential to deploy not 1,700 to 2,200 nuclear weapons, but as many as 15,000.' In this list can anyone make sense of the need for 'spare' warheads?

It is necessary for us to ask ourselves what, outside the skewed logic of military planners, any of this vast catalogue of extra nuclear weapons has to do with keeping ordinary people secure around the world. The Trident nuclear-armed submarine fleet is of particular concern for the whole planet. The US has 18 of the Trident nuclear-armed submarines. Britain has four and is utterly dependent on the US for maintenance, crew training, etc. Bob Aldridge, a leading US authority on the so-called UK Trident fleet, says that the 'Faslane port for the Trident submarines in Scotland simply gives the US a forward base in Europe'. Tridents have a huge range, and at any time could be on patrol under the Indian Ocean or the South China Sea. The missiles were built as first-strike weapons. Moreover the Trident fleet is 'integrated' into Nato's nuclear arsenal. Each Trident submarine can carry warheads with over 300 times the killing power of the bomb dropped on Hiroshima.

The US Trident nuclear-armed submarine programme shows the extent of the real danger the world is in from the nuclear threat. There is, as I have indicated above, the question of global stability, especially in Asia. US nuclear weapons in Asia have played a part in paving the way for the now publicly declared nuclear weapons capabilities of India and Pakistan, two states where tension is high on the borders of Kashmir. Yet the US and Britain continue to denounce the development of nuclear weapons by India and Pakistan while continuing their policies of 'do as I say and not as I do'. Together with plans for Ballistic Missile Defence, the huge US military arsenal, and its military bases around the Pacific, has terrible destabilising effects in Asia.

The hypocrisy of the US and Britain on the question of nuclear weapons in the Middle East is thrown up sharply when one looks at their attitude towards Israel. While both President Bush and prime minister Blair rant on about the nuclear weapons capability that Saddam Hussein might develop, it is a well known fact that Israel is a nuclear weapons state and may have more than 100 warheads. Yet the UN General Assembly agreed a resolution as early as 1974 on the establishment of a Middle East nuclear weapons free zone. This was repeated in the Security Council's Resolution 687 at the end of the Gulf War, which showed that the council was 'conscious of the threat which all weapons of mass destruction pose to peace and security in the area, and of the need to work towards the establishment in the Middle East of a zone free of such weapons'. What has happened since? Nothing. Mordechai Vanunu, who exposed Israel's nuclear weapons programme, was captured by the Israeli secret police in 1986 and jailed for 18 years. He has been treated inhumanely and kept in solitary confinement. He has two years left to serve. Israel's undeclared nuclear weapons arsenal is a real danger in the Middle East.

The dangers of nuclear weapons development are also frighteningly present here in Britain. Warheads, upwards of 100 kilotons, for the US-built Trident missiles are regularly transported for overhaul to Burghfield/Aldermaston and back to Faslane, Scotland. The bomb at Hiroshima was of the order of 'just' 15 kilotons. Is it common sense to be carrying such a devastating weapon around on Britain's roads? Around Aldermaston, where the warheads are manufactured, there is a high incidence of childhood cancers. Of course all the US bases abroad, including Britain, are now also targets for terrorists. Menwith Hill in Yorkshire, the 'spy' base and vital communications link for US world surveillance systems, is extremely vulnerable. So too is Fylingdales, also in North Yorkshire, which is needed for the US Ballistic Missile Defence (known originally as National Missile Defence), the programme that involves the US trying to control the whole planet from space. The US, which dominates Nato, has nuclear weapons based in six Nato countries which include Turkey, an ally despite its list of human rights abuses. In Britain these US nuclear bombs are stored at Lakenheath in Suffolk. Lakenheath is the primary US tactical airbase in Europe, hosting the 48th fighter wing of the USAF, which was heavily involved in attacks on Iraq during the 1990s. There are about 30 nuclear weapons—B61 freefall tactical nuclear weapons, with a variable explosive yield of 0.4 to 80 kilotons. In June 1999 a major nuclear weapons accident exercise, called Dimming Sun, was due to take place in Norfolk. The scenario involved a plane taking off from Lakenheath with nuclear weapons on board and having a mid-air collision with a local (presumably civilian) plane. Dimming Sun was postponed because of the Balkans War in 2001 and was rescheduled for 2003.[4] Can anyone explain how these bases make the British people safer?

Recently, post 11 September, there has been a major, publicly declared change in US nuclear weapons policies. The Pentagon wants more 'usable' nuclear weapons. In the Nuclear Posture Review (revealed in spring 2002) the US called for new emphasis on developing weapons such as nuclear bunker busters which would reduce 'collateral damage'. One such bomb, on which work has already begun, is the Robust Nuclear Earth Penetrator. This is euphemistically called 'low yield', and would probably be under 5 kilotons of power, but if exploded, as intended, against a hardened bunker, it could kill thousands in the vicinity and create radioactive fallout contamination on surrounding land for miles. Who with any shred of humanity could think of a nuclear weapon as 'usable'?

While in some ways this is just an extension of existing policies, it is also a huge shift. It is a breaking of the belief that there is a taboo around using nuclear weapons. Already in the NPR the Bush administration has declared it may, under certain circumstances, use nuclear weapons. Britain followed suit when the defence minister, Geoffrey Hoon, revealed on 20 March 2002 the government's willingness to use nuclear weapons if Britain is attacked by 'rogue states'.

> **The Blair government has assured us that we 'can be absolutely confident that in the right conditions we would be willing to use our nuclear weapons'.**
> **GEOFFREY HOON, 20 March 2002**

Which other governments will follow the US? Perhaps the same governments that followed the US in its 'war on terrorism'. One argument used over the last 60 years from the pro-nuclear lobby has been, 'Ah, but the nuclear weapons will never be used.' The present willingness to use nuclear weapons must surely bring about changes in public attitudes.

Determined groups of people have shown courage and tenacity in opposing the risks. There are strong anti-nuclear groups all over the globe, but their actions are not widely reported in the media. The actions of US groups and individuals are even less widely reported, but across the US there are protesters against the Trident subs, the communication sites for Tridents (Extremely Low Frequency systems in Wisconsin). There are women's anti-militarism actions, non-violent direct action against testing in Nevada, networking groups such as Peace Action, and information groups such as the Western States Legal Foundation. They are not silenced. They see the sense in their arguments and their actions against their own government, and know that eventually there must be changes. In Britain these groups include CND, the Lakenheath Action Group, Trident Ploughshares, Womenwith Hill, the Campaign for the Accountability of American Bases, Aldermaston Women's Peace Camp, the Faslane Peace Camp, and all the hundreds of dedicated individuals in CND. It is now high time that these issues were pushed much higher up the political agenda. People should ask the simple, challenging questions. Why are there so many US overseas military bases? What would we think if China had such bases in Europe? Do the bases bring security or insecurity?

I have only been able to address a fraction of the threat from nuclear weapons, with an emphasis on the US because of its pre-eminent place in the development of nuclear arms. However, there are huge dangers in the developments now going on in other nuclear weapons states. In total this fearful nuclear proliferation is bringing instability to the whole world. There cannot be peace without social justice. It is essential for human security, for everyone on the planet, that we turn away from the massive expenditure of resources on arms, especially on nuclear weapons, and turn our human energy and resources towards bringing health and welfare to the majority of people in the world.

To resist militarism, to raise awareness among the public of the wide implications of nuclear weapons policies in all our countries, we need to use all available outlets for public education and the exchange of information. Just as the US dominates in the world of militarism, so it dominates the world's media. There are some exceptions, but they are in the minority. We need to link campaigns—the campaign against nuclear weapons and against the arms trade needs to be integrated into the anti-globalisation movement and activists' work in the struggle for social justice.

Together we can:

▶ Expose the hypocrisy of states which proclaim they are against nuclear weapons proliferation while practising it themselves.

▶ Reveal the extent to which money and resources which should be spent on welfare go to the arms manufacturers.

▶ Expose the dangers of the US foreign military bases which, far from bringing security, endanger all our lives.

We, the people, call for human security, not military security.

Rae Street is a leading campaigning member of the Campaign for Nuclear Disarmament (www.cnduk.org) **and is a founder member of the Campaign Against Depleted Uranium** (www.cadu.org.uk)

NOTES

1 BAE Systems advertisement, *Guardian*, 7 October 2002.
2 *Nato Review*, Spring/Summer 2000.
3 All quoted in *Guardian*, 21 September 2002.
4 From information supplied by the Campaign for the Accountability of American Bases and Lakenheath Action Group.

If the bomb drops: the British government's official pamphlet of advice on what to do in a nuclear emergency, told you to build a shelter under a table Photographer: Peter Kennard

Camp X-Ray, Guantanamo Bay—the war on terror becomes a war on civil liberties. Over
people from 30 countries have been held here without trial since 2001.

CIVIL LIBERTIES
LOUISE CHRISTIAN

> We have no right to roam the world arresting foreigners we think
> might be dangerous and keeping them in our jails when we cannot
> show them to have committed any crime. (Professor Ronald Dworkin,
> *New York Review of Books*, 25 April 2002)

The war on terrorism which George Bush declared in response to
the atrocities of 11 September was said to be a war which would be
fought in the name of democracy and human rights. Fifty three
years after the adoption of the Universal Declaration of Human
Rights on 10 December 1948, Bush issued a proclamation: 'The terrible tragedies of 11 September served as a grievous reminder that the
enemies of freedom do not respect or value individual human
rights.' He called on 'the people of the United States to honour the
legacy of human rights passed down to us from previous generations, and to resolve that such liberties will prevail in our nation
and throughout the world as we move into the 21st century'. In his
State of the Union address on 29 January 2002 Bush said, 'America
will lead by defending liberty and justice because they are right and
true and unchanging for people everywhere... America will always
stand firm for the non-negotiable demands of human dignity... We
choose freedom and the dignity of every life.'

But these fine sounding sentiments were already being undermined even as Bush expressed them. The transfer of hundreds of

prisoners captured in Afghanistan to a US military base in Guantanamo Bay in Cuba raised questions first about their treatment and conditions, and then more fundamentally about the legal basis for their detention without

The prisoners were being held in wire cages of eight feet by eight feet, open to the elements and lit by floodlights all night

trial or recourse to any court, or access to a lawyer. Also in the US there were reports of hundreds of arbitrary arrests, while in Britain the government rushed through a new terrorism law, the Anti-Terrorism, Crime and Security Act, empowering itself to detain non UK nationals indefinitely without trial. Prisoners have also continued to be detained in Afghanistan in the Bagram air base. Others have been transferred to Diego Garcia, an island in the Indian Ocean leased from Britain. There have been credible reports of torture methods used on prisoners.

Guantanamo, in the furthest south east corner of Cuba, may be best known for its vibrant musical tradition—the song 'Guantanamera', familiar to tourists everywhere, actually comes from there. Now, however, Guantanamo Bay is assured a place in the history of international relations and human rights. Since the beginning of 2001 over 600 prisoners from 30 different countries have been held in the US naval base there who the US government claims are suspected Taliban and Al Qaida fighters. Among them are seven British citizens who have at least been identified. It is not known who many of the other prisoners are, or whether their families have been notified.

In 1903 the Cuban government at the time signed a lease 'for as long as they are needed' to the US government of two territorial areas at Guantanamo and Bahia Honda for the purpose of 'coaling and naval stations'. This agreement followed the ending of the Cuban war of independence from Spain in 1898, US intervention and the notorious Platt amendment of 1901. This was an amendment introduced by Senator Platt before the US Senate about Cuban independence. It provided 'that the government of Cuba consents that the United States may exercise the right to intervene for the preservation of Cuban independence'. Subsequently the agreement was amended to extend substantially the area on lease at Guantanamo Bay in exchange for giving back Bahia Honda to the Cuban government. Today Guantanamo Bay is a vast US naval base inaccessible from the mainland with supplies to US quarters, supermarkets, cinemas and health facilities all being flown in from the US military base in Norfolk, Virginia. The base has been used before to incarcerate prisoners of the US military. In 1994 thousands of Haitians trying to leave in boats for the US were held there, followed shortly afterwards by large numbers of Cubans who also tried to reach US shores.

The conditions at Camp X-Ray caused huge consternation when they first came to light. Prisoners were shown in pictures broadcast around the world arriving at the camp in orange jump-suits, shackled, mittened, hooded, and clearly subject to sensory deprivation. One prisoner was shown motionless on a trolley with his legs shackled. These pictures released by the US government to play to a domestic audience demanding tough action backfired and resulted in international condemnation. It was disclosed that the prisoners were being held in wire cages of eight feet by eight feet, open to the elements and lit by floodlights all night. A hunger strike started in the camp, and two prisoners had to be force-fed after the protest at the forcible removal of a turban

In 2002 the US government was found guilty by the International Court of Justice of violating the Vienna Convention in the case of the execution of the brothers Walter and Karl La Grand. The Vienna Convention states that official law enforcers of any country must advise foreign citizens under arrest of their right to legal help from their own government. In 1999 the La Grand brothers died in a gas chamber in Arizona. The German authorities had not been given time to give legal assistance to the brothers.

from a prisoner during prayer. A British prisoner wrote to his family complaining he had lost three stone in weight, but otherwise letters received from prisoners by their families were short on information. Lawyers were refused any access to the prisoners, but the British government sent MI5 officials to interrogate them in the presence of the CIA as well as Foreign Office officials. On the third such visit, in May 2002, Feroz Abbassi complained that letters from his family explaining they had got him a lawyer had been withheld from him. He said he would not speak without a lawyer. Notwithstanding this, no lawyer was allowed to see him.

The military doctor in charge of the detainees' health was quoted as saying that the suicide attempts were a sign that the detainees were 'finally showing some signs of remorse'

Following international condemnation, cells were built to house the prisoners at Camp Delta, to which they have all now been transferred. Yet these still breach international standards on minimum conditions for humane imprisonment. The cells are tiny—only eight feet by six feet eight inches—and the prisoners are allowed out of them only twice a week for 15 minutes each time. International standards demand prisoners be allowed an hour of exercise a day. It is also said that the cells are lit by bright lights all night as well as in daytime. British officials have admitted that the British citizens have complained at the lack of exercise. The guards at the camp have been reported as saying that the reduction in contact between the prisoners, who are obviously less able to talk to one another than when they were in wire cages, makes their job easier than in Camp X-Ray, where there were hunger strikes and protests. However, the protests have been replaced by suicide attempts, of which there have been reportedly over 30, with some inmates developing serious mental illness. Grotesquely, the military doctor in charge of the detainees' health was quoted in the press as saying that the suicide attempts were a sign that the detainees were 'finally showing some signs of remorse'.

The US defence secretary, Donald Rumsfeld, published an order giving him the power to set up military tribunals with the power to impose the death penalty in order to try suspected members of Al Qaida or persons suspected of terrorism. But none of the prisoners at Guantanamo Bay have actually been brought before such a tribunal or charged with anything. They are being imprisoned indefinitely, incommunicado, without access to a lawyer or to any court or tribunal. This has now been the situation for over a year. International law experts including UN High Commissioner on Human Rights Mary Robinson have been more or less unanimous that this is a gross violation of international law.

The Geneva Conventions govern the treatment of prisoners taken during a war. They provide that if there is any uncertainty the status of a prisoner should be decided by an independent court or tribunal. But this has not happened. If the detainees are prisoners of war then they must be released once the hostilities are at an end (which presumably those in Afghanistan now are), and cannot be prosecuted simply for fighting. They can only be prosecuted for war crimes such as crimes against humanity, genocide and ethnic cleansing. The US government says that the Guantanamo detainees are not prisoners of war because they were not part of the official Taliban army, but are instead 'unlawful combatants'. It is claimed this gives them no rights, but this ignores the provisions of Article 75 of Additional Protocol 1 to the Geneva Conventions which provides for:

> ...an impartial and regularly constituted court respecting the generally recognised principles of regular judicial procedure, which include the following:
> (a) The procedure shall provide for an accused to be informed without delay of the particulars of the offence alleged against him and shall afford the accused before and during his trial all necessary rights and means of defence.

The US has not ratified Additional Protocol 1, but the 1997 Operational Law Handbook of the US army states that it regards it as part of customary international law, which is binding.

On 16 December 2002 the UN working group on arbitrary detention concluded that so long as a competent tribunal is not convened to decide whether the Guantanamo Bay detainees are prisoners of war, then they provisionally enjoy the guarantees provided by the Geneva Conventions to persons taken on the battlefield who are not prisoners of war—ie the right to have the detention reviewed, a fair trial and access to a lawyer. They recalled the decision of the Inter-American Court of Human Rights on 12 March 2002 to urgently request the US government to have the legal status of the Guantanamo Bay detainees determined by a competent tribunal.

In July 2002 an application for habeas corpus by some of the detainees to the United States District Court for the District of Columbia was thrown out on the grounds that the court found that US courts have no jurisdiction over Guantanamo Bay, and that 'aliens' (non US citizens) detained outside the sovereign territory of the US do not have any recourse to a US court to complain of breach of rights. This case has been appealed to the Washington Court of Appeals, but the detainees are also expected to lose there. From there it may be further appealed to the Supreme Court.

In the meantime the family of Feroz Abbasi, one of the British citizens detained in Guantanamo, made an application to the court in Britain asking for an order that the British government make diplomatic protests to the US government. The British government has refused to take any position whatsoever on the legality of the detention, despite being the closest ally of the US in the war and therefore, it might be assumed, having more influence to protect the rights of its citizens. The application eventually went to the Court of Appeal, who delivered judgement in November 2002. Although the Court of Appeal refused to pass the order sought, it did make some unusually trenchant comments about the legality of the detention, describing it as 'objectionable' and an 'arbitrary detention in a legal black hole'. The judgement refers to the common legal tradition in both the US and the UK of the concept of habeas corpus—the principle being that any imprisonment of a person is deemed unlawful unless declared otherwise by a court. This concept goes back to the 17th century and the acknowledged need for the constitution to protect against arbitrary imprisonment ordered by the king. The court quoted Lord Atkin as saying it applies in times of war as in times of peace. The references in the judgement to the proceedings in the US make it clear that the Court of Appeal expect their judgement to carry weight with the US courts in persuading them to overturn the previous finding that they have no jurisdiction.

However, it was not long before the US courts were delivering a judgement in another case, which suggests that they may not be prepared to intervene at all. Initially the US appeared to be

'Aliens' (non US citizens) detained outside the sovereign territory of the US do not have any recourse to a US court to complain of breach of rights

discriminating against non US citizens in that there are no US citizens in Guantanamo. John Walker Lindh—a US citizen detained in Afghanistan—was given a trial and access to a lawyer. (After making allegations of ill treatment he entered into a plea bargain and was sentenced to 14 years.) The appearance of discrimination was one of the arguments that might have meant that the US courts would have to decide that they had jurisdiction over the prisoners in Guantanamo Bay. However, in January 2003 the Richmond, Virginia, appeals court decided that the indefinite detention in the US of Yaser Esam Hamdi without trial or access to a lawyer as an 'enemy combatant' could not be reviewed by the US courts, saying that 'to delve further into Hamdi's status and capture would require us to step so far out of our role as judges that we would abandon the distinctive deference that animates this area of law'.

Hamdi is one of two US citizens now deemed unlawful combatants and arbitrarily detained in the US. He was initially taken to Guantanamo after being held in Afghanistan. When discovered to be a US citizen he was transferred to a navy brig in Norfolk, Virginia, where he is now set to remain indefinitely and arbitrarily detained. The other US citizen deemed an enemy combatant, Jose Padilla, was allegedly planning to construct a radioactive bomb when arrested in Chicago in 2002. A trial court judge ruled in December 2002 that he could have access to a lawyer, but said his indefinite detention without charge in a South Carolina brig 'is not per se unlawful'.

This rolling over of the US courts in refusing to protect fundamental constitutional rights has been mirrored in Britain. The British government has also detained people indefinitely without trial under its new Anti-Terrorism, Crime and Security Act. Eleven non British citizens are currently in this position. Although the Special Immigration Appeals Commission initially ruled that the derogation from Article 5 of the Human Rights Act enabling the

British government to detain 'aliens' (non British citizens) indefinitely without trial was discriminatory because it did not apply to British citizens, this has now been overruled by the Court of Appeal, which did not accept this argument. Both judgements

In the last year the numbers of Palestinians arbitrarily detained by the Israeli forces without trial has risen to well over 1,000

also accepted in its entirety the government's case that there is a state of emergency in this country allowing the derogation to take place, to permit arbitrary and indefinite detention. It is not possible to derogate from Articles 2 and 3 that protect the right to life and to be free from inhuman and degrading treatment, and therefore the right to not be sent back to countries which persecute them. Instead a derogation from Article 5 (the right to access to a court) is relied on to allow arbitrary detention.

The breach of fundamental international law by the US and its allies in the name of democracy sends a message to other countries. In the last year the numbers of Palestinians arbitrarily detained by Israeli forces without trial has risen to well over 1,000, while the phrase 'targeted killings'—used to justify the killing of alleged Palestinian militants—was given legitimacy when the US openly trumpeted in late 2002 that it had carried out a 'targeted killing' of three people said to be members of Al Qaida in Yemen. Arbitrary detention and ill treatment also cause a huge feeling of injustice in the populations of countries whose nationals are disproportionately subject to it. The pressure on the Pakistani government has been sufficient to ensure that it, unlike Britain, has made diplomatic protests about the incarceration of its citizens in Guantanamo. Two of them were released in response.

Meanwhile it is said that the US has arranged for the interrogation of its prisoners held in Afghanistan and elsewhere in countries including Egypt, Morocco, Jordan and the Philippines, where full-blown torture methods are used. In addition, prisoners at Guantanamo have been subjected to sleep deprivation. Harsh lights are shone at them—a practice labelled 'torture lite' by former US navy intelligence officer Wayne Madsen. Solitary confinement and sensory deprivation are also alleged to have been used against the 800 or more mainly Muslims detained in the US on immigration and other charges since 11 September.

Just over a year after George W Bush made the statements quoted at the beginning of this article it is abundantly clear that the agenda of the 'war on terror' is to abrogate fundamental human rights and to perpetrate the very abuses it is claimed we are fighting against. Disturbingly there is little understanding or outrage about what is happening, and this may well be linked to the extent to which the targets are non-citizens or people who are disturbingly not really seen as citizens. In the US anti-Muslim prejudice alone has been enough to achieve this. In Britain hysteria has been whipped up about asylum seekers. In both countries the courts have failed to stand up for liberties, and politicians have whipped up fears about terrorist attacks to justify human rights abuses.

Louise Christian is a human rights lawyer acting for the families of three of the British citizens detained in Guantanamo Bay

EUROPEAN SOCIAL FORUM

I arrived at the Fortezza in Florence (below) in the late afternoon's gloom. The security guards had given up trying to check tickets as thousands of people went through the gates. I was heading for the meeting on whether the movement needs political parties. I couldn't get in. I couldn't even see the speakers over the heads of the crowd. So I stood outside with 100 or so others. Those of us outside strained to hear with our translation headphones.

The front of Saturday's demo left four hours early to make room for the million people who joined it. I marched in a delegation of British socialists, trade unionists and anti-capitalists, through areas of Florence hung with white peace banners from the balconies of flats. We chanted and sang in Italian. People along the route clapped and joined in singing the Internationale. Some had banners with political slogans, some remembering Carlo Giuliani. A few placards just said 'Thank you'.

Walking back into the city centre hours later, my friends and I went down the side streets full of bored looking armed police, and found a marquee put up by Arci, the cultural wing of the Italian Communist Party. We ate, drank, and poured scorn on the owners of the expensive shops that had boarded themselves up because Berlusconi had said we were all coming to riot.

SARAH ENSOR

PALESTINE SOCIAL FORUM

Activists from around the world joined local Palestinian groups in December 2002 for the Social Forum on Palestine. Hundreds of delegates debated the future of the Palestinian solidarity movement only yards from Yasser Arafat's shattered presidential compound in Ramallah. Dr Mustafa Barghouthi, one of the organisers of the conference, told the opening session:

'Today we are achieving a dream. When we were in Porto Alegre last year we proposed that there should be a social forum in Palestine. Many people thought that it would be impossible, but actually we see it as a reality today, thanks to the determination of our friends who believed in us.'

A large delegation of French trade unionists included activists from Attac and a group of teachers. Rachel is involved with twinning French and Palestinian schools. 'The Palestinian issue is such an obvious example of globalisation. If Israel didn't receive so much American help and support, I think that the Palestinians would have their state by now.'

ANNE ALEXANDER

ASIAN SOCIAL FORUM

The Asian Social Forum (ASF), which took place in January 2003 in Hyderabad, India, was attended by 14,000 delegates. The conference was dominated by the threat of war, not just the US war against Iraq, but also the growing confrontation with North Korea and ever-present tensions between Pakistan and India. Speaker after speaker challenged Bush's drive towards war and many described imperialism as the 'military wing of globalisation'. At the conference session on peace and security, one of the largest meetings of the ASF, a debate over the nature of imperialism began to surface.

Although all of the speakers opposed US intervention in Iraq, there was disagreement over the nature of the nation-state. Some speakers argued that some nation-states could be used to challenge US imperialism. Other speakers called for a more radical approach where mass movements from below could challenge imperialism. But all agreed that Bush's 'war on terrorism' was destabilising large sections of the world and should be opposed by the anti-capitalist movement that is developing around the globe.

JOSEPH CHOONARA

REGIONS

The Iraqi healthcare system is in a decrepit state due to sanctions. Children under five are dying at more than twice the rate they were ten years ago

IRAQ
PETER MORGAN

'This is simply a war for oil,' shout the many millions who are opposed to the attack on Iraq, and they are right. But hang on a minute—apart from the huge profits that can be made from oil, what else has the region now known as Iraq given the world? There are a number of things that the dimwit president in the White House, George W Bush, and his buddy in Downing Street, Tony Blair, may not be aware of.

THE CRADLE OF CIVILISATION

In ancient times the area now known as Iraq was almost equivalent to Mesopotamia, the land between the two rivers Tigris and Euphrates. An advanced civilisation flourished in this region long before that of Egypt, Greece and Rome. In about 4000 BC the Sumerian culture flourished—the first of a succession of agricultural and cultural civilisations. Some of the things that developed at the time included a sophisticated irrigation system that created what was probably the first cereal agriculture. The Sumerians were able to pass on complex agricultural techniques to successive generations, which led to marked improvements in agricultural production. By 3000 BC the Sumerians had developed a full syllabic alphabet. The commerce of the times is recorded in great depth, and double-entry accounting practices were found in the records, an innovation still used as a standard for record keeping. Sumerians also developed a maths system based on the numeral 60 which is the basis of the measurement of time in the modern world.

The capital city of Iraq, Baghdad, was created by AD 762. It became an important commercial and cultural city. By the 10th century it was known as the intellectual centre of the world.

Baghdad became a vast area where trade flourished, and it linked Asia with the Mediterranean. Malaria was eradicated—a remarkable thing in its time—and grain production expanded so much that large quantities were exported.

Along with this went important intellectual breakthroughs. An Academy of Wisdom was created (called 'bait-al-hikma') which soon became an active scientific centre. Scholars of all races and religions were invited to work there.

The study of medicine also progressed rapidly and a number of hospitals were established in Baghdad, including a number of teaching hospitals, some of which are still used today.

This is only a very brief and limited recollection of some of the achievements of the area. Of course there were problems, class divisions, poverty, destitution, wars and upheavals. But why is it important to recall some of the achievements of the region? Well, as Edward Said explained recently:

> In the current American propaganda campaign for regime change in Iraq, the people of that country, the vast majority of whom have suffered from poverty, malnutrition and illness as a result of ten years of sanctions, have dropped out of sight. This is in entirely in keeping with Middle East policy, which is built on two mighty pillars: the security of Israel and plentiful supplies of inexpensive oil. The complex mosaic of traditions, religions, cultures, ethnicities and histories in the Arab world is lost to the US and Israeli strategic planners... Since the period before the first Gulf War the image of Iraq as a large, prosperous and diverse Arab country has been replaced in both the media and policy discussions by that of a desert land peopled by virtual gangs headed by Saddam.[1]

I wonder if the father of the current US president was aware of what his army's cruise missiles did when they ploughed into the

Natural History Museum of Baghdad during the last Gulf War. They managed to destroy many original and unique collections that document much of this area's history. It is a hard to find a phrase that best describes this act of cultural barbarism.

OIL

In 1917 the imperialist nations were at war, carving up different parts of the world. The Ottoman Empire collapsed following the British invasion of Baghdad in 1917, and the League of Nations put what was then Mesopotamia under a British administration. The Ottoman Empire was divided up between the imperialist powers. The division was done with little regard to natural frontiers or tribal or ethnic settlements, but according to where the oil was. Hence the straight lines that define many of the boundaries in the Middle East—they were done by the civil servants and world leaders imposing a carve-up on the region according to the allocation of resources. Britain was instructed to establish an Arab government in the territory, but it failed to fulfil its promises of independence, and the country became a British mandate—due mainly to the British interest in the oilfields. Britain also wanted to build a railroad that went through Iraq and down to Kuwait on the Persian Gulf. It would have allowed a more direct trade route to India without having to go round the south of Africa.

In 1920 Britain decided to impose a monarchy on the country. By 1927 the discovery of huge oilfields led to an improvement in the economy, and oil rights were granted to a British multinational. Iraq also joined the League of Nations that year and became recognised as an independent state.

Saddam Hussein, one of the most durable dictators of the late 20th century, has dominated the last four decades of Iraqi history. An army general, he came to power in 1979. He proceeded to consolidate his power by suppressing political opposition centred among the Kurds in the north, as well as other uprisings in the south and east. For much of this time he was supported by the world's powers—including Britain and the US. Bush and Blair talk today about Saddam Hussein as the evil dictator, yet they were quite prepared to put up with him so as long as he defended their interests in the region. Through-out the 1980s the US and Britain gave Iraq military and economic support which helped Saddam Hussein with the war on Iran. The Halabja massacre of March

Iraq's oil production costs are among the lowest in the world, making it a highly attractive oil prospect

1988, which led to the deaths of over 5,000 Kurds, was done with the assistance of the US military.[2] And just before Iraq's invasion of Kuwait, on 2 August 1990, the Bush administration approved nearly $5 million in sales of weapons technology to Iraq. Further arms sales were approved the day before the invasion.

Saddam Hussein's invasion of Kuwait was justified as the reabsorption of a province taken by Britain in 1960. Not surprisingly, this was not how the British and Americans saw it, but then they knew what was at stake—control of the huge amount of oil in the region. They demanded that Saddam Hussein leave Kuwait but he refused, and so the Gulf War (or 'Operation Desert Storm') was launched on 17 January 1991 with the troops of 28 countries, led by the US launching an aerial bombardment on Baghdad.

Around 140,000 tons of explosives were dropped on the country, the equivalent of seven Hiroshima bombs. Probably as many as 100,000 Iraqi soldiers, and tens of thousands of civilians, were killed. Air raids destroyed roads, bridges, factories and oil industry facilities. Electricity, telephone and water services were destroyed. Shopping and residential areas were hit. Diseases spread through contaminated drinking water because there was no electricity to purify the water. The US announced a ceasefire on 28 February 1991 as Iraqi troops fled for their lives—many were butchered on the Basra road.

Iraq has huge reserves of oil and natural gases which the US and Britain are desperate to get their hands on. It contains 112 billion barrels of proven oil reserves, the second largest in the world (behind Saudi Arabia), along with roughly 220 billion barrels of probable and possible resources. Iraq's true resource potential may be far greater than this, however, as the country is relatively unexplored due to years of war and sanctions. Iraq's oil production costs are among the lowest in the world, making it a highly attractive oil prospect. From this evidence it seems clear that all the US and

British rulers have really wanted do about Saddam in recent years is replace him with a more reliable undemocratic puppet regime.

Iraq's proven oil reserves are not distributed evenly throughout the country. In fact, prior to Iraq's invasion of Kuwait in 1990, about two thirds of Iraq's production was coming out of the southern fields of Rumallah, Zubair and Nahr Umar. These are the areas that the US is keen to get into and secure after it launches an attack.

A UN report in June 2001 said that Iraqi oil production capacity would fall sharply unless technical and infrastructure problems were addressed. The problems exist because of the years of sanctions, which have restricted imports of technical and industrial goods to help production. Iraq hopes to counter this by a large-scale programme to drill new wells (417 are planned, most of which are to be carried out by Russian, Chinese, Iraqi and Romanian companies). One of the main reasons why the US and Britain want to get in there now is that the wells are largely being carved out of current oil exploration and production, and so they fear they will not be able to get their hands on future profits. Hence one of the reasons why France has shown a reluctance to support any war—it is wary that the US may get its hands on what it already has access to and from which it is making megabucks.

Recently Iraq has signed a flurry of deals with companies from Italy (Eni), Spain (Repsol YPF), Russia (Tatneft), France (Total-FinaElf), China, India, Turkey and others. According to a report in the *Economist*, Iraq has signed over 30 deals with various oil companies, offering generous rates of return. Russia, which is owed several billions of dollars by Iraq for past arms deliveries, has a strong interest in Iraqi oil development, including a $3.5 billion, 23-year deal to rehabilitate Iraqi oilfields. In total, Deutsche Bank estimates that international oil companies in Iraq may have signed deals on new or old fields amounting to nearly 50 billion barrels of reserves, and an investment potential of more than $20 billion.

There's also the question of gas. US and British companies are missing out here as well. Iraq contains 110 trillion cubic feet of proven natural gas reserves.

Progress on increasing the country's oil output will directly affect the gas sector as well. Generally, Iraq's policy is to award gas and oil concessions to companies from countries supporting the easing or lifting of UN sanctions (ie France, China and Russia). There are other resources which, if extracted, would yield huge profits. Iraq is a country rich in coal, various metals, gypsum, phosphates, salt and sulphur.[3]

On top of the huge profits that are to be made by the victors of war, there are also important geopolitical concerns. The US ruling class sees a military victory in Iraq as sending an important signal to the other imperialist countries such as Russia and China—that the US can dominate the world and impose its will as and when it wants. It sends a similar message to the European states—that they must fall into line and support US foreign policy. It also sends an important signal to less imperialist but no less dangerous nations, such as North Korea, telling them not to try and assert themselves for fear of US military retaliation. Such a strategy is fraught with dangers, however. In the same way that a US victory sends a strong signal to the rest of the world, the same is true if it loses, or gets bogged down in a long, bloody and drawn-out conflict. It would show that the US is not as all-powerful or as strong as it claims to be. In fact, US 'concern' over Iraq is powerfully fuelled by its fear that its old puppet regime in Saudi Arabia is no

£340 million of British taxpayers' money in export credits was given to Saddam Hussein by the Conservative government during the time of the Halabja tragedy. This was when Saddam Hussein massacred Iraqi Kurds using chemical weapons. David Mellor was the Foreign Office minister at the time.

longer stable enough. Due to pressure from the people of Saudi Arabia, Saudi rulers donated $1 billion in aid to the Palestinian intifada in 2002, in addition to donating funds to build houses in Palestinian cities. The fact that the US has propped up so many brutal dictatorships in the Middle East is causing a rise in popular anger across the region as a whole. The US backing of Israel (still a reliable ally in the Middle East) and its designs on Iraq are part of its strategy to try and maintain control in the Middle East. Now that Saudi Arabia, which has the world's largest oil reserves, is a less concrete opportunity for the US in the region it must turn to

Iraq, which has the second largest oil reserves, to ease its dependence on Saudi Arabia.

Finally, what of our own prime minister? What does he think this is all about? Well, on 14 November last year he stated:

> The idea that this is about oil for us is absurd. If all we wanted was greater oil supplies we could probably do a deal with Iraq or any other country on that basis.[4]

Blair seems to have forgotten what the first Gulf War was about. Here's a little reminder for him, taken from a speech on 11 September 1990 by the then US president, George Bush, to the joint sessions of Congress:

> Iraq controls some 10 percent of the world's proven oil reserves. Iraq plus Kuwait controls twice that. An Iraq permitted to swallow Kuwait would have the economic and military power, as well as the arrogance, to intimidate and coerce its neighbours—neighbours who control the lion's share of the world's remaining oil reserves. We cannot permit a resource so vital to be dominated by one so ruthless. And we won't. (Applause.)

THE PEOPLE OF IRAQ

What of the forgotten people, the ordinary Iraqis who have suffered over the years, both at the hands of a despotic leadership, and years of sanctions imposed by the US and Britain?

The plight of ordinary Iraqis over the last decade has been detailed most clearly in two reports written in 1999. Firstly, the UN Security Council itself set up a 'humanitarian panel' to investigate the effects of sanctions. This panel produced a report on 30 March 1999. This is a summary of its findings:

> In marked contrast to the prevailing situation prior to the events of 1990-91, the infant mortality rates in Iraq today are among the highest in the world, low infant birth weight affects at least 23 percent of all births, chronic malnutrition affects every fourth child under five years of age, only 41 percent of the population have regular access to

clean water, 83 percent of all schools need substantial repairs. The...Iraqi healthcare system is today in a decrepit state. UNDP calculates that it would take $7 billion to rehabilitate the power sector countrywide to its 1990 capacity.

The second report was produced by the United Nations Children's Fund (Unicef) in August 1999. It revealed that 'in the heavily populated southern and central parts of the country, children under five are dying at more than twice the rate they were ten years ago'. Unicef executive director Carol Bellamy 'noted that if the substantial reduction in child mortality throughout Iraq during the 1980s had continued through the 1990s, there would have been half a million fewer deaths of children under the age of five in the country as a whole during the eight-year period 1991-98'.

Denis Halliday, the former UN humanitarian coordinator in Iraq, said after resigning his post in protest at the sanctions regime, 'We are in the process of destroying an entire society. It is as simple as that. It is illegal and immoral.'

I am writing at a time when Bush and Blair have not yet launched an all-out war against Iraq. If they launch the war then the process of destroying Iraqi society will be almost complete. The military plans are frightening. More than 3,000 missiles will be launched in the first 48 hours of war. This is more than the total used throughout the whole of the last Gulf War. The use of nuclear weapons has even been suggested. A presidential directive, signed last September and now leaked to the press, has given the US military the green light to use nuclear weapons if they feel them necessary to win the war. 'A list of targets has been drawn up in a "Theatre Nuclear Planning Document" by Stratcom, the Pentagon's nuclear planning wing,' reports the *Guardian*.[5] New Labour's defence secretary has stated that it will support the use of nuclear weapons if necessary. This will be followed by a land invasion, one aim of which will be to secure the oil, the other to head towards Baghdad to depose Saddam Hussein. The fact is that tens of thousands of ordinary Iraqis will be killed and the country devastated.

Bush and Blair have made clear their contempt for the views

of the majority of people throughout the world. The more they try to make the case for war, the more opinion is turning. The conclusion that millions of people are coming to is that there is only one power capable of stopping this war—the power of the masses of ordinary people that are already taking to the streets in protest before the war has even begun. We need to send Blair and Bush a message—that they do not act in our name, and that if they don't stop this war then we'll stop them.

Peter Morgan works on the monthly magazine
Socialist Review
sr@swp.org.uk

NOTES

1   *London Review of Books*, 17 October 2002.
2   *Los Angeles Times*, 13 February 1991.
3   Information on Iraq's energy resources is available on the Energy Information Administration website: www.eia.doe.gov
4   *Guardian*, 15 November 2002.
5   *Guardian*, 3 February 2003.

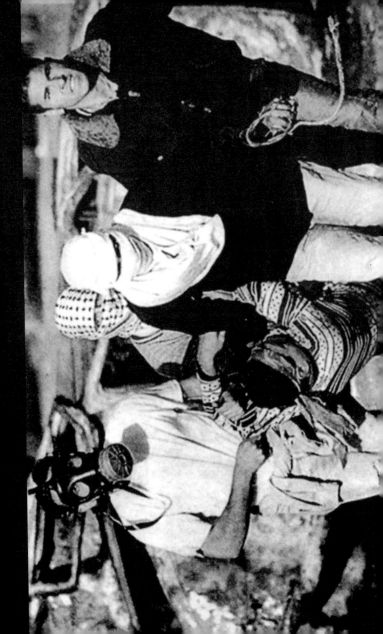

PALESTINE
GEORGE GALLOWAY

I used not to use the word imperialism. I thought young people wouldn't even know what it meant. Then Robert Cooper [former foreign policy adviser to Blair] writes a pamphlet in which he openly calls for what he describes as a new imperialism. Suddenly I find that everyone is using the words imperialism and anti-imperialism, and I think that is a jolly good thing. If something looks like a duck and walks like duck, the chances are it is a duck. That's exactly what we've got going now—a new imperialism. All sides are using its real name.

In what sense do you think that the Palestinian struggle can be seen as an anti-imperialist struggle?
Israel was planted in the Middle East as an imperialist vanguard, and it has been a very successful one. It was the plantation of many European people in a mainly Arab region, and one of its core purposes has been discharged splendidly. It built itself into the most powerful potential gendarme that the region could currently have. It was built at a time when the big imperialist powers probably imagined that the days when they could physically and directly occupy a region were coming to an end. Of course, as we enter a new century almost 100 years after the Balfour declaration, we are actually seeing the big imperialist powers moving back into physically occupying territories. But they hoped—and it worked for a

long time—that the corrupt king- doms, puppet presidencies and the Balkanisation of the Arab region into divided and weak mini-states, together with an ever more powerful Israel, would do the job. And it did for a very long time. I think we are now moving into a Sykes-Picot II

The purpose was that the Arabs should always remain divided and weak, so that they would never be united and strong enough to control their own destinies

because the settlement—the Balfour, Sykes-Picot settlement—is no longer stable, no longer sufficient. Israel of course, armed to the teeth with rockets pointed at every Arab capital, could destroy Arab capitals, but cannot physically control such a vast region with the resources available.

I have always regarded Israel as a settler state, as an advance guard of imperialism and its interests in the region. That is not to say that the Israelis have no national rights. Israelis were born there, so I believe they have inevitably acquired national rights. I am certainly not one of those who believe that the settlers should be sent home. But settlers they are, and an advance guard of an empire I'm sure they are.

In this very building where you are interviewing me, parlia- ment, Sykes and the others were once discussing the future of the Arab regions in a committee room . Mr Sykes was the British For- eign Office official and Picot the French official. They were tasked with the job of poring over the maps of the Arab region and divid- ing it up between the imperialist powers—not between just Britain and France. Other powers were also to be given a role in different parts of the region. The purpose was that the Arabs should always remain divided and weak, so that they would never be united and strong enough to control their own destinies. For even back then the main Western powers knew that the Middle East, the Arab region, would become strategically speaking vastly important to the future development of the world, and so it turned out, perhaps even more than they imagined.

Sykes-Picot II is also taking place in this building, in parlia- ment. I could tell you that in here, if not physically on the drawing board, discussions are being conducted about dividing existing Arab countries and creating new Arab countries—replacing unstable puppets with more stable puppets. For example I was approached by a former minister not long ago in the corridor, and was engaged in a conversation about Saudi Arabia. He spoke of whether Saudi Arabia really was one country, and whether it wouldn't be better as two countries, perhaps even three countries. He made the point that the 'West' (the Anglo-American axis) had no interest in the holy places in Saudi Arabia, and they were aware that it was a standing provocation to have soldiers in the holy places—so why shouldn't we have a division of Saudi Arabia? Lo and behold, he seemed to have discovered that there was a Shi'ite majority in the eastern province of Saudi Arabia and also rather a lot of oil. He had been told that the Shi'ites in Saudi Arabia were an oppressed minority, and wouldn't it be a good idea if a separate state for the Shi'ites in Saudi Arabia were created? He seemed to imply, though it was unspoken, that it would be militarily occupied, or at least dominated, by the big powers with an interest in the oil in the eastern province.

Sudan is already effectively partitioned on the utterly bogus lines that Christianity must be defended in the south of Sudan. Again, just by chance, the oil in Sudan is in the south of the country, and I suspect that Sudan may never again be united.

The same minister—or ex-minister, now—later talked to me about what might become of the Sunni and Christian minorities in Iraq in the new dispensation. He suggested it would be better if Jordan were effectively extended into the centre of Iraq, with perhaps a Hashemite on the throne in Baghdad, united with the Hashemite family in Amman. Because, after all, the poor Sunni and Christian populations would find it difficult to live under the Shi'ite majority in Iraq. It would, apparently, be a way of avoiding civil war.

So you see what I call the Yugoslavisation of Iraq and the rest of the Arab world being created amongst the smoke of the battlefield.

How do you feel about the Israeli-Palestinian peace conference that Blair organised in January 2003, and also Israel's role in the future reordering of the region?

I'm glad that the conference was a fiasco because I believe the conference was aimed against the Palestinians, not for them. It was part of an ongoing attempt to create an alternative quisling leadership within the Palestinian ranks. It was an attempt to find a leadership that will say yes to what Arafat has already said no to in the past. Basically, the thesis is that an alternative Palestinian leadership might say yes to the Camp David proposals that Barak and Clinton made but Arafat rejected. All this requires finding someone of sufficient weight to emerge as an alternative leadership. Of course these things are contradictory, because Arafat said no because Barak and Clinton's offers did not satisfy even the minimum requirements of as elastic a figure as he. It follows that anything less than Camp David, or even Camp David again, is going to be less than acceptable to the national movement in Palestine. The issues are the scope of the territory, its contiguousness, its lack of an Arab border, the continued presence of the Israeli settlements, the lack of any satisfactory conclusion to the situation of Jerusalem, and in particular the Al Aqsa and the utter lack of any proposals for the millions of Palestinian refugees—their legal and moral right to return to the homes from which they were driven.

> Israel is an undeclared nuclear weapons state, even though the UN decided long ago that the Middle East should remain a nuclear weapons free zone due to the antagonisms in the region.

Arafat said no because these issues were insufficiently addressed by Barak's proposals. So the London conference was partly about throwing sand in the eyes of Arab public opinion as they build up to the invasion of Iraq. They were hearing what the Arabs are saying about the double standards whereby Israel is endlessly rewarded for its breaches of international law, while Iraq has to be endlessly punished for breaches of international law which took place for a few months 12 years ago. They are aware that the double standard is a potentially fatal flaw in their policy toward the Arab world. So they partly launch these initiatives to throw sand in the eyes of Arab public opinion, as in the Madrid process. But its parallel purpose was to help the process of undermining Arafat, which is going on apace.

For example, Joseph Lieberman was in Jerusalem just a few weeks ago. He announced in advance that he would not meet President Arafat. Lieberman was the vice-presidential candidate with Al Gore—a very influential man in the US. In the very recent past this refusal would have meant that no Palestinian would agree to meet Lieberman. The standard response to all those visitors to Jerusalem who made that statement in the past was, 'We have one address. Our address was Jerusalem, now it is the compound in Ramallah. If you want to speak to the Palestinians you have to speak to our leadership at that address.' On this occasion, however, a steam of potential alternative leaders went to meet Lieberman.

You may say to me, 'Isn't this odd?' because I'm arguing that Israel is an indispensable part of the imperialist camp—and yet it is not following orders. It would have been in the interests of Britain and the US if Israel did not have such a belligerent, ugly leadership, which is so provocative in terms of international public opinion. Yet the powers are unable to bring such a leadership about. There's no doubt that it would have been helpful to imperialism if Israel had not thrown this boulder in the way of the Palestinian delegates leaving the West Bank. It is a rather odd case of the tail wagging the dog, but this is what happens when you create a satellite like Israel and arm it to the teeth. It then has a certain limited capacity to decide to confound your plans. That is what is happening. But I don't think this changes my essential thesis that the real axis of evil in the Middle East begins in Pennsylvania Avenue and ends in Sharon's cabinet.

Some people say that Israel is pushing America to take action on its own, exaggerating Israel's weight and the Zionist lobby in America. How do we address that?
It's a very common view in the Arab world. I don't myself share that view. Most Arabs believe that the Zionist lobby—or for some of them, even more crudely, America's Jews—control the state. This engenders a kind of defeatism and helplessness. Of course the Israel lobby is an important domestic political factor, and of course

the bizarre development of this alliance between the Christian right and Zionism is a domestic political factor in US politics—even though a very small number of those Christian rightists probably have any real time for Jews. I always joke that if you think George Bush likes Jews then you've obviously never been to his golf club. These are political factors and may become from time to time more important, but I believe that Israel is not a strategic liability to the US, which is what some Arabs argue. It is ultimately still a strategic asset of imperialism. Its purpose is to be an armed advance guard of imperialism in the region. It fulfils this purpose well, and therefore there's no point in hoping that the US might switch its allegiance away from the extremely powerful settler state of Israel to the extremely ramshackle and unstable medieval monarchy in Saudi Arabia. They realise that their interests cannot be guaranteed by the monarchy of Saudi Arabia, but they have been and will continue to be guaranteed by the bristling marshal state of Israel.

One way of proving Israel is not a liability but is a strategic asset is the destruction of Nasser in the 1967 war. The whole Arab national movement took such a battering then.

Any Arab leader who has emerged in however deformed a way, like the Iraqi leader, will be smashed. If necessary they will be smashed by Israeli power. If there were any requirements for it, Baghdad could be levelled through the use of a tactical nuclear bomb with the push of a button. We know this thanks to Vanunu, who is now in his 18th year of solitary confinement. That was his punishment for telling us that Israel has undeclared illegal nuclear weapons. But you are right—the destruction of Nasser was a setback from which the Arab national movement has never really recovered. The apparently imminent destruction of what the big powers may see as a mini-Nasser in Baghdad in the form of Saddam Hussein is intended to be a discouragement for the others. I suspect it will suppress resistance among the Arabs for a time but not for long.

The Arab national movement is now metamorphosing into something much tougher and harder to beat. The movement of

Islamic fundamentalism will be historically the biggest gainer from the period into which we appear to be now entering.

When you are talking about the reordering of the Arab states, do you think they have a function for Israel, and do you think they've thought that through?

They hope that these quisling states will eventually finally bow the knee and allow Israel to economically dominate them. That has not happened yet, and this is an indication that the Arab masses are not yet defeated. For example, I have just been in Egypt for nearly three weeks. The plan of the big powers was that Israeli capital, know-how and visitors would be all over Egypt by now. But I saw that they are not. There are no Israelis in Egypt other than intelligence officers. The only shop in Cairo that sells Israeli newspapers has to be guarded by three men with machine-guns. The feeling against so-called globalisation on the Egyptian street means that even the minimal amount of Israeli capital being invested in Egypt has to be heavily disguised.

The same is true to a lesser extent in Jordan. But in the post-Iraq period, if Mubarak and the dwarf Abdullah II can keep their seats, and especially if strengthened by a redivision of Iraq, the Western powers would hope that Israel would economically begin to dominate the region. Ironically this would stretch Israeli power from the Nile to the Euphrates, which is course the original promise that the great estate agent in the sky apparently made to the Jewish people in the Bible. This is, at least reputedly, the reason for the two lines on the Israeli flag. They symbolise the Nile and the Euphrates.

Tell us about the spirit of the intifada and how you feel about the fact that a whole new generation across the world are taking up the Palestinian cause?

I compare the Palestinian phenomenon to the process of labour that a woman has to go through to give birth. Once it begins, it cannot be stopped. It must go forward to new life or to death. I believe the Palestinian people have made this decision, and cannot be turned back from it. The intifada will continue. Today's intifada is being fought by the children of those who fought the previous intifada, and the next intifada may be fought by their children. But the struggle—and this is not leftist rhetoric—will continue until a liberation of some kind, or death.

I have been very close to the Palestinian cause for over 25 years. I have seen the movement wax and wane, and move from one theatre to the next. The first time I visited the Occupied Territories, in 1980, there was no resistance and no sign of Israeli soldiers. I was shocked. I had come from the revolution in Lebanon, from Beirut—'Fatah [victory] land'—to the Occupied Territories. But this has all changed utterly. The sacrifices that have been made by Palestinians have been momentous. They are too great in number and strength now for the Palestinians to turn back. What I think is regrettable—and we ourselves are responsible for—is that its character may begin to change from its secular, nationalist, socialist hegemony to an Islamicist one. I think that is regrettable. This shift is, I believe, already well under way. The discrediting of left wing and nationalist forces has been profound. But that has not meant a waning in the determination, or slackening of the armed struggle. On the contrary, it has taken the intifada to even more militant heights. Israel has made a very big mistake. They could have made an arrangement with a moderate nationalist leadership, and the arrangement might have helped, and been more reasonable. But instead their policies have radicalised and Islamicised the Palestinian movement. I didn't fight all this time to see Sheikh Yassin inherit the Palestinian national movement. I am sorry that he is inheriting it. But I have no doubt that Israel will find him even harder to defeat than the PLO.

The wider feeling for Palestine in the Arab world, the Muslim world and around the world is stronger than ever before. It's become a global issue—I think it could go beyond the Islamic solution because of the involvement of these wider forces.
I think that wider forces in the world have made it a universal issue. This was also true of the Algerian struggle. The Algerian leadership had an Islamic leadership, but progressive people all around the world supported the Algerian Revolution. If you see

the film *The Battle of Algiers*, you can see that the struggle had a very Islamic profile. The same, I think, will be true for the Palestinian cause. I think the only nationalist leader left in the Palestinian struggle of any weight is Barghouti, and his imprisonment for a very long time would appear to be guaranteed. Israel has constantly undermined the very secular nationalist leadership that they actually could have reconciled with. This guaranteed the growth in strength of the feeling among Palestinians that the negotiations don't work, and a movement that will not be reconciled with Israeli leaders—a very, very foolish policy for the Israelis to have pursued. I can understand why people like Sharon have done it. It may have favourable short term effects, by putting Israel so vividly on the side of 'anti-terror', and polarising the situation in a way that suits them. But I do not understand why Israel's friends in the West, and a proportion of Jewish people in the West, have supported Sharon's terrible policies.

The increasingly Islamic character of the Palestinian resistance will not detract from Palestine's emblematic importance around the world. When I see these huge demonstrations in Florence and Genoa and other places, the salience of the Palestinian flag is remarkable. It is a heart-warming thing for me. It was a very hot potato indeed to say you were with the PLO in 1974—the time of my first engagement with the issue. You would invite the kind of condemnation you would get today if you said you were with Osama Bin Laden. We have moved a huge way from 1974 to 1982—the beginning of the turning point, Israel's invasion of Lebanon and the massacres in Sabra and Shatila. These began what we can now see is a big turning point in international opinion. The idea that injustice has been done to the Palestinians, that there is a need to find a solution based upon justice for them, is an idea that is now hegemonic among a large proportion of people throughout the world. I am perfectly sure that the struggle for liberation will continue.

In regards to the growth of Islamism, in the late 1980s all the universities where the nationalist leadership was in power in the student unions, and hegemonic in terms of the street, were closed down because they were hotbeds of the PLO. In contrast, the

Islamic University in Gaza was never closed throughout the first intifada. In a sense, Hamas and Islamic Jihad were helped into being by the Israelis—though obviously they were not agents of the Israelis. They were helped in the way that the Muslim Brotherhood in Egypt was greatly empowered by Britain acting as the cat's paw against Arab nationalism. Bin Laden himself was an agent of the West against the Najibullah government in Afghanistan. So the Islamic formations in the Palestinian movement were aided and abetted by Israel. Their universities were allowed to stay open, their buses were allowed to run, they were allowed to hire halls, and they were allowed to become powerful because the Israelis thought this would create a fatal division in the Palestinian national movement. This division didn't exactly happen because both sides performed more skilfully than Israel had hoped, and avoided civil war.

Now I hope I'm wrong in saying that the Islamists are on their way to domination of the national movement because of the failure of the others. Israel will discover as we did with Bin Laden that the point about Frankenstein's monster is that it turned out to be a monster. Holding a tiger by the tail is never a good policy, because tigers are too powerful to be kept by their tail.

George Galloway is a Labour MP and a leading member of the Stop the War Coalition (www.stopwar.org.uk)

He was interviewed by John Rose

INTIFADA
NUMBER TWO
ISRAELI BRUTALITY AND
PALESTINIAN RESISTANCE

Israel's reaction to the intifada which began in September 2000 reveals its agenda for the Palestinians. It has demonstrated a lust for more and more land while denying Palestinians any hope of the right to return. The talk of 'peace with the Arabs', which was a theme of the 1990s, is now plainly no more than a new version of war.

At the same time the intifada has revealed a deep commitment by Palestinians to resistance in our homeland. It has been a continuation of our long struggle, and shows how Israel will not last if it maintains its character as a settler and colonial state in the region.

The first intifada, which began in 1987, was a mass popular revolt. The current intifada has a different character, with a small number of militants engaged in military operations from the West Bank and Gaza. Nonetheless the Israelis are determined that no resistance should take place—not even that of a single individual.

As a result 3.5 million people are subject to intense repression. During the first intifada Israel sent patrols of individual soldiers into the West Bank and Gaza—now they routinely despatch tanks to our towns and villages.

The current repression involves every sort of aggressive measure: assassination of militants (and those who happen to be in the area when killings take place); demolition of homes; mass deportation; collective punishment; arrests of tens of thousands of people; and closure of all of the West Bank and Gaza—every city, town and refugee camp.

This has had a profound effect upon Palestinian society, most seriously upon the local economy and infrastructure. There has been a severe shortage of local materials and a loss of crops, and hence a failure of manufactured products to reach the market and the local population. Palestinians have been forced to consume Israeli products which find their way into every single village, undermining the basis of local productive networks.

There has been a rapid rise in unemployment and underemployment. The only two groups able to maintain their incomes have been those working for the Palestinian Authority (PA), which employs nearly 160,000 Palestinians, and those working with non-governmental organisations (NGOs). This has had the effect of guaranteeing employees' loyalty to the PA and to the Oslo accords in much the same way that in many Arab countries ruling regimes secure the loyalty of a large bureaucratic apparatus. It also guarantees the loyalty of those employed by NGOs to the Oslo 'peace' agreement—the mission of most NGOs has been to achieve normalisation between Arab countries and Israel.

These developments are the outcome of a definite Israeli strategy which serves the main purpose of Zionism—removal of the remainder of the Palestinians from Palestine. The fact is that Israel has so far failed to evict a mass of Palestinians as it did in 1948. Its policy is now to encourage Palestinians to leave by themselves, to discourage Palestinians of the *shahat* (those outside the homeland) from returning to Palestine, and to encourage those who returned to the West Bank and Gaza after the Oslo accords to leave again.

Despite these pressures Palestinians remain steadfast. This is evident in the readiness to bear all the forms of the enemy's brutality, and in the tireless attempts to maintain 'normal life'. With the exception of a few intellectuals, and those in the PA who called for the cessation of struggle and abandoned the right of return, the level of resistance remains that of a people's war.

There is a well used comment after military operations: 'All right, they will break our bones, it is expected, but with this enemy there is no other way.' This has not changed with the re-election of Sharon as prime minister. Palestinians know fully that Sharon does not have new methods of oppression—only what he has used and we have faced.

A NEW MORAL IMPULSE

There is another very significant development evident among Palestinians on the streets, in coffee shops, in the villages and refugee camps. This is the interest taken in the anti-war and anti-globalisation movements outside Palestine, and the attempts to participate in them. Palestinians believe that these movements are opposed to Zionism, and this has given them a new moral impulse.

Political Islam continues to exert an influence. It was not the Islamists who betrayed the first intifada but the secular political forces. Organisations such as Hamas began to gain support in the early 1990s when organisations of the PLO abandoned military struggle and soon fell into the trap of the imperialist 'peace' settlement. Military operations brought the Islamists growing backing, and it was only when some secular organisations renewed military action that their monopoly over these operations was broken.

Israeli brutality against the Palestinians did lead many people to express hope in the military strategy of the Islamists. Israel realises this and believes that the attachment of Palestinians to 'the mosque' will help its policy by presenting the entire Palestinian people as ardent fundamentalists. We need to recall that for Zionism and its main supporter, the US state, it has been the secular left which has been the main enemy, not Islamism.

a further factor pushing the people towards Islamism has been a well financed Western-backed current in the West Bank and Gaza—the NGOs that work for normalisation with Israel and work hand in hand with those who demand reforms of the PA like those demanded by the US. These reforms are entirely different from those the people aspire to.

What prevents domination by the Islamists over Palestinian political life is the secular culture of the Palestinian people, their struggle, their openness to the world, and the historically positive role of secular forces in the struggle.

The Islamists have been able to build some economic structures for their supporters. They have been unable, however, to expand this to the whole society—and indeed this is not their aim. The social dimension of their work is also lagging behind secular developments, especially in relation to women's issues. What is necessary is that questions of social justice, development, democracy and plurality should be tackled by the secular forces and debated openly, including with the Islamists.

In February 2003 Palestinian organisations met in Cairo. Their talks were directed towards ending popular resistance, even in its political forms. Participation of the Islamists points to a new development in their position—an acceptance of the mediatory role of their hosts (the Egyptian capitalist state) and a readiness to compromise by exchanging the sacrifices of the people for a political deal. There may also be pressure upon them from Saudi Arabia, from Syria and from Iran—states concerned that US aggression against Iraq may have its effects upon them too.

In this situation it is vital for the left to grasp the moment—a moment when people's readiness for struggle is high. The left should commit itself to a firm and principled position on the right of return, on struggle against corrupt capitalism, and for a socialist Palestine in a united socialist Arab state.

ADEL SAMARA, Ramallah,
occupied West Bank

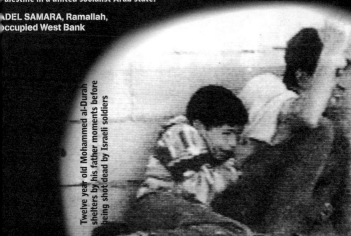

Twelve year old Mohammed al-Durah shelters by his father moments before being shot dead by Israeli soldiers

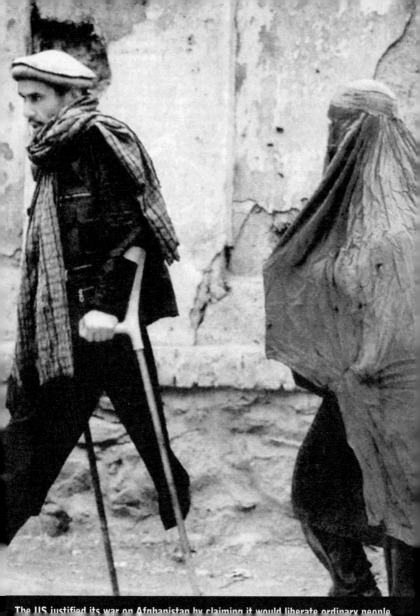

The US justified its war on Afghanistan by claiming it would liberate ordinary people

AFGHANISTAN
JONATHAN NEALE

THE HISTORICAL CONTEXT

To understand the American war in Afghanistan we need to go back to the 1970s.[1] I spent two years doing anthropological field research in Afghanistan in the early 1970s. It was a land of desert and bare mountains. Only 2 percent of land could be farmed, and most of that required irrigation. The great majority of the population lived from agriculture and pastoralism, and power lay with great landlords who lived in large forts in the countryside.[2]

At the head of the government were the royal family—King Zahir Shah until 1973, and then his uncle Mohammed Daoud. There was no taxation on land or livestock. Most of the central budget came from foreign aid from the US and the Soviet Union. That aid was not spent on economic development, because industry, and an urban capitalist class, would destroy the power of the feudal lords and the king. So the money went on education and a national army largely staffed by conscripts.

That created, however, a new class of educated people who became teachers, civil servants and army officers. Because the old feudal class was so small, this new class was drawn from the children of small farmers in the countryside. They brought with them to the cities their parents' hatred of the big landlords and the king. In their new jobs they were frustrated and angered by the corruption and backwardness of the old regime, and dreamed of development.

By the early 1970s the predominant politics in this new class were Communist. They looked to the Soviet Union as a model for development into a modern industrialised economy run by people like them. The Communists and idealists were brave. Two things were central to their dream—land reform and women's liberation.

The competing trend among the new educated class was Islamism. The Islamists took their ideas mostly from Al Azhar University in Cairo. During the early 1970s the Communists and the Islamists fought for leadership of the opposition. The fight centred on Kabul University and the high schools around the city. There were demonstrations, and fights with axes and at times with guns. But the critical thing was endless political argument, and the Communists largely won those arguments among the students and the new educated class. They did not win the argument in the countryside, however. There the grip of terror exercised by the landlords was simply too strong.

In April 1978 the Communists launched a military coup. It was almost bloodless—the royal family had little support in the country. The new Communist government's first action was two decrees. One shared out the land of the great landlords. The other called for various rights for women.

Both these decrees were symbolic. The new government controlled the cities. In the countryside, however, it could not enforce the decrees. The coup was the work of young educated officers in the army and the air force. But the rank and file of the army were conscripts, and the Communists had not won them over. They were trying to make a revolution from the top down.

Risings began almost immediately in the rural areas, led by local mullahs. Without enough popular support, the government reacted to these risings with jailings, torture and bombing. The risings spread. Within a year it was clear the Communist government would soon fall.

In December 1979 the Russian tanks rolled into Kabul. The reason was oil. The Soviet Union bordered Afghanistan to the north. The Central Asian provinces of the Soviet Union had much

The Russian war was fought along the lines of the American war in Vietnam of the country's oil and gas. Their population was also at least nominally Muslim. The rulers in Moscow were afraid that the fall of a Communist government on their border to a Muslim insurrection would encourage unrest across Central Asia.

After the invasion the Communists lost most of their support in the cities. In Herat, Kandahar and Kabul, all over the city men and boys climbed up onto the roofs of their houses at night and shouted, 'God is great!' into the darkness. The students at the main girls' high school in Kabul had demonstrated often for the rights of women and against the veil. Now they gathered in the school yard and chanted slogans against the Russians.

The Russian war lasted seven years.[3] The resistance was the Afghan peasantry in arms. Each community, in each valley, fought on its own to defend its own territory. There was no national guerrilla army, and no centralised campaign. Each group fought when the Russians came to their valley. If they lived near a road they attacked Russian convoys on that road. They all fought under the banner of Islam. This was only natural. The Afghans had fought and won three wars against British invaders between 1838 and 1919 under the banner of Islam.

The nominal leadership of the resistance lay with seven separate Islamist parties with headquarters over the border in Peshawar, in Pakistan. These seven parties were funded by Pakistan, Saudi Arabia and the US. The controllers were Pakistani Inter-Services Intelligence (ISI), Saudi intelligence and the US Central Intelligence Agency (CIA). Most of the leading figures in the seven parties were former leaders of the Islamist students. Their parties were not simply American or Pakistani puppets. Like the Afghan Communists, they represented a real movement inside Afghanistan.

The Russian war was fought along the lines of the American war in Vietnam. There were helicopter gunships, mines, napalm and free-fire zones. Something like half a million or a million Afghans died (all the figures are guesses). Roughly another million were maimed, largely by mines. From a population of 20 to 25 million, 3 million were driven into exile in Pakistan, 2 million into Iran, and another 2 million took refuge in the Afghan cities.

For 40 years Afghanistan had been polarised politically between Islamists and Communists. Now the only basis of organising left was ethnicity

Many individual Communists, probably a majority, were appalled by the Russian invasion. Some joined the resistance, some went into exile, and many were imprisoned and killed. The Communist Party as an organisation, however, supported the Russians, fought alongside them, and tortured for them.

The local resistance groups across the country depended on the parties in Peshawar for guns, surface to air missiles and money. Within three years, by 1983, there was deep cynicism about the Peshawar parties in the resistance, and among refugees in Pakistan. The party leaders were stealing a good part of the money intended for refugees, and selling off a lot of the arms. But there was no alternative leadership to the resistance.

Inside Afghanistan, the old feudal lords had fled. Power in rural areas now lay with the local commanders of the resistance. They used that power to gain control for themselves and their families of much of the land that had belonged to the old lords.

In 1987, after seven years of war, the Russians withdrew beaten. For the next eight years the various Islamist parties fell out among themselves.[4] Their leaders formed shifting, and utterly unprincipled, alliances. Kabul had been the one city not bombed by the Russians. Now the Islamist factions set up artillery on the heights above Kabul, shelled the city, and fought each other through the neighbourhoods. The city turned to rubble. Across the country local commanders competed for land, and control of the burgeoning opium and heroin trade.

Most Afghans lost all faith in any alternative. Hundreds of thousands had supported the Communists. Millions had fought for the Islamists. Now they believed in nothing. For 40 years Afghanistan had been polarised politically between Islamists and

Communists. Now the only basis of organising left was ethnicity. The south and east were largely Pashtuns, speakers of the Pashtu language. The centre was largely Hazara, the north and east Persian-speaking Tajiks and Turkic-speaking Uzbeks.

After the Russians left, the CIA withdrew support to the Islamist parties. The resistance had served the CIA's purpose in weakening the Soviet Union, and it now did not want to be the sponsor of any new Islamist government. But in 1995 the Americans returned. The reason, again, was oil and gas.

After the collapse of the Soviet Union in 1989 the Central Asian provinces had become independent countries—Kazakstan, Uzbekistan, Kyrgyzstan, Turkmenistan, Azerbaijan and Tajikistan. All but the last had oil and gas. New oil and gas fields had also been discovered in northern Afghanistan. Russia, China, the US, Iran and Turkey competed for control of all this oil. The winner would be the country that controlled the pipelines out of Central Asia. The old pipelines ran to Russia, and the Russians paid much less than the market price. The obvious place for a short new pipeline was down through Iran to the Gulf. But Iran was an enemy of the US. An American oil company, Unocal, planned a short pipeline a couple of hundred miles to the east, through Afghanistan and Pakistan to the Indian Ocean.

THE TALIBAN

The pipeline would not work, however, without peace and a strong central government in Afghanistan. In 1995 the local Afghan commanders and Islamist parties were still at war with each other. That year Pakistani intelligence set up a new army, the Taliban, with money and support from the US and Saudi Arabia. The Taliban were hardcore right wing Islamists, and overwhelmingly Pashtuns. Their officers were drawn from the Pakistani army, and from Pashtun ex-Communists who had been army officers for the Russians. The soldiers were mostly boys who had grown up in the refugee camps in Pakistan and been educated in the religious schools there ('Taliban' means 'students of religion').

The Taliban invaded from Pakistan into southern Afghanistan. They promised peace, an end to corruption, suppression of the local commanders and harsh but fair justice. Wherever they conquered they disarmed the local population, something never done in Afghanistan before. Most Afghans had strong reservations about the Taliban. But they had turned against the Islamist parties and the local commanders, and the yearning for peace was strong.

In the Pashtun villages the great majority of women still went unveiled, and girls went to school. Had the Taliban tried to stop this, they would have faced the fury of the villagers

American support, in particular, led people to hope that the Taliban might actually be able to deliver peace and the rule of law.

The Taliban were thus able to conquer most of the country quickly, but not all. In the city of Mazar in the north, the last to fall to them, they tried to disarm the Hazara migrants to the city. The Hazaras, from the central mountains, had always been at the bottom of the ethnic pecking order in Afghanistan. In the last 100 years Pashtuns supported by the government had taken much of their land and pastures, and many had been driven to work as unskilled labour in the cities.[5] Now, faced with a Pashtun Taliban army, they fought back. The urban population of Mazar rose with them. The Taliban recaptured Mazar a year later, but they could never gain control of the whole north. It became clear that the Taliban central government would never be able to deliver a safe pipeline. The US withdrew support, though the Pakistani and Saudi governments did not.

The Taliban did deliver law and order in most of the country, and were less corrupt than the local commanders and the Islamists. They too were Islamists, of course, but of a more right wing kind. Much of their propaganda focused on the modesty of women, and enforcing veiling in the cities. In this they were trying to follow the example of their Saudi sponsors. But there was another dynamic at work. NGOs funded by the UN and the European Union did most of the actual work of government in the towns and cities—the schools, roads and hospitals, and the delivery of flour and bread. All the Taliban did, in practice, was hold show trials and be Islamists. Precisely because their dependence on the US and the West was known to everyone, they had to emphasise their Islamic purity.

In doing so, they were not expressing a primordial Afghan or Pashtun culture. When I lived in Pashtun villages in the early 1970s only a few rich families in each village veiled their women, perhaps four or five households out of 200. The rest had to send their women out to work in the fields and with the animals. Under the Taliban the new dress rules were enforced in the cities, and girls were forbidden to go to school. But in the Pashtun villages the great majority of women still went unveiled, and girls went to school. Had the Taliban tried to stop this they would have faced the fury of the villagers.

The Taliban's insistence on women's dress cannot be understood separately from the experience of the Russian invasion. The Afghan Communists had been fierce, and principled, supporters of women's rights. Women had been Communist agitators from the start. Then they had supported the Russian bombers. To use an analogy, if all American feminists had supported and fought alongside a foreign invader that killed 10 million Americans (the same proportion of the population), it would be difficult to argue for women's liberation in the US.[6]

BIN LADEN

In the 1980s Bin Laden had been the young man chosen by the Saudi government to organise foreign Islamist volunteers to fight with the resistance of the Afghans.[7] He worked out of Peshawar. His organisation of volunteers, called Al Qaida, was funded by the CIA. In 1989 he lost that funding and left Afghanistan, shocked by the infighting among the Islamists. For a time he returned to Saudi Arabia, and at first supported the American alliance against Iraq in the first Gulf War. But the bombing of Iraq was too reminiscent of the Russian bombing of Afghanistan, and he was outraged that the Saudi royal family allowed US troops to be stationed in Saudi Arabia permanently after the Gulf War. He decided that the Americans were just like the Russians, and became a leader in the underground opposition to the Saudi dictatorship. Bin Laden went into exile, first in Sudan and then in Afghanistan. He still had an organisation called Al Qaida. When it was implicated in bombings of US embassies in Kenya and Tanzania, the US air force bombed an alleged training camp for Al Qaida in southern Afghanistan, and demanded that the Taliban turn Bin Laden over to them. The Taliban government replied that they would do so, but first the US would have to provide evidence to an Afghan court to justify extradition. The US government refused to do so, probably because it didn't have any evidence.

11 SEPTEMBER AND THE AFGHAN WAR

Then came 11 September 2001. Here I will deal only with the consequences for Afghanistan.

11 September was a major challenge to US power in the world. In the Middle East, in particular, US influence and power depended more on fear than consent. Fear, and US power, had to be restored. Someone was going to pay.

There was debate in the Bush administration about where to strike first. Iraq and Saudi Arabia were possibilities. But both might provoke internal resistance and demonstrations or uprisings across the Middle East. The Taliban, however, were widely despised in the Middle East for their right wing attitudes to women, and many in the Arab world looked on Afghans as backward anyway. Moreover, the Taliban had little support inside the country. Millions of Afghans had fought for Communism and Islam. Now there was widespread cynicism about both. With a million dead by now, after 23 years of war, few Afghans were likely to resist the US.

The economy was also shattered. Much of the agricultural land was still full of mines. Most of the refugees in Pakistan, Iran and the cities decided not to return. There had been a drought for three years, many nomadic pastoralists had been forced to kill their herds for lack of water, and famine threatened much of the country. Without regular shipments of food aid, many would starve. Farmers in many areas had survived by growing opium. But then the Taliban had prevented poppy farming in the hope that this would appease the Americans. Precisely because Afghans had suffered so much, and were so helpless, they would now suffer more.

The US government also saw possible gains if it invaded Afghanistan. First and foremost there was the Central Asian oil. A

A victory in Afghanistan could not only guarantee a pipeline, but tip the balance of power away from Russia across Central Asia

victory in Afghanistan could not only guarantee a pipeline but tip the balance of power away from Russia across Central Asia.

There was a broader reason too. In economic terms the US was increasingly competing with the European Union, a roughly equivalent power. In military terms US superiority was overwhelming. Washington had learned from the war against Iraq in 1991 that a military victory could be translated into superpower domination of the world economy.

And so the invasion began. The justification was that they would 'regime change' the Taliban, free Afghan women and capture or kill Bin Laden, thereby getting justice for 11 September.

There were problems, however. The US did not dare invade with ground troops in force, for two reasons. The first was that ever since the Vietnam War there had been strong resistance inside the US by ordinary working class people to letting their children die abroad for American foreign policy. This was usually called the 'Vietnam syndrome', as if it were a sickness, when in fact it was a healthy reaction. The American elite hoped that after 11 September they could get round this, but they were still wary of committing troops in force. The other reason was that US tanks and infantry would recall still bleeding memories of the Russian war inside Afghanistan.

So the US sent special forces, paratroops and CIA agents, but not infantry or tanks. Kandahar was heavily bombed, and so were many rural areas. Roughly 3,000 civilians were killed, and perhaps as many Taliban troops. Many more people died of hunger and disease as they fled, and because relief supplies could not get through. We have no idea how many. But there were limits to the American war. The sort of saturation bombing of Kabul necessary to destroy the Taliban regime would quickly lead to an outcry across the world.

The US government was particularly worried about the effects of bombing in Pakistan. The military dictatorship there was backing the American invasion. The US had to use Pakistani airspace for the bombing, and any invasion force would have to go through there. Once the Afghan War began, there were demonstrations in Pakistan, particularly near the border. These were

Roughly 3,000 civilians were killed, and perhaps as many Taliban troops. Many more people died of hunger and disease as they fled

called mainly by the Islamists, and the crowds were tens of thousands, not hundreds of thousands. There was also considerable support for the Islamists inside the Pakistani military, which after all had created and organised the Taliban.

All this meant that the Bush administration calculated that they would have to work through Afghan allies on the ground. They had two possibilities. One was to work through the Northern Alliance, an ethnically based coalition of Islamists and former Communists in the north. They had a few thousand troops in the field, who suddenly received new uniforms and shoes from the Americans. There were political problems here, however. In the north east the main force in the alliance was the Panjshiri Tajiks, who had been funded by and allied to India and Russia. In the north the main commander was Dostum, an Uzbek who had been a Communist general. He was funded by and allied to Russia and Uzbekistan. In the east the main commander was Ishmael Khan, a Communist officer who had gone over to the Islamists after the Russian invasion. He was allied to Iran. What all this meant was that a victory for the Northern Alliance might not be a victory for the Americans, but for competing powers.

The Americans did have their own candidate leader in the wings, and had been pushing him in meetings of the Afghan opposition abroad. This was Hamid Karzai, a Pashtun Afghan who had long lived in the US, and had worked for the American oil company trying to get the pipeline. All Afghans, of all political persuasions, believe Karzai is a career CIA officer. The CIA's hope was that Karzai could win support among rural Pashtuns, and that would balance the foreign ties of the Northern Alliance.

Pakistani military intelligence officers were sent into Afghanistan to try to organise rural risings against the Taliban, and failed. Abdul Haq, an American-backed Islamist, was sent into eastern Afghanistan, where the local people betrayed him and the Taliban killed him. Karzai was sent into his tribal homeland in southern Afghanistan, and had to be airlifted out by helicopter.

The Taliban were not collapsing. They even held Mazar, which had once risen against them. And they held Herat, where people had fought the Taliban, and Taliban dress codes could only be enforced on the main thoroughfares. The bombing was not rallying Afghans to the Taliban, but it was clearly making them unwilling to support the Northern Alliance or the Americans. The war had begun in October. By December it was clear that it would take serious bloodshed to take Kabul. The political consequences of saturation bombing, though, might have been serious in Pakistan. There had demonstrations of 100,000 in London and 200,000 in Italy. Within America, too, people were asking questions about a war that seemed to be going nowhere.

The Northern Alliance troops were also clearly reluctant to fight. Like all other Afghans, they had had enough of real war.

So a deal was done in December between the Taliban, the Northern Alliance, and the US and Pakistani governments. The deal is common knowledge inside Afghanistan. The general shape of the deal is clear. The Taliban rank and file, and most of their leaders, would be allowed to return to rural southern Afghanistan in peace. Their senior leaders would be given refuge in the Pashtun tribal areas of Pakistan. Hamid Karzai would be installed at the head of a government in Kabul.[8]

Most of this deal worked. Some of my Afghan sources claim that the Taliban leaders were actually flown to Pakistan in American and Pakistani helicopters. This may or may not be true. Certainly the Taliban were allowed to escape. Their senior leader, Mullah Omar, was even able to ride out of an American-held village in southern Afghanistan on the back of a motorcycle.

But in two places the deal broke down. In Mazar, in the north, Dostum was the local leader of the Northern Alliance. As Mazar fell, Dostum was in the nearby city of Kunduz, negotiating the surrender of the Taliban there. He sent back to Mazar several hundred foreign, largely Pakistani, Islamist volunteers who had fought with the Taliban, promising them safe passage home. US defence secretary Donald Rumsfeld, however, was publicly baying for the blood of Al Qaida on television, saying that they should be shot when captured. In Mazar the foreign volunteers came under the control of CIA operatives, who led local Afghans in slaughtering most of them. The hundred or so who survived were holed up in the basement of a fortress. Dostum, furious, returned to Mazar from Kunduz, accompanied by the Taliban leaders. With the help of the Taliban leaders, he was able to negotiate the surrender of the surviving foreign volunteers. The CIA, however, then took them as prisoners to a new American air base in the south. From there they were flown to Guantanamo Bay, an American military enclave on the Cuban coast. There they were tortured. The American military even took pictures of prisoners in cages and black hoods, and of one prisoner being carried on a stretcher to his next interrogation. The military then released these pictures, probably to frighten both people in the Middle East and Americans.

The deal also broke down outside Kabul. The Northern Alliance had promised the Americans they would not take Kabul on their own. But as the Taliban left the capital, the Northern Alliance troops commanded by Tajiks flooded into the city from the north. The Americans began flying in troops to Bagram, the old Russian air force base just north of Kabul, and were able to install Karzai as president. But the ministries of foreign affairs and of the interior were run by Northern Alliance Tajiks, and so was much of the machinery of government. Their strategy was to wait out the Americans, who they were pretty sure would tire and leave.

The authority of the new government did not stretch beyond Kabul, and not even over much of the city at night. Osama Bin Laden had fled to the eastern mountains along the Pakistani border. The American troops pursued him there, but the local people and the local Afghan commanders allowed him to escape to Pakistan.

In the north east the real power now lay with the Tajik commanders, in the north with Dostum and around Herat in the east with Ishmael Khan. In the south and east power lay with shifting coalitions of Taliban leaders and former commanders of the resistance to the Russians. The American media called all of these people warlords, a stigmatising word for commanders. From the point of view of the US government, almost all of Afghanistan was now controlled by Taliban or by people allied to competing foreign powers.

At first, the US reacted partly by bombing many parts of rural Afghanistan. The region around Herat was particularly badly hit, because of Ishmael Khan's links to the Iranian regime. Considerable numbers of special forces wandered around looking for Mullah Omar. But the American forces did not dare touch the local Taliban commanders in the Northern Alliance. The one time they did so in force they bombed a wedding party, killing dozens, and it turned out that both bride and groom were related to Karzai.

One incident in particular highlights the US weakness. When the first foreign prisoners were flown out of an American air base in the desert, about 100 miles south of Kandahar, someone outside the base fired on the helicopter taking the prisoners away. It was at night, and the American troops on the base had to wait until morning to leave the base to investigate the shooting. When they did so, they did not dare go more than 400 metres from the base.

However weak the American grip looked inside Afghanistan, the fall of Kabul was an important victory for the US on the world stage. There was almost no media coverage of its weakness inside the country, and none at all of the deal it had made. The lesson for most people across the world was that the US regime could 'regime change' anyone it wanted. And during the war the US had gained bases in Pakistan, Afghanistan and every Central Asian country except Turkmenistan. It now controlled the oil and gas of Central Asia. Flushed with confidence, the Bush administration could now turn its attention to Iraq, and hope for even greater victories.

AFTER THE WAR

This was no consolation for the Afghans. Karzai's job, Afghans knew, was to bring the Pashtun south and east under the control of the central government. After all, he was himself a Pashtun, and his father had been an important CIA-backed leader in the

Torture, murder, ethnic cleansing !!! Welcome to Israel

The Muslim Association of Britain

Two million say no to war in Britain's biggest ever protest on 15 February 2003

resistance to the Russians. It was clear by the end of 2002 that he had failed in this job.

Karzai was able to convene a 'Lowe Jirga', a big tribal council. The kings of Afghanistan had called such a council at important turning points in the country, summoning the great rural lords. This new Lowe Jirga was not elected. Most of the people who went were local commanders, tribal elders and big landlords, but there were some government officials, some ex-Communists and some women as well. As they met, ex-king Zahir Shah had just returned from exile. The majority of the council wanted to elect Zahir Shah as president. He may have had few friends when he was a brutal dictator, but in the light of what had happened since his rule was fondly remembered. And at least, they thought, he isn't Karzai. The CIA stepped in and compelled Zahir Shah to refuse the office. Karzai was then elected without opposition.

As Karzai spoke to the council, one white-bearded rural elder listened. When Karzai began to talk about god, the white-bearded man said quietly, but loud enough for everyone near to hear, 'Now he's lying.' The people around him knew what he meant—any Afghan politician who talks about Islam is using you.

Karzai's position was increasingly insecure. In the summer of 2001 his deputy, Abdul Qadir, was shot dead as he left his offices in Kabul, possibly by Islamists or possibly by business rivals. Qadir was a major figure in the heroin trade in eastern Afghanistan. After that, US special forces replaced Karzai's Afghan bodyguards. There were no Afghans left he could trust.

By the late summer there were attacks on the US military almost every day—53 in October alone. It is not certain who were responsible for these, but people suspected former Taliban and/or former Islamists from the resistance to the Russians.

There were also constant small fights between local commanders in the countryside. This was partly because the Americans were funding and arming them heavily. In some instances there were even American military advisers on both sides of these fire fights. But the deeper reason for these small battles was structural. The old landlords had left their land at the beginning of the resistance to the Russians. The new commanders had used their military leadership to get control of much of this land. The new pattern of land tenure was complicated. In some areas commanders had led their own ethnic group to drive out another group and take their land. In other areas the commanders had taken control of land owned by their tribal brothers. Control of land in rural Afghanistan had always been based on force, and every big landlord had his retinue of armed men. But now the new claims to land had almost no legitimacy. The land had been won by force. It could only be held if the fear that force created stayed in place. A commander who looked weak would lose the land. A strong central government, too, would threaten his, or his group's, control of the land. The only way to hold onto the new land was to continue to demonstrate your force and your brutality. That created a constant push towards local bloodshed.

In the cities Karzai's government was losing legitimacy quickly. People had expected that the Americans would pour money into the reconstruction of the country. It didn't happen. Less than a fifth of the money promised was allocated. Most of that went on foreign aid workers, whose salaries and overheads consume an average of $110,000 per person per year. This was not the aid Afghans needed. Afghans have always worked hard, and a thousand Afghans could have worked for the cost of one American or European. For the owners of the few substantial houses that had survived the wars in Kabul, the aid wages were a bonanza, and rents were higher than in London. For ordinary people, such conspicuous wealth in the midst of such poverty was obscene. Karzai's government, and the ministers of the Northern Alliance, were also very publicly corrupt.

When Karzai first took office, many educated former refugees from the Afghan diaspora in the West had come home, most of them hoping to reconstruct and 'modernise' their homeland. By November 2002, even those of them with high office in ministries were appalled by the corruption. They were particularly angry at the corruption in the Western NGOs, which they had not expected. The foreign workers in the NGOs, meanwhile, were agitating strongly for US and allied troops to patrol the whole country. They wanted the troops to protect them from Afghans.

The comparison with Palestine is telling. In the West Bank

and Gaza, the NGO workers do not ask for foreign protection, because the Palestinians know the aid workers are on their side.

Kabul University, dear to the memory of many educated Afghans, had been looted and turned to rubble during the fighting between the Islamist factions. Karzai's new government restored it and began classes. There were no books, but teachers read from the precious notes they had taken in lectures 20 years before. The new students had desperately high hopes. They too turned against the government. The government and the NGOs were feeding them, as they still had to feed much of the urban population. One day in early December, during the fast of Ramadan, the students gathered at sundown to eat. There was no food, so they demonstrated. Policemen, dressed in full Western Darth Vader style riot gear, opened fire on the students, killing four.

When the invasion of Afghanistan began, the US government said that it intended to change the regime, restore stability, and leave. Through 2002 its policy had been to use allied British, Turkish, German and other troops to patrol Kabul. American troops occupied their own bases, and made some forays into the countryside. By December 2002 it was clear that if the Americans withdrew Karzai would be killed. That month the US changed policy. It now refused to supply more arms to the local commanders, and said it was going to extend US and allied patrols across much of the country. The immediate targets were Dostum in the north and Ishmael Khan in the east, but this was a general plan to gain control of the whole country.

I write this in late December 2002. Much of Afghanistan's future will be determined by what happens in Iraq. But some things are clear.

The US plan to take real control in Afghanistan may well work to some extent for a time. No one should underestimate how weary ordinary Afghans are of war. But in the longer term any American occupation will meet resistance by Islamists, and that in turn will produce brutal reprisals. There is also a large question about how many American deaths the American public will tolerate.

For 164 years, since 1838, Afghanistan has been a pawn for foreign powers in various versions of what Kipling called the

'Great Game'. It's a droll phrase, but less amusing if your child's head is the football. If the US occupation fails, we will be told that Afghanistan is a 'failed state'. And it may be, in the same sense that if you cut off a man's legs just before the race he will be the last to finish the 100-metre sprint. The devastation that Afghans have lived through for 24 years, and the oppression they suffered before this time, comes from foreign powers who will give no real aid in the future but flood the country with arms. On their own, there is no way Afghans could afford to kill each other on such a scale. And whatever you may read in the writings of their enemies, Afghans are not bloodthirsty savages. They are people, like you and me, worried about food and their children. Left to themselves, they would not build a paradise. But they are deeply sick of war, and would make some sort of peace. They should have that chance.

Jonathan Neale is a writer and anti-capitalist activist. His most recent books are *The American War: Vietnam 1960-75* **and** *You Are G8, We Are 6 Billion: The Truth Behind the Genoa Protests*
findjonathan@hotmail.com

NOTES

1   I have provided notes here to alert readers to good books. Much of this chapter, however, is based on two years of field research in Afghanistan between 1971 and 1973, and on many conversations with Afghans and foreign researchers on Afghanistan since. Given the current situation in Afghanistan, I cannot footnote these sources. More detailed references are in Jonathan Neale, 'The Afghan Tragedy', *International Socialism* 12 (Spring 1981); Jonathan Neale, 'Afghanistan: The Horse Changes Riders', *Capital and Class* 35 (1988); and Jonathan Neale, 'The Long Torment of Afghanistan', *International Socialism* 93 (Winter 2001). All three articles are available on the net at www.marxists.de

2   For Afghanistan in the 1970s see Jonathan Neale, 'The Afghan Tragedy'; and Nancy Tapper, *Bartered Brides: Politics, Gender and Marriage in an Afghan Tribal Society* (Cambridge, 1991).

3   For the Russian war see Jonathan Neale, 'The Afghan Tragedy'; Jonathan Neale, 'Afghanistan: The Horse Changes Riders'; M H Kakar, *Afghanistan: The Soviet Invasion and the Afghan Response, 1979-1982* (Berkeley, 1995); Raja Anwar, *The Tragedy of Afghanistan* (London, 1988); and Oliver Roy, *Islam and Resistance in Afghanistan* (Cambridge, 1986).

4   For the period from 1988 to 2001, the best sources are Barnett Rubin, *The Fragmentation of Afghanistan: State Formation and Collapse in the International System* (New Haven, 1995); Ahmed Rashid, *Taliban: Islam, Oil and the New Great Game in Central Asia* (London, 2000); William Maley (ed), *Fundamentalism Reborn: Afghanistan and the Taliban* (London, 1998); Michael Griffin, *Reaping the Whirlwind: The Taliban Movement in Afghanistan* (London, 2000); and Jonathan Neale, 'The Long Torment of Afghanistan'.

5   See Sayed Mousavi, *The Hazaras of Afghanistan: An Historical, Cultural and Economic and Political Study* (New York, 1997).

6   For the lives of Afghan women in the 1970s, and the complex relation between gender and class inequality then, the best source is Nancy Tapper, *Bartered Brides*. For the gender politics of the Taliban, see Nancy Lindisfarne, 'Starting from Below: Fieldwork, Gender and Imperialism Now', *Critique of Anthropology*, December 2002.

7   The best source on Bin Laden and Afghanistan is Michael Griffin, *Reaping the Whirlwind*.

8   The account of the deal, and what happened in 2002, is based partly on following press reports in the *Guardian*, *International Herald Tribune* and *Le Monde*, but mainly on conversations with Afghans.

COLOMBIA
MIKE GONZALEZ

THE GENESIS OF PLAN COLOMBIA

As the United States issues its threats right and left, sheltering behind a 'war against terrorism' that seems to apply to all the enemies of George W Bush and his coterie, there is one long-running war that has faded into the background. Yet it continues as intensely, and as destructively, in 2003 as it had for several years before the destruction of the Twin Towers—though then it was called 'the war against drugs'. Colombia remains a testing ground for the US's ability to crush popular resistance and make sweeping attacks on living standards that masquerade behind the neutral terminology of 'structural adjustment' and 'economic globalisation'.

Plan Colombia was presented to the Colombian Congress by its then president, Andres Pastrana, in 1999. It was strongly rumoured that the Spanish document was a translation of a version written originally in English and discussed during an earlier visit to President Clinton in Washington. Whatever the anecdotal truth, there is no doubt that 'Plan Colombia is both a continuation and an escalation of US politico-military policy adapted to new global realities'.[1] That was not how it was represented, needless to say. Pastrana's justification for the plan was that it offered a strategy for restoring stability and peace to Colombia, a country whose modern history has been violent and conflict-ridden. The centrepiece of the policy, ostensibly at least, was a drugs eradication programme, enabling Clinton to argue that the plan was not a military in-

Plan Colombia is both a continuation and an escalation of US politico-military policy adapted to new global realities

tervention but an extension of domestic drugs containment policies. In fact the $1 billion of aid that Clinton sought from Congress was overwhelmingly devoted to arms and military spending. The only other measure was a large-scale programme of defoliant spraying intended, it was alleged, to eliminate coca and poppy production while leaving other crops unscathed.

The world's media (and the British government) bought the drugs eradication story and accepted the idea that the confrontation between the Colombian state and the guerrilla organisations (now renamed 'narco-guerrillas') was an extension of the drug war. The US State Department was able to report on 30 June 2001 that 'the US Congress gave final passage June 30 to an $11,200 million spending bill that includes $1,300 million in emergency aid designed to *help the government of Colombia battle the illegal drug trade*'.[2] In fact the US government knew that eradication programmes would have a negligible impact on drug use.

The Colombian government, however, was devoting most of its energies to the defeat of the guerrillas. The net effect was the increasing militarisation of Colombian society, the displacement of well over 2 million people, and the creation of a deepening economic crisis whose victims included the small farmers, trade unionists and urban refugees who repeatedly demonstrate their concerns in the streets of Colombia's cities. In reality the plan has only served to legitimise a whole range of assaults on democratic rights, to militarise all aspects of civil society, and to subordinate the interests of the majority of Colombians to the geopolitical concerns of global capitalism.

DRUGS: MYTH AND REALITY

Plan Colombia therefore allowed both the US and Colombian governments to confuse public opinion and conceal their real purposes behind the veil of a 'war on drugs'. Ostensibly this 'war' was waged on two fronts—the eradication of the coca fields and a frontal challenge to the power of the drug barons. The counter-guerrilla campaign hovered in the background as the guerrillas were deliberately confused with the drug cartels.

The Colombian drugs boom began in the 1960s when the northern regions around Santa Marta provided a marijuana much prized in the booming US market. The result was a kind of gold rush along Colombia's Caribbean coast. When US authorities began to control that trade the weed was replaced by cocaine, which was much more profitable and less bulky.[3] The raw material was the coca leaf, grown by peasants and small farmers in Bolivia and Peru, then collected in unmarked planes and taken to small laboratories and processing plants in the Amazon regions before export to the US and, in smaller quantities, Europe.

Medellín became the centre of this new drug trade. It was dominated by people like by Pablo Escobar,[4] who had emerged from the slums and shanty towns. The scale of profits involved in the trade gave the drug cartels the ability to buy and sell politicians, lawyers, judges and generals—and to murder those who refused to comply—as well as dispense largess in the poor districts which provided their bodyguards and runners. In 1990 the Medellín cartel murdered three presidential candidates, and Escobar boasted that he could pay off the national debt, or take on the Colombian army and win.

The Colombian ruling classes were deeply divided and crosshatched by regional power bases, and the state was a point of negotiation between them. In 1990 Escobar was throwing down a gauntlet to that class as a whole. And even if those classes had been corrupted and controlled by the drug cartels, they could not tolerate an alternative power within the nation-state. In 1990 Escobar was jailed in a prison of his own design, then fled into hiding before his death at the hands of the security forces. His place was then occupied by a new cartel based in Cali. Its leader, Rodriguez Orijuela, was later arrested, just as the extent of their involvement in, and control of, the government of Ernesto Samper—the very government that had proclaimed its resolve to crush the cartels—began to emerge with mounting supporting evidence. Longer term, the effect would be to lead to a reorganisation of the production of and trade in cocaine as the larger cartels shifted their attention to heroin, leaving cocaine to smaller-scale producers inside and outside Colombia.

The trumpeted eradication measures, and the spectacular assaults on coca and poppy growing areas, only affected the smallest cog in the system—the peasant growers. Since the coca plant gives a crop in 60 days, it took very little time for new crops to be grown elsewhere.

> According to a 1999 General Accounting Office report, 'Despite two years of extensive herbicide spraying [in Colombia], US estimates show [that] net coca cultivation actually increased 50 percent'.[5]

In fact:

> Even if 'successful' eradication were actually achieved in Colombia, there are 1.6 billion acres in the rest of the biophysically hospitable Amazon. That is more than 2,000 times the 740,000 acres needed to fulfil the complete international demand for cocaine. *In the entire history of the use of force against illicit crops, not one effort has succeeded in reducing the supply of natural drugs needed to fully supply the world market.*[6]

The reality, then, is that the fundamental issue is the demand, not the supply—and the US government, while willing to disburse tens of millions in spectacular interventions in the affairs of supplier countries, refuses to address the issue of why drugs are so widely used in the US. Meanwhile an estimated 50 percent of the half a trillion dollars of profit that drugs yield every year remains within the financial system of the US itself, reinvested and manipulated by some 500 or so economic actors.[7]

The US continues with its policy of spraying crops under the aegis of Plan Colombia. For nearly two decades the use of the herbicide glyphosate, it is claimed, has eliminated some 150,000 acres of land devoted to the cultivation of coca and poppy plants. In recent times the fields have been sprayed with a different agent—the myoherbicide *Fusarium oxysporum*—whose effects are far-reaching and indiscriminate. It kills a wide range of plants, and will almost certainly have catastrophic effects on the fragile ecology of the region.[8] The irresistible conclusion is that the drug eradication programme which ostensibly lies at the heart of Plan Colombia is incapable of realising its own goals. We must assume therefore that the 'war on drugs' has very different purposes.

STRATEGIES IN THE BACK YARD

Plan Colombia, as Petras emphasises, is the latest chapter in a long narrative of counter-insurgency—the succession of policies and strategies whereby the US protects the economic interests of its home-based capital.[9]

The Cuban Revolution of 1959 ushered in a new period of US-led counter-insurgency which combined military, economic and ideological interventions under the twin banners of the Alliance for Progress and the Inter-American Security Treaty. The objectives were to isolate Cuba, provide alternative routes to reform within the imperial context, and impede any growth in the development of guerrilla warfare across the continent. The iron fist emerged from the velvet glove of reform in September 1973, when Chile's experiment in radical transformation through parliament was destroyed by a US-supported military coup led, among others, by Augusto Pinochet. The Chilean coup was not just a local matter, but a strategy of militarisation and enforced economic integration. The 'Chilean miracle', proclaimed by Thatcher and others, effectively subjected workers to the laws of the market in their most brutal form while destroying their organisations of self-defence. It was ironic to hear the mock horror expressed by Western leaders when the coordination of repression by the military regimes of the southern cone (Plan Condor) emerged into full public view during the Pinochet trial. The regionalisation of the conflict and the coordination of strategies between the new military governments was the hallmark of US thinking throughout this period.

US 'low intensity operations' in Central America in the 1980s were prompted by a need to contain and limit the political impact of the Nicaraguan Revolution of 1979:

> Through the application of a flexible mix of aid blockades, trade sanctions, economic sabotage, political and psychological pressures, civic action 'pacification' programmes, military warfare and electoral intervention, Reagan-Bush policy has attempted to consolidate or install in power in Central America elected governments willing to accommodate White House objectives—not least in the economic sphere.[10]

Petras's definition does not capture the human costs of the policy—the tens of thousands of dead, the destruction of the economy, the displacement of millions towards the slums around the capital cities, the creation of monstrous corps of murderers like the Nicaraguan Contras with their specialities in the dismemberment of living bodies, the creation of a kind of counter-reform in the countryside where large swathes of land are restored to the landowners, often through the actions of peasant militias. The militarisation of society, and the implantation of terror in the countryside, render any and all forms of self-organisation or self-defence extremely dangerous. The role of the US was to support internal counter-revolutionary forces, reinforce the military through direct military aid and the provision of trainers, use international financial and other agencies to isolate and undermine the local economy, and mobilise a massive propaganda apparatus across the world.

It is those same geopolitical imperatives that impel US policy in Colombia today, though the scale of things has changed. Clinton's legacy to Latin America—Plan Colombia—both continues and develops. Significant new resources are added, and the right to intervention is reinvoked by redefining the issue as a domestic US matter (the campaign against drugs), and emphasising its international and

Colombian society is becoming increasingly militarised under the umbrella of Plan Colombia

regional nature. To that must be added the reality of a world entering the 21st century in an era of globalisation on the one hand, and mounting resistance to globalisation on the other.

The original outlays envisaged by Plan Colombia amounted to $1.3 billion. The distribution of that finance was revealing—82 percent was devoted to directly military purposes, divided between helicopters for the anti-drugs batallion of the Colombian army (47 percent), sea and river operations (27 percent), and 7 percent to the national police. Of the remainder just over 11 percent would be dedicated to alternative development projects and 7 percent towards the defence of human rights![11] This leaves very little room for doubt as to the repressive purposes of Plan Colombia. It is a *military* project whose objective is control over the southern regions of Colombia. Furthermore it is not limited to Colombia itself. The six-year projection within the plan assumes the progressive involvement of what are there described as 'partner nations'. The real significance of the term soon emerged, as the Ecuadorean government was 'persuaded' to cede to the US the Manta air base and its hinterland near the Colombian border.[12]

As the new more aggressive spraying policy begins to affect other crops, and as the confrontation between the military and the guerrilla forces grows more intense (for what other purpose can the cascade of new military material into the area have?), tens or hundreds of thousands of peasants will join the fleeing columns making for the larger cities. They will not only be escaping the increasingly generalised violence—they will also be moving because their very livelihood has been destroyed. Others, however, will swell the ranks of the guerrillas for identical reasons, and provide legitimacy for a mounting and increasingly costly military campaign.

Colombian society is becoming increasingly militarised under the umbrella of Plan Colombia—not only because the armed forces now have enormous logistical and ideological support from the powerful northern neighbour, but also because the priorities of the Colombian government are increasingly military ones. As the tide of refugees grows and the availability of basic foods declines, so the repression currently focused on the areas under

Those who came in from the cold to negotiate and became candidates in the elections of 1990 were almost all murdered

guerrilla domination has intensified. In the latter half of the 1980s, it did appear that a political space was opening in parallel with the settlements reached between the leaderships of the armed struggle and the state in Central America. But as elements in the Colombian state opened dialogue with the M-19 and the Farc guerrillas, many within the military establishment were demanding a repressive solution. Those who came in from the cold to negotiate and became candidates in the elections of 1990 were almost all murdered. Trade union leaders and militants in social movements were assassinated in growing numbers. The assault on the cocaine barons, by contrast, yielded almost nothing. Some were captured, some killed, but the structures of their invisible order remained intact.

The reality was that the Colombian state was powerless to impose any kind of national solution or to initiate a process of reform. While the army complained bitterly that it was perpetually being restrained in its counter-guerrilla activity, and darkly criticised the political agenda and the concept of peace as essentially the concession of victory to the guerrillas, the political class was so compromised and corrupt that it could not seize the window that had briefly opened before it.[13] The army's frustration expressed itself in the growth of the paramilitary organisations who terrorised populations, and waged a private and undocumented war against the rural population. It is quite clear that these were the irregulars of the Colombian army, and that in many cases their connections with the military were intimate and immediate.[14] On the other hand, they were also directly connected to the drug cartels—or were instruments of rival factions. This did not stop them enjoying the covert support of sections of the army, the political class, and indeed US agencies like the CIA.

It is bitterly ironic that one of the principal leaders of the para-military gangs, Carlos Castaño, is now offering himself as a bro-ker between the Colombian government, the drug barons and the US government.[15] The new Colombian president, Alvaro Uribe, continued the long tradition of sustaining two contrary positions at once when, towards the end of 2002, his government both announced a crackdown on the paramilitaries and contin-ued the policy of 'peace negotiations' with them.

For any who imagined that Plan Colombia would bring the paramilitaries under control, or limit their activities, this is the most public of replies. The paramilitaries will become effectively absorbed into a strategy of military containment and control. Their leaders, like Carlos Castaño, will be incorporated into the structures of a new, militarised state.

When Alvaro Uribe assumed office in August 2002, almost his first act was to announce the creation of a million-person network of spies and informers culled from the ranks of the displaced and the unemployed. In addition, weapons would be supplied to a net-work of armed peasant militias, the very sectors who had provided the social base for the AUC and other paramilitary organisations. These would operate in support of an expanding military cam-paign, as the accords with the guerrillas reached by Pastrana were abandoned, and open war engaged.

THE WIDER FRAME

What are the perspectives that inform US policy in Latin America? The framework for Plan Colombia is marked by two key dates as far as economic policy is concerned. In January 1994 the long-prepared North America Free Trade Area (Nafta) was announced, drawing Canada, Mexico and the US into 'a tariff-free zone of eco-nomic activity'. This was the first stage in a new phase of global economic integration. The second was the creation of the Free Trade Area of the Americas (FTAA), which was finally agreed, with sirens and the explosion of teargas canisters as background music, at Quebec City in April 2001. This would complete the absorption of Latin America into a global economic system.

Venezuela (now no longer necessarily a 'partner nation') was

COLOMBIA & THE IMF

The Colombian government reassured the IMF that the government had initiated roundtable discussions with unions and the business community about 'restructuring and downsizing...the public sector...to increase efficiency and minimise duplications'. It added, 'The government remains committed to a liberal trade regime...agricultural sector protection and import tariff dispersion will be set in accordance to Andean pact rules, and will meet the deadlines set by the WTO.'

THE PEOPLE'S RESPONSE

AUGUST 2001

Farmers cause widespread protests, frustrated in their efforts to persuade the government to give them financial aid and to end food imports. Thousands of small farmers, organised by the Movement of Farm Salvation, join rural communities in setting up roadblocks across the country. At least two protesters die when the police use teargas and armoured vehicles to break them up.

Trade unions in the capital, Bogota, go on solidarity strike in support of bus and taxi drivers, who are protesting against increased taxes. Hector Fajardo, secretary general of the United Workers' Federation, says, 'We shall go on to the streets to support Bogota's drivers and protest against the neoliberal programme emerging in Colombia.'

DECEMBER 2001-JANUARY 2002

Municipal workers from the Sintraemcali union occupy the 17-storey Central Administration Building of Colombia's water, electricity and telecom companies (Emcali). Workers demand an end to privatisation plans. The union successfully closes the building for a month and negotiates a peaceful settlement, which involves shelving plans to privatise the company and promises to maintain low prices for the poor. Outside the building over 800 people support the occupation. Despite police aggression they provide food for the people inside. Marches and concerts are organised to support the action, which attract thousands more people. The occupation ends after over ten months of 'local action', mainly comprising of 'mingas', where workers provide services to the poor for free on weekends.

From a report by MARK ELLIS JONES of WDM www.wdm.org.uk

the key supplier of oil in the region, but Colombia possesses major deposits of oil and natural gas, currently exploited by foreign multi-nationals and distributed through the state oil enterprise Ecopetrol. The scale of deposits means that Colombia will become a powerful player in the world oil trade. To a lesser extent, so too will neighbouring Ecuador. Control of these resources—as well as other important export areas like flowers and other commodities—is crucial to the growth and expansion of the regional 'free trade' area. Ecuador's economy has already been 'dollarised'—that is, integrated into a global economy. Venezuela, on the other hand, is now run by the nationalist-populist Chávez regime, its rhetoric clearly rooted in a politics of national liberation and anti-imperialism. As I write, Chávez's future is uncertain, as a coalition of business-led interests lead the country into the fifth week of a national strike. Colombia's role, as a political focus and as an oil producer, becomes even more central.

It would be tempting, as James Petras does for example,[16] to see the struggle between the guerrilla organisations and the Colombian state as the core of the conflict. Sections of both right and left describe it that way. And it is certainly true that the Farc's control of a very large area, as agreed with the previous president, Pastrana, was wholly unacceptable to the imperialists and their domestic allies. After all, in an era of globalisation, capital's freedom of movement is of the essence. There can be no liberated territories in such a scheme.

There is not, as some commentators have suggested, a direct parallel to be drawn between Colombia and Vietnam. There is no long history of colonial war, no national liberation struggle as such, no international power struggle reflected in the specific arena. The liberated territories under Farc control do not correspond to the existence of a state (North Vietnam) with its own mass military organs. If, on the other hand, the reference is to the possibility that the US may find itself compelled to commit large numbers of troops in the face of the collapse of its local surrogate and the decomposition of the military command (as in South Vietnam), then I think this unlikely too. The Colombian army is numerous and well organised, all the more so with the high level of training and support it has received throughout the 1990s (and not just since the implementation of Plan Colombia) from the US. What Plan Col-

61 percent of 44 million Colombians live in absolute poverty

ombia does represent is an escalation of that involvement—and a clear perception on the part of the US that the Colombian state cannot coordinate or impose a political solution across the national territory without the support and the direct involvement of the US military.

But can the guerrillas be defeated? The major guerrilla organisations—the Farc (Revolutionary Armed Forces of Colombia), the ELN (National Liberation Army) and the ERP (People's Revolutionary Army)—have long, albeit different, histories. The Farc, under its legendary leader Manuel Marulanda (or Tirofijo, meaning 'Sureshot'), emerged during the years of La Violencia, the 14-year period during which all political life in Colombia was played out in armed conflict. La Violencia began with the assassination in the capital, Bogotá, of a trade unionist and Liberal presidential candidate, Jorge Eliécer Gaitán. The violent reaction to his death set in motion a process in which social struggles 'degenerated into local party feuds'.[17] In some areas the Communist Party began to organise armed peasant defence organisations and to introduce the land issue into their demands. But the irony was that this was a boom time for the Colombian bourgeoisie. Industrial production rose while wages fell—small wonder when all forms of independent organisation were repressed in both city and countryside.

In the second half of the 1950s successive governments tried to negotiate an end to the violence, yet each amnesty or ceasefire produced more violence and death. In any event, the amnesties did not apply to the Communist Party, which had now grouped several thousand peasant families into areas of the south known as the independent republics, like Marquetalia. In 1963 these were invaded and crushed by the Colombian army. Those who escaped the subsequent repression formed mobile guerrilla groups which met (for the second time) in 1966 to form the Farc.[18]

The Farc is indelibly marked by the circumstances of its birth. It emerged first as, and has remained in essence, an organisation of peasant self-defence. In the anarchic conditions of the Colombian countryside, it has in many ways constituted both a form of local administration and, as Jenny Pearce puts it, 'virtually a rural civil guard'. As violence, official and paramilitary, has continued to characterise daily life for most of Colombia's rural population, organised self-defence has increasingly become the major issue, but the base of the Farc is among small farmers living in precarious conditions. Many of them grow coca—and the Farc has taken a tax from this as from all other activities in the areas under its control. This has allowed the US and its allies to coin the term 'narco-guerrillas'—and to lump the Farc together with the drug producing cartels as if they were two faces of the same phenomenon. Their profits seem to be modest—they have very few of the trappings of the servants of the drug cartels, no AK-47s or Russian second-hand submarines. They also appear to be highly disciplined and punish any violation with some ruthlessness. Their attempts in the 1980s to move into parliamentary politics were met with a murderous response in which many of their leaders were killed by death squads almost certainly rooted in the army. Petras states that 'in most of their dealings with the rural population, the Farc represents order, rectitude and social justice'. The repression that followed fell equally on the other armed organisations.

The Farc's rival, the ELN, was founded in the mid-1960s by students, intellectuals and left wing priests. Its methods have continued to rest on the perception of the guerrillas as substitutes for the masses—kidnappings, particularly of oil company employees, have gained them the resources for survival. By 1993 the Farc declared a renewed military offensive in the face of stagnation in the peace negotiations, just at the time when the ELN for the first time was opening discussions with the government of Ernesto Samper. Later, under Pastrana, the talks with the ELN remained in suspension, while he reopened discussions with the Farc.

But all that is history now, as President Alvaro Uribe launches a new initiative to prepare for the imposition of the programmes and projects of global neoliberalism. Negotiations with the Farc have ended, and the creation of new civil militias together with an intensification of direct military repression leaves little doubt as to the general conditions he is setting out to create.

What then is driving Plan Colombia? If it is not drug eradication or a counter-insurgency war, what is the long term strategic direction of the succession of Colombian presidents, and of the newest in the line, Uribe? The key is in the testimony of the trade unionists and activists who are in the forefront of the battle against economic policies that faithfully reflect the long term aims of the FTAA. Some 3,500 trade unionists have been murdered in the last ten years. In recent months the military, the police or the paramilitaries have attacked marches against education cuts, against privatisation, against the failure to fulfil the promise of land reform, and in favour of human rights.

Behind the veil of the counter-guerrilla war, Plan Colombia has done nothing to address the rising debt problem, the deepening unemployment and the crisis in human and civil rights which have afflicted the country in recent times. All it has done is reinforce the machinery of repression that is increasingly directed at those who are fighting neoliberalism. In Cali, the public sector workers' union has been subjected to constant assault, and its leaders move constantly from refuge to refuge as the death threats follow them and their families. Hundreds of thousands of Colombians have fled the country. Today 61 percent of 44 million Colombians live in absolute poverty, and 60 percent of the economically active population live from hand to mouth without jobs or in occasional employment.

This has been the achievement of Plan Colombia. It has enriched the tiny minority who head the state, and provided the means for that state to crush resistance to the economic strategies that promise only poverty. The extraordinary and inspiring thing is that the struggle for human rights, public ownership and the right to a decent life continues even in the face of repression—just as it has in Ecuador and Bolivia. That struggle is sure to continue.

Mike Gonzalez is a senior lecturer in Hispanic studies at Glasgow University. He was the co-author of *The Gathering of Voices: The Twentieth Century Poetry of Latin America* and edited *The Routledge Encyclopedia of Latin American Culture*. He is an active member of the Scottish Socialist Party (www.scottishsocialistparty.org)

NOTES

1 James Petras, 'The Geopolitics of Plan Colombia', *Monthly Review*, vol 53 no 1 (May 2001), p31.

2 US Department of State website, 'International Information Programs', 30 June 2001, my emphasis.

3 See Colin Harding, *Colombia: A Guide to the People, Politics and Culture* (London: Latin America Bureau, 1996), pp28-36. For a general discussion, see Jenny Pearce, *Colombia: Inside the Labyrinth* (London: Latin America Bureau, 1990), chapter 2.1, 'Colombia's Two Economies', and in particular pp103-115.

4 Escobar's story is most powerfully told by Gabriel García Márquez in his *News of a Kidnapping* (London: Jonathan Cape, 1997).

5 Winifred Tate, 'Repeating Past Mistakes', *NACLA Report on the Americas*, vol XXXIV, no 2 (September/October 2000), p17.

6 Ricardo Vargas Meza, 'Biowarfare in Colombia?', *NACLA Report on the Americas*, vol XXXIV, no 3 (September/ October 2000), p21, my emphasis.

7 This conclusion of an OECD report is quoted in the document 'Plan Colombia: Máscaras y artificios' by Belén Vásconez of the Comisión Ecuménica de Derechos Humanos of Ecuador, published on the web by the Pulsar Agency on 27 November 2000.

8 Documented in convincing detail by Ricardo Vargas Meza in 'Biowarfare in Colombia?'

9   For a general picture of that relationship Eduardo Galeano's classic *Open Veins of Latin America* (New York: Monthly Review Press, 1967) remains unsurpassed.

10 James Petras and Morris Morley, *Latin America in a Time of Cholera* (London/New York: Routledge, 1992), p63.

11 These figures are quote by Ricardo Vargas Meza in a fine piece called 'Plan Colombia: ¿construcción de paz o sobredosis de guerra?' on the Equipo Nizkor website, www.derechos.org/nizkor/colombia/doc/vargas.html

12 In January 2003 a new president of Ecuador, Lucio Gutiérrez, will take power. He represents a coalition which includes the indigenous organisations, and his nominee for foreign minister is an indigenous woman.

13 It is interesting now to return to Jenny Pearce's characteristically thorough and insightful study *Colombia: Inside the Labyrinth*, completed in 1989 and published the following year. She ends her book with this perspicacious question: 'Can an economy that has created only 500,000 jobs in manufacturing, which a leaked World Bank Report (July 1989) describes as closed and meeting the needs only of a minority, provide the majority of its population with a humane existence and the means to a livelihood? The archaic political order that has kept that minority in power has proved incapable of taking on this responsibility. The bomb will carry on ticking until it does, or until the left proves itself able to unite the people around an alternative social and political project' (p287).

14 Nazih Richani, 'The Paramilitary Connection', *NACLA Report on the Americas*, vol XXXIV, no 2 (September/October 2000), pp38-41.

15 See Nazih Richani, 'The Paramilitary Connection'.

16 See Garry M Leech, 'The Drug War: An

Exercise in Futility', *Colombia Report*, 16
April 2001, www.colombiareport.org

17 'Plan Colombia has to be seen as an
attempt to behead the most advanced,
radicalised and well organised opposition to
US hemispheric hegemony'—James Petras,
'The Geopolitics of Plan Colombia', p35.

18 Jenny Pearce, *Colombia: Inside the
Labyrinth*, p47.

19 See Jenny Pearce, *Colombia: Inside the
Labyrinth*, pp49-68.

Popular protests from Serbian workers and students successfully toppled Milosevic in October 2000

BALKANS
DRAGAN PLAVŠIC

The bloody break-up of Yugoslavia during the 1990s has been viewed in the West as the inevitable result of longstanding hatreds among the nations that inhabit the Balkans. By contrast, Western intervention in the region by the United States, Britain and the European Community[1] has been viewed as an anti-nationalist force for multi-ethnic tolerance and democracy. This chapter is an attempt to explain why the widespread belief that Western intervention has played a positive role in the Balkans cannot be sustained by the evidence.

It is possible to separate out three major phases of Western intervention during the break-up of Yugoslavia. The first phase encompassed the 1980s, when intervention appeared primarily in its economic form in the shape of the International Monetary Fund, or an early version of what is today commonly called 'globalisation'. The economic measures imposed by the IMF laid the groundwork for the rise of nationalism and the collapse of Yugoslavia. The second phase, spanning the early 1990s, was marked by the leading political role played by the European Community as war consumed Yugoslavia. In this phase the policy of arbitration between the warring parties adopted by the EC had the effect of reinforcing nationalism and entrenching ethnic divisions. The third phase began with the run-up to the Dayton accords of 1995 in Bosnia, a watershed marked by the decisive military intervention of the US, which was ultimately to reach its high point with the bombing of Serbia in 1999. In this phase US policy moved to backing one set of nationalists against another.

FIRST PHASE: IMF ECONOMIC INTERVENTION

The first phase marks the prelude to the break-up of Yugoslavia. Tito's Yugoslavia had borrowed heavily from abroad to fuel growth in the 1970s, but its failure to keep up with repayments when the world economy went into recession in the late 1970s resulted in Yugoslavia falling victim to one of the earliest 'structural adjustment programmes' imposed by the IMF. As elsewhere, the IMF's anti-inflationary policy involved severe measures such as cuts in public sector spending together with the liberalisation of trade and prices. The effects were disastrous. By the mid-1980s the situation for ordinary Yugoslavs had become critical. As Susan L Woodward has observed, 'By 1985-86 the preconditions for a revolutionary situation were apparent. One million people were officially registered as unemployed. The increasing rate of unemployment was above 20 percent in all republics except Slovenia and Croatia. Inflation was at 50 percent a year and climbing. The household savings of approximately 80 percent of the population were depleted'.[2] The result was a massive growth of strike militancy across Yugoslavia. In 1983 there were less than 100 strikes; in 1985, 699 strikes; in 1986, 851 strikes. And in 1987 there were 1,570 strikes involving 365,000 workers, or one tenth of the workforce.

The pressure of mass social unrest from below meant that Yugoslavia's leaders, who had faithfully implemented the IMF's market reforms, could not carry on ruling in the old way. The depth of the economic crisis led directly to political crisis, as each national government within Yugoslavia sought out new sources of ideological legitimacy. The slogans of the Tito years now appeared obviously ineffective. They found this new political 'legitimacy' in the form of nationalism. In Serbia, Slobodan Milosevic defused social unrest with his nationalist campaign against the Albanians of Kosovo. On one occasion, confronted in Belgrade by 20,000 angry Serbian workers, Milosevic cajoled them with nationalist

One million people were officially registered as unemployed. The increasing rate of unemployment was above 20 percent in all republics except Slovenia and Croatia myths. As one commentator observed at the time, the 'workers arrived at the protest as workers but they left as Serbs'.[3] In Croatia, Franjo Tudjman rose to power by intimidating the Serb minority and proudly proclaiming that his wife was 'neither a Serb nor a Jew'. In Slovenia, Milan Kucan, the head of the Slovenian Communists, promised prosperity with the slogan of 'Europe, now!' In Bosnia nationalist parties came to lead the Muslims, Serbs and Croats.

By the late 1980s the consequences of this first phase of Western intervention were clear. The IMF-imposed model of market-based restructuring—or globalisation—served as the *economic* precondition to the initial collapse of Yugoslavia. The mass social unrest it provoked and the rise to power of leaders who used nationalism to defuse it then served as the *political* precondition to the further slide of Yugoslavia into full-scale war. The very countries in the West whose economic policies had failed so disastrously in Yugoslavia now sought political solutions to the crisis they had helped to create. They were to succeed only in adding fuel to the fire.

SECOND PHASE: EC POLITICAL INTERVENTION

The second phase of Western intervention takes us from the economic to the political plane, to the response of the European Community to war in Yugoslavia.

The EC's own Badinter commission had advised that Croatia did not fulfil the requirements for recognising its independence because of its failure to respect free speech and the rights of its large Serb minority. Despite this, Germany pre-emptively recognised Croatia and Slovenia in December 1991 in the hope of gaining influence in the region by stealing a march on its EC partners and the US. The rest of the EC swiftly followed suit in January 1992. By this time war between Croatia and Serbia was well under way, but recognition did nothing to assuage the conflict, as advocates of it had argued it would. On the contrary, recognition only ensured the spread of war to Bosnia. The then UN secretary general, Perez de

The West tried to act as arbiter between the claims of competing nationalists, but not in any sense as an opponent of them

Cuellar, said that he felt 'deeply worried that any early, selective recognition would widen the present conflict and fuel an explosive situation especially in Bosnia-Herzegovina and also Macedonia, indeed serious consequences could ensue for the entire Balkan region'.[4] The referendum on independence in Bosnia held shortly after EC recognition of Croatia disastrously pitted Bosnia's Muslims and Croats against each other. They voted almost unanimously in favour of independence against the Serbs, who overwhelmingly boycotted the vote. In short, premature EC recognition of Croatia forced Bosnia into an impossible referendum that led directly to war.

It is in the bloody and brutal conflict in Bosnia that we can see a main role that Western intervention played in the Balkans during the first half of the 1990s. The West tried to act as arbiter between the claims of competing nationalists, but not in any sense as an opponent of them. This policy entailed nothing less than tacit acceptance of the very logic of the nationalists, whose overriding goal was to carve out the largest possible territory for their own ethnic group. In practical terms, the EC colluded with the nationalists in order to facilitate a negotiated division of Bosnia along ethnic lines. This would ultimately become acceptable to all three sides. This policy opened the door to the destruction of the intermixed demographic structure of Bosnia by one round of ethnic cleansing after another, and its replacement by ethnically exclusive enclaves.

The interminable rounds of diplomacy the EC conducted in the early 1990s all followed this strategy. From the Lisbon plan of 1992, which proposed cantonising Bosnia into Bosnian Muslim, Serb and Croat enclaves, to the Vance-Owen plan of 1993, which proposed ten ethnic enclaves, to the Owen-Stoltenburg plan of

1993 and the Contact Group Plan of 1994, which both reverted to the idea of three ethnic cantons, all of the plans paid only lip service to the idea of a multi-ethnic Bosnia. As the Sarajevo journalist Tihomir Loza wrote of the Lisbon plan, it was 'a programme of division and will produce permanent instability. It will fuel rather than satisfy the Great Serbian and Croatian territorial claims in Bosnia... Ultimately the EC proposal will fail because it is a foreign solution... And it is foreign to the Balkans, in terms of historic ethnic borderlines and the Bosnian tradition of coexistence'.[5]

Contrary to the EC's stated goals, the result was not to weaken the forces of nationalism but to strengthen them. Each so-called 'peace plan' legitimised the claims of the nationalists, and fuelled ethnic cleansing for territorial gain to reinforce the machiavellian bargaining over borders that each side undertook at the negotiating table.

This is the essential context of the terrible massacre of Muslims by the Serbs at Srebrenica. But Srebrenica was also the base from which, according to Misha Glenny, the Muslims had launched offensives to regain territory from the Serbs, moving 'swiftly through Serbian villages, slaughtering a large number of civilians on the way'.[6] Elsewhere Bosnian Croats and Muslims fought no less bitterly over control of central Bosnia and over devastated towns such as Mostar. This context only fuelled the plans Milosevic and Tudjman had secretly discussed of dividing Bosnia between them. Thus otherwise bitter enemies, such as the Bosnian Serb leader Radovan Karadzic and his Bosnian Croat counterpart, Mate Boban, met secretly in Austria to discuss the carve-up of Bosnia. Tudjman himself sat down to dinner one infamous evening in London in 1995 with Paddy Ashdown, leader of the British Liberal Democrats. He brazenly drew out on the back of a menu card his vision of a Bosnia divided between Croatia and Serbia.

The conclusion to be drawn from this tragic history is clear. The EC was not an anti-nationalist force—its plans legitimised and fuelled nationalism. The EC did not save multi-ethnic Bosnia—it helped to bury it. Paying only lip service to the ideal of multi-ethnicity, the EC oversaw the bloody partition of Bosnia into mutually hostile ethnic enclaves.

THIRD PHASE: US MILITARY INTERVENTION

The third phase of Western intervention was marked by the decisive entrance of the US on the Balkan scene. The continued bloodletting in the Balkans represented a serious obstacle to US plans to extend its power into Eastern Europe through the medium of Nato. These plans would reach fruition in the late 1990s at the time of the bombing of Serbia. The Clinton administration came to realise that the opportunity that had arisen in the late 1980s of expansion eastwards into the vacuum created by the collapse of the Russian Empire and the Warsaw Pact could not be successfully exploited without a decisive demonstration of US power in the Balkans. The strategy the US adopted to achieve this demonstrates the other main way in which imperialism has intervened in the region, not as an arbiter between the warring parties, but as a partisan sponsor of one nationalist group, or groups, against another. This led to direct US complicity in the crimes of the nationalists it chose to back.

CROATIA AND BOSNIA

The first step the US undertook was to forge the Washington accords of March 1994. It brought about an unholy alliance between the Croat president, Franjo Tudjman, and the Bosnian Muslim president, Alija Izetbegovic, whose forces had until then been fighting bitterly in Bosnia. In forging this alliance, the US explicitly chose sides in the civil war. As the former EC negotiator David Owen commented later, 'After the Washington accords the US appeared increasingly to join Germany in seeing Tudjman's government as a strategic as well as a political ally against the Serbs. This relationship made it easier for the Croatian government to defy the UN in Croatia, and to some extent the EU, as well as to risk attacking the [Krajina] Serbs living in Croatia'.[7] In fact the US broke the UN Security Council weapons embargo on the former Yugoslavia, and began covertly supplying arms to the Croats and the Muslims. Meanwhile 15 'retired' senior US officers, employees of a US company, Military Professional Resources Inc, arrived to help train Croat and Muslim soldiers, and to assist in military planning.

The complicity of the US in this act of mass ethnic cleansing received relatively little attention from the Western media

The US backing of Croatia led to the single most successful act of ethnic cleansing in the Balkan wars of 1991-95. In August 1995 Tudjman launched Operation Storm, a mass offensive against the Krajina, ethnically cleansing 150,000 Serbs from their homes within a few days. US naval aircraft bombed Krajina Serb missile positions. With some understatement, Ivo Daalder, a former National Security Adviser to President Clinton, has written that Operation Storm 'did not catch Washington by surprise'.[8] In fact, he records how one senior administration official he interviewed characterised Clinton's policy towards a Croatian attack on the Krajina as 'an amber light tinted green'.[9] Richard Holbrooke, the principal US envoy in the Balkans, met Tudjman one month later and 'indicated [his] general support for the offensive'.[10] When some US officials questioned Tudjman's cleansing of the Serbs, Holbrooke's aide, Robert Frasure, wrote him a note which read, 'We hired these guys [Tudjman and the Croatian army] to be our junkyard dogs because we were desperate. We need to try to control them. But this is no time to get squeamish about things'.[11]

The complicity of the US in this act of mass ethnic cleansing received relatively little attention from the Western media. Its complicity in the event was the inevitable result of its backing of Croatia's nationalists. Such complicity flies in the face of the claim that US intervention in the Balkans has been an anti-nationalist force for multi-ethnic tolerance. Operation Storm was but a prelude to a wider offensive against the Bosnian Serbs by combined Croat-Muslim forces supported by decisive US air attacks, during which a further 60,000 Serbs were ethnically cleansed. The extent to which the offensive was US-sponsored was revealed when the Clinton administration ordered the Croats and Muslims to halt their offensive before reaching the Serb-held city of Banja Luka, which they duly did. Holbrooke told Tudjman and Izetbegovic that the city was 'unquestionably within the Serb portion of Bosnia'.[12] Thus, although the US broke with the EC's policy of arbitration between the warring sides by backing its own chosen nationalists, it did not break with the logic of partition that had dominated EC diplomacy in the early 1990s. On the contrary, the Dayton accords of 1995, which followed the successful Croat-Muslim offensive and the defeat of the Bosnian Serbs, sounded

In no sense, then, have ethnic divisions in Bosnia been overcome. On the contrary, they have been entrenched, reinforced and institutionalised by Western intervention

the final death knell for multi-ethnic Bosnia. In order to seal the accords and the version of partition favoured by the US, the Clinton administration sought the assistance of none other than Slobodan Milosevic, one of the architects of the bloody division of Bosnia. At the US air force base in Dayton, Ohio, Izetbegovic, Milosevic and Tudjman pored over the map of Bosnia and thrashed out where the new borders between the Muslims, Serbs and Croats would henceforth run, under the imperial gaze of the US.

The Dayton accords divided Bosnia yet again into three ethnically exclusive enclaves, only this time with a reduced Serb share of territory. A UN protectorate was also imposed, guaranteed by the US and the West. As a result, Bosnia today is a grotesque caricature of multi-ethnicity and democracy. Since 1995 it has been governed by four successive International High Representatives, each one directly appointed by the West. As one authority on Bosnia has explained, 'It is a powerful job, very similar to that of a colonial governor, with the authority to sack elected presidents and prime ministers, and to impose legislation by decree'.[13] The present incumbent is none other than Paddy Ashdown, who assumed the post in May 2002. Since that time he has already sacked one Croat and one Serb minister. The irony of the situation is glaring—a Western liberal politician exercising dictatorial powers to prevent Bosnia imploding from the bitter divisions between the Muslims, Serbs and Croats that the West helped to inflame. In no sense, then, have ethnic divisions in Bosnia been overcome. On the contrary, they have been entrenched, reinforced and institutionalised by Western intervention.

KOSOVO

The second decisive intervention the US made in the Balkans was Nato's 78-day bombing of Milosevic's Serbia in 1999. The alleged humanitarian purpose of the bombardment was to put an end to the repression of the Albanians of Kosovo at the hands of the Serbian government. Serbian repression was certainly fierce, but notably less fierce in scope and intensity than Turkey's repression of the Kurds or Indonesia's repression of the East Timorese, both humanitarian disasters the West did nothing to stop. The US and Britain continued to supply Turkey and Indonesia with military hardware during the 1990s even at the height of the repression. Of the 20 or more conflicts raging across the globe at the time, why did Kosovo become the focus of the military attentions of the US, Britain and Nato?

It is impossible to provide a rational answer to this question without setting the bombing in a broader geopolitical context. Just as the disintegration of the Turkish Empire in the Balkans in the 19th and early 20th centuries created a power vacuum that the Russian and Austro-Hungarian empires tried to fill, thereby provoking the First World War, so the US has tried to fill the vacuum created by the collapse of the Russian Empire and the Warsaw Pact by expanding Nato membership eastwards. Unlike other areas of the world, except the Middle East where oil is the crucial factor, the Balkans became a geopolitical hotspot of critical importance for the US strategy of expansion eastwards and the containment of Russia.

Thus in March 1999, the same month that the bombing of Serbia began, the Czech Republic, Poland and Hungary joined Nato. At Nato's Washington summit in April, Georgia, Ukraine, Azerbaijan, Moldova and Uzbekistan, all formerly part of the Soviet Empire, formed Guuam, an alliance with close economic and political ties to the West. Continuing instability in the Balkans over Kosovo was as much a threat to these plans of expansion as it was an opportunity to demonstrate the power of the US and Nato to crush a Balkan ally of Russia and, by implication, any other recalcitrant state that stood in their way. The fact that Nato embarked on the first 'out of area' military campaign of its 50-year history, while the US and Britain simply ignored the UN Security Council, signalled the depth of US determination to take advantage of this historical opportunity for imperial

The option of a peaceful solution to the Kosovo crisis was pushed aside in the rush to wage war

expansion. In short, the war against Serbia was a classic act of US geopolitical opportunism that exploited the plight of the Kosovan Albanians as a Trojan horse for the far greater prize of imperial expansion eastwards.

Entangled with this drive eastwards was a subsidiary economic motive for the bombing. This involved plans for the construction of a trans-Balkan pipeline via Bulgaria, Macedonia and Albania from the Caspian Sea, where massive capital investment by Western oil multinationals has taken place over the last decade. On 2 June 1999, one day before Serbia sued for peace, the US ambassador to Bulgaria, Avis Bohlen, signed an agreement with the Bulgarian deputy prime minister, Evgeni Bakardjiev, which awarded the country $588,000 to help fund a feasibility study on such a pipeline. The director of the US Trade and Development Agency, J Joseph Grandmaison, stated that 'the competition is fierce to tap energy resources in the Caspian region... This grant represents a significant step forward...for US business interests in the Caspian region'.[14]

The option of a peaceful solution to the Kosovo crisis was pushed aside in the rush to wage war. This became only too clear during the Rambouillet negotiations that the US presided over in early 1999. The terms put to Serbia were clearly not intended to bring about peace, but to ensure their rejection as a pretext for war. Annex B of the Rambouillet accords provided for the virtual military occupation of Yugoslavia. Nato would be entitled to enter any part of Yugoslavia, move military equipment freely through Yugoslavian airspace, ports and roads, use water, gas and electricity free of charge, and be immune from all Yugoslavian laws. Lord Gilbert, Britain's second most senior defence minister during the bombing, later told the House of Commons defence select committee, 'I think certain people were spoiling for a fight in Nato at that time. I think the terms put to Milosevic at Rambouillet were absolutely intolerable—how could he possibly accept them? It was quite deliberate'.[15]

The humanitarian claims made for the war were resoundingly hollow, even on their own terms. Rather than prevent a humanitarian catastrophe, the bombing actually created one, as Serbian paramilitaries responded to Nato's air attacks by embarking on the mass ethnic cleansing of some three quarters of a million Albanians from Kosovo. Even Nato's commander, General Wesley Clark, admitted that the cleansing was an 'entirely predictable' consequence of the bombing.[16] The BBC's foreign editor, John Simpson, who was expelled from Serbia by Milosevic during the war, later wrote that the bombing 'gave Slobodan Milosevic's thugs an excuse to murder even more ethnic Albanians'.[17] The US backing of the Albanian nationalists of Kosovo, the Kosovo Liberation Army (KLA), followed their earlier strategy adopted in relation to the Croat-Muslim alliance in Bosnia. In both cases local nationalists served as Nato's troops on the ground, while Nato provided decisive air support, with tragic consequences. At the end of the war, as Albanians returned to the homes that they had fled to escape Serb retribution over the bombing, some 200,000 Serbs and Roma suffered reverse ethnic cleansing at the hands of the KLA. Few have since returned. As in 1995, Western support for one set of nationalists against another entailed direct complicity in their crimes.

The other direct consequence of the war was to provoke conflict in neighbouring Macedonia in early 2001. There the Albanian nationalists of the National Liberation Army, modelled on the KLA and emboldened by US backing for the Albanian cause, began a guerrilla campaign for minority rights that provoked the ire of Macedonian nationalists and threatened the partition of the state into ethnically exclusive zones. Nato's bombardment of Serbia and its backing for the KLA ensured the spread of conflict even deeper into the Balkans. It left an explosive balance between two sets of nationalists in Macedonia, which the West has so far only just managed to control.

Inevitably, the Kosovo that emerged from the war against Yugoslavia, like Bosnia before it, is not the multi-ethnic democracy the West claimed it wanted to establish. The remnants of the

Serb and Roma minorities are shut up within their mini-enclaves and require round the clock UN protection from hostile Albanians. As in Bosnia, it is the UN special representative, a Western appointee, and not the Albanians themselves, who holds real power in the province. This includes the power to dissolve the Kosovan assembly, to control the police and the judiciary, to decide on economic policy and even to conduct foreign affairs.[18] One anonymous Albanian official has commented that 'they listen to us, they'll hear our views, but there's no way that we can actually participate in formulating policy. This colonial approach is not what we expected'.[19] The military guarantor of this 'colonial approach' is Camp Bondsteel in southern Kosovo, the largest military base the US has constructed abroad since the Vietnam War. By any objective standard, Kosovo today is not a multi-ethnic democracy. It is altogether more accurate to call it by its proper name—a Western colony.

THE SERBIAN REVOLUTION

The one beacon of hope amid this tragic history of Western intervention was the Serbian Revolution of October 2000 that brought down the regime of Slobodan Milosevic. Having lost the presidential elections to Vojislav Kostunica, Milosevic tried to fix the results, only to be confronted by a mass uprising against him across the length and breadth of Serbia. There was a general strike, led by 7,500 defiant miners of the giant Kolubara mining complex in central Serbia, and a million-strong demonstration in Belgrade on 5 October stormed the federal parliament. They overthrew the Milosevic regime within a matter of days. Noam Chomsky subsequently observed:

> What happened was a very impressive demonstration of popular mobilisation and courage. The removal of [Milosevic] is an important step forward for the region, and the mass movements in Serbia— miners, students, innumerable others—merit great admiration and provide an inspiring example of what united and dedicated people can achieve.[20]

There is no starker contrast in the history of the Balkans of the last decade than that between Western intervention and the Serbian Revolution. Where the West brought colonial rule to Bosnia and Kosovo, the revolution brought democracy to Serbia. Where the West sanctioned ethnic cleansing on a mass scale in Croatia, Bosnia and Kosovo, the revolution ethnically cleansed no one. Where the West failed to secure Milosevic's overthrow with 78 days of bombing, the revolution felled him within a few days. Where the West brought death to hundreds of innocent civilians, the revolution cost three lives.[21] And where the West's bombs wrought $30 billion worth of economic damage to Serbia, the revolution succeeded without destroying one factory, bridge, hospital or school.[22] As with the Romanian Revolution of 1989 that overthrew the tyrannical Nicolae Ceausescu, and the Albanian Revolution of 1997 that brought down the autocratic Sali Berisha, the Serbian Revolution demonstrated that real progress in the Balkans can only be secured when it is the work of the people themselves.[23] As one Belgrade University student told the BBC, 'We did it on our own. Please do not help us again with your bombs'.[24]

Dragan Plavsic is a regular contributor to *Socialist Review* **on Balkan affairs**
dragan@plavsic.freeserve.co.uk

NOTES

Thanks to Nicolai Gentchev and Andreja Zivkovic for their comments on this article.

1 I refer to the European Community (EC) throughout. The EC did not become the European Union until 1 November 1993 when its initial political intervention in the Balkans was already drawing to a close.

2 Susan L Woodward, *Balkan Tragedy: Chaos and Dissolution After the Cold War* (Washington DC, 1995), p73.

3 Quoted in Zoran Stojiljkovic, 'Budjenje radnicke Srbije' ('Working Serbia Awakes'), in the Belgrade weekly

Blicnews, no 25 (19-25 April 2000). My translation.

4   Quoted in David Owen, *Balkan Odyssey* (London, 1995), p376.

5   Tihomir Loza, 'Separation Anxiety', *Yugofax Journal—Breakdown: War & Reconstruction in Yugoslavia* (London, 1992), p30.

6   Misha Glenny, *The Fall of Yugoslavia: The Third Balkan War* (London, 1996), p221.

7   David Owen, *Balkan Odyssey*, p386.

8   Ivo H Daalder, *Getting to Dayton: The Making of America's Bosnia Policy* (Washington DC, 2000), p120.

9   Ivo H Daalder, *Getting to Dayton*, p122.

10   Richard Holbrooke, *To End a War* (New York, 1998), pp159-160.

11   Richard Holbrooke, *To End a War*, p73.

12   Richard Holbrooke, *To End a War*, p160.

13   David Chandler, 'Bosnia's New Colonial Governor', *Guardian*, 9 July 2002.

14   US Trade and Development Agency website, http://www.tda.gov/trade/press/june2_99.html

15   House of Commons Defence Select Committee—Fourteenth Report, 23 October 2000. Appendix 2 of the report contains the text of the infamous Annex B to the Rambouillet accords. Lord Gilbert responds to Question 1086 in the Minutes of Evidence on 20 June 2000 at http://www.parliament.the-stationery-office.co.uk/pa/cm199900/cmselect/cmdfence/347/0062005.htm

16   *Sunday Times*, 28 March 1999.

17   John Simpson, 'The Shame of the Nation', *New Statesman*, 26 March 2001.

18   See the United Nations website at http://www.un.org/peace/kosovo/pages/regulations/constitframe.htm for the full text of the Constitutional Framework for Provisional Self-Government in Kosovo. Chapter 8 sets out all the powers reserved to the UN special representative.

19   Quoted in Helena Smith, 'The Do-Gooders Flood Into the West's New Colony', *New Statesman*, 27 March 2000.

20 Noam Chomsky, 'Comments on Milosevic Ouster', http://www.zmag.org/chomskyonelec.htm, 16 October 2000. A lucid and comprehensive account of the Serbian Revolution can be found in Lindsey German, 'Serbia's Spring in October', *International Socialism* 89 (Winter 2000). Lindsey German was a member of the Committee for Peace in the Balkans that organised the anti-war campaign in Britain.

21 The bombing of Serbia killed 503 civilians, 240 Yugoslav army members and 147 Serb policemen, according to the Serbian government, figures supported by organisations such as Human Rights Watch (*Guardian*, 19 September 2000). Tony Blair's claim that 'it was never a quarrel with the Serbian people' requires no comment.

22 The estimate of $30 billion ($29.6 billion to be exact) is that of the G17 group of anti-Milosevic, pro-market Serbian economists. Their calculations are set out in their paper, 'Economic Consequences of Nato Bombing: Estimates of Damage and Finances Required for Economic Reconstruction of Yugoslavia', June 1999. This is rather more plausible than the figure put out by the Milosevic government of $100 billion.

23 Both Ceausescu and Berisha were Western favourites in their day. Ceausescu was given an honorary knighthood by the queen in 1978 on the recommendation of the then Labour government and its foreign secretary, David Owen. She managed to withdraw it only hours before Ceausescu was shot during the revolution. Berisha was favoured for his free market zeal. The collapse of Albania's savings pyramid schemes led to his downfall.

24 Quoted in Noam Chomsky, 'Comments on Milosevic Ouster'.

1870s

Russia goes to war with the Turkish Ottoman Empire, which governs the Balkans. Other European powers intervene, setting different groups against each other, including the Serbs and Albanians. Britain uses the excuse of atrocities against Christians in Bulgaria to get involved in 1878. Intervention leads to wars between the Balkan states themselves—between Serbia and Bulgaria in 1885, for example.

1912

War erupts again. Serbia, Montenegro, Bulgaria (below, circle) and Greece attack the decaying Ottoman Empire. The Balkan states then go to war with each other. The European powers scramble to back competing sides.

The Great Powers sign the treaty of London, which recognises an independent Albania but leaves half of the population outside the new state.

1921

The Kosovans petition the League of Nations (the United Nations of its day). They beg for reunion with Albania. The league refuses.

1912-13

Balkan Wars—a prelude to the First World War, which begins when the Austro-Hungarian Empire declares war on Serbia. Once again the Great Powers encourage the repatriation of states.

1919-20

Britain backs the seizure of Kosovo and the formation of the Kingdom of the Serbs, Croats and Slovenes. The Great Powers give Italy a mandate over central Albania as reward for fighting against Germany.

1915

Western Allies make secret pact of London. They agree to carve up the two year old Albanian state between Italy and Greece.

THE BALKANS

SECOND WORLD WAR

During the war the region is torn apart as Nazi-backed Ustashe forces in Croatia systematically kill Serbs and Jews. Serbian Chetniks turn on Croats. A Communist—Tito (right of picture), who is half Croat and half Serb—succeeds in building a multi-ethnic anti-Nazi movement.

END OF SECOND WORLD WAR

Workers revolt in Greece. Britain crushes this movement and makes the Balkans a front line in the Cold War.

AFTER THE WAR

Yugoslavia is run by Tito. He uses the language of socialism but in reality maintains a strict regime of state control with its own ruling class. However, under his regime different nationalities manage to live together in peace. Towards the end of Tito's rule he grants Kosovan Albanians certain national rights. Milosevic reverses this as he drives to succeed Tito.

1990s

The West's intervention in the Balkans makes the situation worse. It enshrines the idea that different ethnic groups who have often lived side by side now must be forced to live apart, policed by Nato forces.

1995

The Dayton agreement is imposed by the US, and divides Bosnia into two separate zones, giving 51 percent to the Croats and Muslims, and 49 percent to the Serbs. This 'peace deal' involves driving Serbs, Croats and Muslims from one area to another, which in turn creates festering discontent. It also gives Milosevic control over Kosovo as 'compensation' for accepting the forced removal of Serbs from Krajina in Croatia.

Kosovo is one of the poorest areas in Europe— so poor that the Serbs who were driven out of Croatia in 1995 refused to be settled there.

5 OCTOBER 2000

Revolution! The Serbian people revolt and topple Milosevic for themselves. The Zastava car workers, miners at Kolubara, refinery workers at Pancevo and transport workers of Belgrade are at the forefront of the struggle. The idea that Western intervention in the Balkans was necessary for 'humanitarian reasons' is discredited.

Delegates at the Asian Social Forum declare, 'Another world is possible'

A World without Poverty and Hate ...
A World without Bombs ...
A World as much of Women as of m...
A World of Freedom ... ... and
A World we must Today Fight for and Win...

IT IS POSSIBLE.

Another
worldie
possible

INDIA AND PAKISTAN
BARRY PAVIER

At the end of 2003 the news magazine *India Today* published an editorial which accused the Bush administration of double standards in refusing to declare that Pakistan was a terrorist state:

> America refuses to accept...that victimhood and vengeance can't be America's prerogative alone. Musharraf is a promoter of international terror and India continues to suffer. America indulged him because he was a useful ally during the Afghan War. America makes a mockery of its post-9/11 morality by indulging him further...discovering America and getting out of the Cold War mindset was the major policy triumph of the BJP government. The relationship is still healthy, and for all rhetorical purposes they stand together on the right side of history. Ideally, no third party should be allowed to spoil the moment. By romancing the general, idealistic America has let down its natural ally.[1]

This magazine reflects opinion among that section of the Indian ruling class that wishes to project Indian capitalism into the global economy, and the influence of the Indian state beyond South Asia into the Middle East, Africa and South East Asia. Specifically, for many years it has had close links with the general staff of the armed forces and with the foreign ministry.[2] In the context of the Bush administration's aggressive foreign policy, the editorial revealed how states and their ruling classes can attempt to use the US government's policy to promote their own maximum objectives—promoting them, moreover, far beyond the limits of what might otherwise have been possible.

The Indian ruling class is not unique in this. The Israeli government of Ariel Sharon had been increasing its violent assault on the Palestinian National Authority for months under the cover of the 'war on terror'. Closer to home, Pervez Musharraf had spent all of his time since 11 September 2001 frantically manoeuvring to obtain some concessions from the US government. These were to be compensation for the fix he found himself in from the US-enforced cooperation with the assault on the Taliban. The failure of the US government to condemn him for supporting acts of violence against Indian rule in Kashmir, which was part of the compensation, was what inspired the editorial.[3]

This shows that the advocates of a solution by violence for the India-Pakistan confrontation had become very assertive by the end of 2002. Dangerous enough in itself, the situation has been made even more so by the practical certainty that both countries possess operational delivery systems for their nuclear weapons. From this point on, any conflict which seems to be heading towards a decisive success for either state will be likely to cause an exchange of nuclear weapons in densely populated areas. The horror of this prospect has not been made less likely by the most recent political developments in both countries.

RAMPANT COMMUNALISM IN THE STATES OF PARTITION

Elections never tell you everything that is happening in the politics of a society. Very often they can be downright confusing, usually by offering so narrow a choice to an electorate that it has little meaning.[4] On other occasions they reflect significant movements within societies. This happened in the Pakistani general election of October 2002, and in the Gujarat state election in India in December 2002. Both demonstrated two connected and disturbing phenomena—the collapse and marginalisation of socialist and working class organisations, and the consolidation and predominance of communalist politics.

Large-scale attacks on Muslim residential and business areas happened in 13 districts of Gujarat state, killing at least 2,000 people and making tens of thousands refugees

In early March 2002 an anti-Muslim pogrom swept Gujarat after activists of the Vishwa Hindu Parishad (VHP) were involved in a violent affray at Godhra railway station on 27 February which left 58 dead when one carriage of the train was firebombed.[5] Over the next week large-scale attacks on Muslim residential and business areas happened in 13 districts of Gujarat state, killing at least 2,000 people and making tens of thousands refugees inside their own towns. This massacre seems to have been partially orchestrated by activists of the Rashtriya Swayamsevak Sangh (RSS), but especially by members of the VHP-affiliated Bajrang Dal, since it was their activists who had been killed at Godhra. The state government, run by the Bharatiya Janata Party (BJP) under RSS full timer Narendra Modi, reacted very slowly to suppress the pogrom. Even when it did do so it began to promote its own line on the event. Godhra was the major incident, the ensuing violence was simply an understandable reaction, and anyone who said otherwise was a part of 'anti-Hindu forces out to bury Gujarat's pride'. In other words, the Muslims were the aggressors and deserved what they got.

Modi soon decided that this card should be played for all it was worth and called early elections to the Gujarat state assembly. After a bureaucratic confrontation with the chief election commissioner about the possibility of holding elections given the disturbed nature of the state, the elections were held on 16 December 2002.

Modi went on an all-out communalist platform, standing a Bajrang Dal activist in the Godhra constituency just in case anyone had not got the message. The only potential alternative put forward was the Congress Party. The party of Mahatma Gandhi and Jawaharlal Nehru has become a hideous mutation of its past as an anti-imperialist party, and stood on a platform of counter-communalism. It persuaded Muslim community leaders to endorse them, while it played the caste card in candidate selection for specific constituencies. It headed its campaign with the rene-gade former RSS chief of Gujarat who had split away on personal grounds in 1998. The result was a 51 to 38 percent win for the BJP, which gained two thirds of the seats.

This was the worst possible outcome. The BJP government had previously lost 15 state elections on the trot. It was coming under heavy criticism from the RSS and the VHP for making too many concessions to its coalition partners and to various interest groups. Now the perfect solution appeared. Modi's communalist campaign possessed the potential to sweep the country, especially in the atmosphere created by constant tension and violence gen-erated by the conflict in Kashmir and the 'war on terror'. Modi himself now appeared as a potential alternative national leader to the ageing prime minster, Atal Behari Vajpayee, and his deputy, L K Advani. But Modi only has one real policy—a solution by violence.

The other face of the Gujarat debacle has been the complete marginalisation of the left. This simply repeats on a more emphatic scale what has been happening across India for over a decade. It was obvious what was going to happen for months in advance, and this should have made Gujarat a priority for the left. On 28 Sep-tember 2002 there was a 'Peace March for Communal Harmony' in Ahmedabad, the state capital. This was organised by most of the major left political parties, and by local trade unionists, activists and community groups. At the end of the march a convention was held that issued a declaration against communalism.

The declaration made general condemnations of communal-ism, and demanded the arrest of the perpetrators of the pogrom and compensation for the victims. But it then laid out no set of actions to achieve this. It made hopeful statements:

> The majority of people, as their struggles unfold, will see through communal fascism, and the incompatibility of their economic and political interests with communal politics... This convention calls upon people to combine their struggle for economic and social demands with the struggle against communal fascism in order to build a new society, new democratic, secular and egalitarian India.[6]

This does not answer the most basic question which all activists have to be prepared to answer—so what is to be done? The statement reflects the residual influence of Stalinist determinism on the Indian left—somehow the masses must come to realise their true interests. The consequence of this attitude was seen in the election. The largest party on the left, and a participant in Ahmedabad, the Communist Party (Marxist) stood a candidate—as a result of an electoral pact with the Congress. He lost. Most community activists ended up campaigning for the Congress, and so have become complicit in both its 'soft communalism' and its debacle. In other words, the position of the left is now worse than it was in September 2002, because it has not created an alternative to ruling class ideas.

The elections in Pakistan in October 2002 were intended to produce democratic legitimacy for the military government of Pervez Musharraf. He had seized power from prime minister Nawaz Sharif in October 1999 to prevent himself from being sacked as army chief of staff. Nawaz Sharif had been hoping to come to terms with India over Kashmir so that he could create new links with dynamic sectors of the Indian economy, especially IT. In this way it could 'piggyback' the Indian economy to higher growth and so solve the problem of economic backwardness. This strategy was wrecked by the army's adventure in the Kargil area of Kashmir in the winter and summer of 1999, which led to a major localised war. This explains Sharif's keenness to get rid of Musharraf.

This coup of self-preservation only created new tensions. For a start, it revealed the basic split in the officer corps. Musharraf is the leading figure in the 'modernist' wing (a great admirer of Mustapha Kemal Ataturk, creator of the Turkish republic and its anti-Islamic army). This set him against the Islamic revivalist wing of the officer corps, which had grown in strength during the Afghan war against the USSR in the 1980s. This wing is strongest in the covert operations centre, the Inter-Services Intelligence (ISI). This tension has produced a surreal and dangerous situation. While Musharraf supports US operations in Afghanistan, ISI field officers have certainly facilitated the escape and concealment of significant numbers of Taliban and Al Qaida personnel. By itself this is an unstable and dangerous

RESISTANCE

STRIKES

Indian workers have an inspiring tradition of struggle to draw on. During the freedom struggle against British rule, strikes were seen as an important weapon against both imperialism and economic exploitation. For example, in 1928 around 31 million working days were lost due to strikes. This movement continued throughout the Second World War, with a number of political strikes against the war. In the final year of British rule, an estimated 1.8 million workers were involved in strikes.

In recent years industrial action has again played an important role in fighting against the drive towards greater deregulation and privatisation of the economy, which has been relentlessly pursued by successive governments with the support of institutions like the IMF, World Bank and WTO. A one day general strike in 2000 involved around 30 million workers and incorporated opposition to both neoliberalism and attacks on the Muslim minority. In April 2002 opposition to the wholesale privatisation of banks, ports and other sectors of the economy led to a 10 million strong general strike.

PROTESTS

Few areas of the world have been as badly ravaged by imperialism and globalisation as the Indian subcontinent. A number of movements have erupted in recent years that have challenged both the nation-states and multinational corporations in this region.

Massive protests against the Narmada Valley dam scheme, which threatened the displacement of over half a million people and threatened the livelihood of 21 million more, forced many investors, including the World Bank, to withdraw support. The pressure applied by companies like Monsanto and the WTO for Indian farmers to use GMO crops, including those which use the notorious 'terminator gene', has created outrage in the Indian countryside. Impoverished farmers in some regions have attacked test fields and organised large demonstrations, including a 'laugh in', where 1,000 farmers laughed for a whole day outside Bangalore's town hall, and which was reported around the world.

Recently there has also been growing opposition to militarism and war. The 14,000-strong Asian Social Forum, which took place in India in January 2003, issued statements opposing both war with Iraq and any confrontation between India and Pakistan. Even in Pakistan, where the left is much smaller than in India and operates under severe repression, activists managed to call protests in 20 cities to coincide with the international day o situation, where a random encounter could produce a violent incident that could rapidly escalate out of control.

On top of this Musharraf was faced by the 'routine' condition of Pakistan's political life. The main parties of the ruling class—the Pakistan Muslim League (PML) of Nawaz Sharif and the Pakistan People's Party (PPP) of Benazir Bhutto—were alienated from his regime, with both leaders exiled due to corruption charges. The economy was facing falling growth rates, and the temporary approval that had been obtained from a reduction in some of the more obvious aspects of corruption, such as those practised by customs and immigration officers at airports, was quickly running out. Additionally there were demands from his international supporters for a return to at least a semblance of democracy.

A referendum in April 2002 failed miserably in legitimising the regime. Pushed into holding a general election, he managed to engineer a split in the PML to produce a pro-government party, the PML (Q). The 'Q' stood for the founder of Pakistan, Mohammed Ali Jinnah. In itself this was a verdict on the ease with which ruling class politicians can be bought by government patronage. He hoped that this would produce a government dominated by his supporters. In fact, what he did not calculate on was the support gained by a coalition of six Islamic revivalist parties, the Muttahida Majlis-e-Amal (MMA—roughly translated as the United Party of Hope). Normally such parties have had a marginal impact electorally, not least because they resemble a bunch of squabbling cats in a sack. This time hostility to the US government and the perceived anti-Muslim nature of its 'war on terror' was enough to get them into a block which held together for the elections.

The results were instructive.[7] A 40 percent poll indicated lukewarm confidence in the process. Overall the PML (Q) got home first with 28.25 percent, with the PPP second on 23 percent. The MMA came in third at 16.7 percent. Fourteen other parties plus independents shared the other 32 percent.

In the North West Frontier Province (NWFP) bordering Afghanistan, where hostility is at its greatest towards the US, the MMA won 82.8 percent of the votes for the national assembly. In the vote for the NWFP provincial assembly the MMA vote went down to 47.4 percent, with the rest of the vote splitting eight ways. In Baluchistan the MMA vote was 50 percent for the national assembly and 25 percent for the provincial assembly. The MMA vote fell away in the two most populous provinces—9.8 percent and 7.7 percent in

In the regions where the 'war against terror' is having a pervasive impact on everyday life the majority of the populations hate the US and hate their own government

Sindh, and 2 percent for both in Punjab, where the PML (Q) managed to easily top the poll.

The MMA has now been able to form governments in both the NWFP and Baluchistan. Tactical manoeuvring and the attractions of office are producing a willingness to coexist with Musharraf. This has also led them to enter a PML (Q) led national coalition. This was eventually stitched up after a couple of months bargaining which engineered a split from enough PPP MPs to secure a majority.

The results clearly show that the MMA vote was an anti-US vote. Apart from chucking the US out of the country, the MMA had no other real policy apart from land reform, itself a commentary on conditions in the NWFP and Baluchistan. But again the left and the working class movement were dangerously marginalised. One Trotskyist managed to get elected to the national assembly on a PPP ticket. This shows the existence of a pool of support for socialist politics, and at the same time the futility of this support, buried in a party dominated by and organised for a corrupt faction of bourgeois and landlords. This initiative did not create anything more than a local impact, and gave no alternative national focus.

What the elections do show is that in the regions where the 'war against terror' is having a pervasive impact on everyday life the majority of the populations hate the US and hate their own government. They see the Islamist parties as providing the only effective alternative focus. What makes this even more of a catastrophe is that this has not always been the case in the NWFP. For 30 years after partition it was dominated by a party descended from the Khudai Khitmatgars. This pro-Congress mass movement of the pre-independence period opposed partition and the creation of Pakistan. In 2002 the party representing this tradition, the National Awami Party, got just 8 percent of the vote for the NWFP provincial assembly. There is very little left of the support for the Communist Party in Sindh and Punjab, which was built up before 1947 and was seen to be massive by the support organised for the decisive 1946 mutiny of the Royal Indian Navy. But, as in India, the Pakistani left have squandered this inheritance over the past 50 years to a point where they now have little influence on national events at a time when the national and international crisis is creating a massive constituency which is asking, 'What is to be done?' Conceding the field to the Congress and PPP has not been a satisfactory answer for them.

The immediate danger is that an unstable civilian government may prompt an initiative by the section of the Pakistani army which created the Kargil War in 1999. The extra danger this time not only comes from the existence of operational nuclear weapons on both sides, but the Kargil War clearly demonstrated the superior resources that are available to the Indian armed forces. In a war of attrition they will win. This is a consequence of the increasing divergence of the two economies in the 1990s, which is currently accelerating. For the Pakistani military, therefore, there is the constant pressure to fight before the gap becomes insurmountable, and an increasing pressure to rely on nuclear weapons to tip the balance in their favour.

The Pakistani economy was constantly overshadowed by that of India in the 1990s. In the 1980s it actually slightly outperformed India by an average of 6.3 percent to 5.8 percent per annum. In the 1990s the gap swung violently the other way to a Pakistani average of 3.7 percent and an Indian one of 6 percent.[8] This trend has continued into the 21st century.[9]

The most dynamic, 'globalised' sections of the Indian bourgeoisie have realistic expectations of entering a mutually profitable relationship with the US ruling class. It explains their desire to bring the US administration around to a wholehearted commitment to India. The expansion into software writing has been followed by a rapid growth of Business Process Outsourcers (BPOs—

call centres to the rest of us)—336 were created in India in 1997-2002. Current growth in BPOs would by itself add 3 percent to India's total GDP by 2008, and employ 2 million people.[10] This is

In November 2002 Bill Gates of Microsoft made a tour of India that resembled that of a head of state

before any expansion generated by the association of software producers such as Wipro and Infosys.

In November 2002 Bill Gates of Microsoft made a tour of India that resembled that of a head of state. Apart from distributing $100 million from his Aids charity, Gates spent three days in the leading IT centres of Mumbai, Hyderabad and Bangalore. His main aim was to pre-empt the penetration of the Indian market by his main competitor, Linux. He signed a BPO deal with Wipro and a portal deal with the Karnataka state government. In other words, for the US information technology sector, India is not only a central market but also a key business partner. Pakistan is nowhere in this scene. There is practically no Pakistani lobby among US capitalists, but a mighty powerful Indian one.

THE FUTURE

Normally speaking, the Sangh Parivar and the governmental allies of the BJP are in competition with the globalisers in the Indian ruling class. Simply, this is because their dominant supporters come from the petty bourgeoisie and regional capitalists who historically have had little interest in the global market. In fact, they look to the state to subsidise their enterprises, which is why they have been resisting privatisations in the huge state sector.

However, at this moment they are united on the central issue of pressurising the Bush administration to make a commitment to India. This, they calculate, would open the way to the achievement of their maximum objectives. It would also potentially lead to full-scale war.

The pity is that the left in both countries ought to be in a position to create a serious alternative. In Pakistan the position of the workers and peasants has been desperate for years. In one of his most recent writings Tariq Ali recounted how a Pakistani civil servant burned himself to death in protest at being impoverished by the government and the ruling class."

In India rapid growth in some sectors has simply increased existing social tensions. These exist on regional lines, as some states, such as Bihar, have missed out on the boom and had negative growth in the 1990s. They exist on class lines inside the boom areas, partly as the sections of the working class which aren't part of the expanding sectors are driven down into intermittent employment in the 'informal' sector. They exist on 'normal' lines inside the boom sectors as workers who, despite enjoying rising standards of living, suffer levels of exploitation which are not only increasing, but are the highest in the country due to the high value of the commodities they produce.

Quite apart from the multitude of strikes, apart from long-standing campaigns such as that against the Narmada dam, the Ahmedabad march in September 2002 showed that the capacity exists for organising a fightback against communalism and the ruling class. But the habitual lack of clarity among the Indian left threw that chance away by the way that, for the most part, they ended up supporting the Congress campaign. The election catastrophe was the result.

Posing an alternative means just that—an alternative to the two states that create never-ending conflict, both between themselves and internally. Global imperialism in 2003 quite happily contains this communalism within itself. In South Asia the Indian ruling class is attempting to compel US imperialism into making an unconditional commitment to it. Once done, it intends to fully enter the global capitalist system as a major partner with an expanding influence. To achieve this it is willing to risk all-out war and a nuclear exchange. The Pakistani ruling class is in danger of disintegration. Several factions would then be liable to seek a solution by violence, again with nuclear weapons in their armoury. Socialists and the left could pose a serious alternative, but only if and when they grasp the nettle of opposing the very existence of the two communal states, which by their very nature generate conflict without end.

Barry Pavier teaches history and politics at Bradford College in West Yorkshire. He has participated in anti-imperialist campaigns since 1968, and has been a member of the Socialist Workers Party since 1973 (www.swp.org.uk)

NOTES

1   'Dual Morality', *India Today*, 23 December 2002.
2   So, for instance, the same issue contained details of how the Indian armed forces almost went to war with Pakistan on two separate occasions in 2002, complete with war-gamed outcomes.
3   These included an attack on the Indian parliament building in December 2001 and an attack on a major Hindu temple in Gujarat in September 2002.
4   Such as the US Congressional elections in 2002, where most of the electorate behaved as normal and stayed at home.
5   The best explanation of what happened at Godhra seems to be that some drunken VHP activists roughed up Muslim snack vendors. They did not realise that the adjoining Muslim slum is dominated by particularly violent criminals.
6   www.labourfile.org/cec1/labourfile/News%20Update2/link%20page.htm
7   Results, plus later developments, can be found on http://www.votesmart.com.pk
8   World Bank, *Development Indicators*, August 2002.
9   IMF, *World Economic Outlook*, April 2002.
10 'Housekeepers to the World', *India Today*, 18 November 2002.
11 Tariq Ali, 'In the Dog House', in *On the Abyss: Pakistan after the Coup* (New Delhi: HarperCollins India, 2002), pp4-5.

Indian strikers demand justice, January 1995

PLAYERS

Spanish protesters take to the streets against Bush

THE BUSH DOCTRINE

ANDREW MURRAY

The 'Bush Doctrine' is more than the basic strategic formulation of US foreign policy under its present, reactionary, administration. It is also the template for the operation of the whole 'new world order' first proclaimed by the president's father in the wake of the end of the Cold War in 1991. That is to say, it is a doctrine for the ordering of the entire world, rather than simply a guideline for the intervention of the US within it. That one doctrine can play both these roles is testimony to the unique opportunities the present moment presents for the US establishment and the big business interests for whom it operates.

Three factors condition this moment. First, the collapse of the USSR has removed any perceived systemic alternative to the free enterprise capitalism for which the US is the standard-bearer. This makes it easier for it to present the brazen pursuit of its own interests as the pursuit of general human wellbeing in a way that could not have been so easily accomplished 20 or more years ago.

Second, the US enjoys an overwhelming military hegemony. Again, the collapse of the USSR removed from the scene the only power able to restrict Washington's freedom of operation by military strength, at least throughout the eastern hemisphere. Today the US military budget is greater than that of the next ten states put together, and its military technology appears to be at a qualitatively higher level as well.

The third factor is that the first two factors outlined above are wasting assets. The underlying relative position of the US politically and militarily can only grow weaker over the next 20 to 30 years, even without allowing for dramatic turns in the international situation which could accelerate this process.

The most compelling fact is the gradual decline of the US share of world production. This peaked at around 50 percent (including the then-socialist countries) in 1950, but fell to 22 percent by the start of the 1990s. It has recovered somewhat since as a consequence of the prolonged stagnation of the Japanese economy, but on any reasonable projection this decline is likely to be resumed, the more so with the popping of the dot.com and telecom bubbles on the US stockmarket. US savings are at very low levels, making a fall in investment over the coming years all but inevitable, and prolonged federal budget deficits may ultimately become unsustainable too.

Military power cannot outstay economic power indefinitely. Even if US arms spending does not decline absolutely (clearly the US right will try to cut everything else to the bone first), other powers, growing relatively stronger in economic terms, will eventually be in a position to challenge it.

Likewise, the growing discontent around the world at the development (or non-development) of the capitalist economy in the post Cold War era, the growth of the anti-globalisation movement, the multiple signs of a recovery in the strength of the international working class movement and, indeed, the massive upsurge of opposition to George Bush's war policy itself, all mean that the ideological hegemony of 'US values' is not likely to be preserved for very long either.

These three factors together make this a window of opportunity for the US ruling class which will not remain open indefinitely. Now is the moment for the US to reach for a 'once and for all' reordering of the world structured around its own priorities. This sense infuses many of the basic documents of the 'Bush Doctrine'. One does not need to be a fully paid-up conspiracy theorist to suspect it is not accidental that it is at just this moment that the senior George Bush's hand-picked judges decided to impose their sponsor's son on the US people, the presidential election result notwithstanding, at the head of the most aggressively right wing administration in the country's post-war history, sharing Ronald

The underlying relative position of the US politically and militarily can only grow weaker over the next 20 to 30 years

Reagan's ideological predilections with the bonus of the absence of the restraints that the world of the 1980s still imposed on the Hollywood ham actor's freedom of manoeuvre.

Apprehension coexists with chauvinism and chest-beating aggression at the heart of the 'Bush Doctrine'. The long term fear is not of terrorist attacks or of weapons of mass destruction, but of the US ruling elite losing its privileged place in the sun to some or all of Russia, China, Japan or the European Union in the future.

The 'Bush Doctrine' was codified and summarised in the administration's new National Security Strategy, presented to the US Congress in September 2002. It has, however, been a long time in development, and its main lines long pre-date not merely 11 September 2001, but even the advent of the present president to office.

In 1992, when George Bush Sr was still in the White House, a Pentagon defence planning document argued that the US should ensure that no rival be allowed to emerge to challenge its hegemony in the post Cold War world. To ensure this, the US should, it asserted, retain sufficient military power to deter such a development while ensuring that US policy accounted 'for the interests of advanced industrial nations to discourage them from challenging our leadership or seeking to overturn the established political and economic order'.

This policy, styled the 'benevolent domination by one power' (no prizes for guessing which), was clearly aimed at forestalling challenges from other capitalist rivals. Integrating Germany and Japan into a US-dominated security system which looked after their interests as well would prevent such powers from developing their own nuclear weapons, for example. 'Nuclear proliferation...could lead Germany and Japan and other industrial powers to acquire nuclear weapons to deter attack from regional foes. This could start them down the road to global competition with the US and, in a crisis over national interests, military rivalry.'

The US should also, the document urged, act to prevent the

development of European-only security arrangements outside Nato (ie US) control, and should extend Washington's military hegemony into Eastern Europe.

The 'Bush Doctrine' is, in large measure, an extension of US foreign policy as it has been evolving for 11 years or more

This policy was broadly followed by the Clinton administration. For example, the US involvement in the 1999 war against Yugoslavia, in which direct US interests were only marginally concerned, can be explained in large part as designed to prevent Germany leading an EU military intervention outside of US control, and to remind the European powers who is 'boss' as far as armed might is concerned.

The Clinton administration was also frank in its 'US interests first' position, even though it was generally more concerned to sugar the pill with 'internationalist' rhetoric than its successor has been. And 'regime change' in Iraq was first adopted as official US policy in 1998, under Clinton, although it was not then suggested that all-out invasion was to be the means to effect this.

So the 'Bush Doctrine' is, in large measure, an extension of US foreign policy as it has been evolving for 11 years or more, rather than a new departure. The new elements are threefold.

First, the sheer public brazenness with which it is expressed—offered to the world on a 'like it or lump it' basis. Second, there is an increased willingness to use military force to achieve its objectives as, if not a first, then clearly not a last resort. Third, there is an unwillingness to make more than the smallest cosmetic concessions to the interests of US 'allies' when they do not align precisely with Washington's own. Bush's 'America first' trade and environmental policies illustrate this, and represent the biggest departure from Clinton administration attitudes.

All these trends were clearly at work before 11 September. In January 2001, for example, as the new administration was preparing to take over, the conservative think-tank Project for the New American Century sent a hair-raising blueprint for a Bush foreign policy to vice-president Dick Cheney, defence secretary Donald Rumsfeld and others.

This document argued, among other things:

> The United States has for decades sought to play a more permanent
> role in Gulf regional security. While the unresolved conflict with
> Iraq provides the immediate justification, the need for a substantial
> force presence in the Gulf transcends the issue of the regime of
> Saddam Hussein.

The plan adds that, even should Saddam depart from the
scene, bases would need to remain in the region on a permanent
basis because 'Iran may well prove as large a threat to US interests
as Iraq has'.

The remarkable document also frets that Europe could eventually rival the US and, in chilling rhetoric reminiscent of the Nazis,
urges the development of 'advanced forms of biological warfare
that can target specific genotypes [which] may transform biological
warfare from the realm of terror to a politically useful tool'.

Likewise, a Pentagon strategic document, prepared before 11
September, identified the Far East as a zone of critical US interests
on account of its potentially dynamic role in the world economy,
noted the lack of US military infrastructure there, and urged the
government to seek ways to establish bases throughout the region.

Small surprise, then, that the first country to be targeted for
US military intervention in the 'war against terror' after Afghanistan was the Philippines, where a fairly obscure Muslim insur-
gency became the pretext for the US establishing its first foothold
since the enormous bases at Clark Field and Subic Bay were shut
down by the Manila government after the end of the Cold War.

US bases were also established throughout the former Soviet
republics of Central Asia. These have the dual function of helping
guarantee US access to the vast (and non Opec controlled) energy
reserves in that area, and of encircling China with Pentagon
bases. We can be sure that these outposts of Washington's might
will remain in place long after the ostensible reason for their
establishment—the conflict in Afghanistan—has faded away.

The National Security Strategy issued roughly a year after 11
September pulls all these threads and more together. The terror

attacks on the US are used as a means of mobilising domestic opinion behind the goals of the administration, but the latter have not in any sense emerged as a response to those dramatic events. As argued earlier, it is not merely a programme for the use of US power, it is a charter for a 'new world order'. There is, it argues, 'a single sustainable model for national success—freedom, democracy and free enterprise'. Only nations following that model will be able to enjoy prosperity. America, it says, stands for certain 'non-negotiable demands', including the rule of law, limits on the power of the state, respect for women, religious and ethnic tolerance, free speech and 'respect for private property'.

The strategy dwells at length on the dangers of 'terrorism', which is, however, given no exacting definition beyond 'premeditated politically motivated violence perpetrated against innocents'. This may sound unexceptionable, but it begs a number of questions when applied to any particular situation and could, of course, cover almost all circumstances of armed struggle.

In relation both to terrorism and 'weapons of mass destruction', the US reserves unto itself 'the option of pre-emptive actions to counter a sufficient threat to our national security... To forestall or prevent such hostile actions by our adversaries, the US will, if necessary, act pre-emptively.'

This doctrine replaces the existing formulas of international law with the subjective judgement of the US administration as to what is a threat or not. And what might constitute such a threat in Washington's eyes? The very next paragraph is instructive:

> The lessons of history are clear—market economies...are the best way to promote prosperity and reduce poverty. Policies that further strengthen market incentives and market institutions are relevant for all countries—industrialised countries, emerging markets and the developing world.

In relation to 'emerging markets', the US security strategy insists on the necessity of 'international flows of investment capital' to expand 'productive potential'. Free trade is asserted as a 'moral principle' and a measure of 'real freedom'.

Descending from such cloudy moralising, a more practical concern is expressed—and a solution advanced to deal with it. The US needs to strengthen its 'energy security', and will therefore work with its allies and trading partners 'to expand the sources and types of global energy supplied, especially in the western hemisphere, Africa, Central Asia and the Caspian region'.

These and other strategies will be implemented by the US 'organising coalitions, as broad as practicable, of states able and willing to promote a balance of power that favours freedom'. Nato, for example, 'must build a capability to field at short notice, highly mobile, specially trained forces whenever they are needed to respond to a threat against any member of the alliance'—using the new and expanded definition of threat, presumably.

Here a note of uncertainty creeps into the document. It 'welcomes our European allies' efforts to forge a greater foreign policy and defence identity with the EU, and commit ourselves to close consultations to *ensure* that these developments work with Nato [my emphasis].' Bear in mind here that the main pre II September foreign policy issue for Bush was opposition to the autonomous development of a EU-wide army, which the leaders of France, at least, wish to ensure has as little to do with Nato as possible.

Russia is then warned over its 'uneven commitment to the basic values of free market democracy', which remains 'of great concern', while China is scolded for 'pursuing advanced military capabilities that can threaten its neighbours'.

Yet the very next section of the strategy asserts that 'it is time to reaffirm the essential role of American military strength. We must build and maintain our defences beyond challenge.' So while China should not even have region-wide military capabilities, the US can and will retain worldwide capacities.

Those forces 'will be strong enough to dissuade potential adversaries from pursuing a military build-up in hopes of surpassing, or equalling, the power of the US.' It is entirely fair to assume from the document that those 'potential adversaries' include the European Union, Russia and China.

It is perhaps unfair to Tony Blair that this comprehensive world plan for unending capitalist domination should be known as the 'Bush Doctrine'. The British prime minister has, after all, been at the forefront in developing the ideological underpinnings of the doctrine and propagating them internationally at times of crisis when US presidents have been disqualified either on grounds of moral turpitude (Clinton) or stupidity (Bush Jr).

In May 1999, at the height of the bombardment of Yugoslavia, undertaken in full defiance of international law, Blair flew to Chicago to observe Nato's 50th birthday celebrations and delivered a landmark speech in which he set out the circumstances under which 'the international community' could intervene in a sovereign state. These included, he made it clear, failure to open up markets and observe the rules of a free market economy.

In 2001 he used his speech to the Labour Party conference to proclaim his 'passion for Africa'. Those African states to be blessed with British assistance would have to open up their markets to world capitalism, he emphasised.

And at the 2002 Labour Party conference he celebrated Britain's role in an international coalition for 'free trade, free markets and free enterprise'. Following a diplomatic row with French president Jacques Chirac shortly afterwards, he said that 'the world is moving in one direction, and that is liberalism'. Obviously he was referring to economic liberalism rather than political liberalism, which his government at least is in full flight away from.

Blair has said that Britain must pay a 'blood price' to stand shoulder to shoulder with the reactionary US administration. Clearly, this blood is to be spilt in the cause of imposing freebooting capitalism on the world, whether it likes it or not. And just to underline the point, Blair has had his erstwhile foreign policy adviser, Robert Cooper, author a pamphlet calling for a return to imperialism and colonialism in the 21st century. Blair's own policies towards Africa, the Middle East and the Balkans indicate that this is not just rhetoric.

As this is written, Iraq is in the Bush-Blair doctrine's sights. Next year it may be Iran or North Korea, and beyond that Syria or Cuba. And there is no reason to believe that there will ever be an end to the 'threats' against which the doctrine is mobilised, from countries wishing to order their own affairs or control their own resources.

As this is written, Iraq is in the Bush-Blair doctrine's sights. Next year it may be Iran or North Korea, and beyond that Syria or Cuba

However, even this programme for more or less endless imperialist war is only the beginning of the problem. Inter-imperialist conflict will increasingly become the focus of international relations. The conditions which gave rise to the suppression of these rivalries—solidarity against the USSR, the overwhelming economic power of the US—have been eroded.

On one issue after another—the European army, 'Star Wars', trade and even the projected war against Iraq—diplomatic clashes between the big powers have become the norm. Indeed, German chancellor Gerhard Schröder won re-election on the basis of criticisms of US policy, bringing relations between the two countries to their worst pitch since 1945.

And will Russia indefinitely acquiesce in the expansion of US power up to its frontiers, and even beyond? China seems clearly indisposed to have any limits to its regional authority set down in Washington. If Japan's economy revives, three powers will be contesting for control of the economies and markets of the Far East.

These are the ultimate targets of the 'Bush Doctrine', the ultimate objects of its warnings. It is an attempt to utilise the one area in which US relative power has not been eroded—military might—to reorder a capitalist world hierarchy with the US permanently at the top, Britain at its right hand, and the other big powers each enjoying their Washington-allotted place in the sun, content to share in the feast of the world's resources at the expense of the world's poor, and with never a thought of challenging the ultimate authority of the one superpower.

However, it is a castle built on shifting sands. Already the attempts to impose the 'Bush Doctrine' have raised international tensions to a post-war peak. Already other powers are chafing against their subordinate position.

The anti-war movement has already justly characterised the present conflict as an 'endless war', with a seemingly inexhaustible lists of countries to be targeted by one means or another. That is quite bad enough. But the experience of history is that the actual end of such a policy generally lies in a major war between the big powers for world hegemony. The main lesson which we can draw from the vast worldwide movement which has developed against the 'Bush Doctrine' and its early outings in practice is that such an conclusion is far from inevitable—but averting it will require still greater mobilisations than even those which have happened so far.

Andrew Murray is communications officer for the train drivers' union Aslef. He is the author of *Off the Rails: The Crisis on Britain's Railways* and *Flashpoint: World War Three*. He is chair of the Stop the War Coalition (www.stopwar.org.uk)

An artist against the 'war on terror' depicts the warmonger Bush and his 'poodle', Blair

Bomber Blair

BRITISH STATE

JOHN NEWSINGER

There are two interrelated dimensions to British imperialism. First, the British state's competitive relationship, military and economic, with other rival imperialist powers. This dimension is characterised by wars and alliances, whereby the ally of one day (Japan in the First World War, for example) can became a mortal enemy on another day (Japan in the Second World War). This competition between the Great Powers cost the lives of hundreds of thousands of British, mainly working class, people in the two world wars. The Cold War was a later episode in this Great Power competition and it continues today, with the British state finding itself pulled between its satellite relationship with US imperialism and being part of an emerging rival European imperialism.

The second dimension concerns the British state's exercise of domination—political, economic and military—over those parts of the globe incorporated by trade and war into its sphere of influence. In the 19th century this included both those countries like India forcibly incorporated into Britain's formal empire by military conquest and ruled directly by British officials and soldiers, and those countries like China that remained politically independent but were in reality part of Britain's informal empire. Even this informal empire required the regular use of military violence as a tool of policy to persuade recalcitrant governments to do what Britain wanted. Britain's three opium wars with China are a good example of this. Today's American Empire functions primarily as an informal empire, but once again one that routinely uses military force as a tool of policy.

At the end of the First World War, after the terrible carnage of the Western Front, the British state emerged as the world's strongest imperial power, ruling more of the world than ever before. Much of the Middle East (Palestine, Jordan and Iraq) was taken from the Ottoman Empire, and Germany's African colonies (Namibia and Tanganyika) were seized. Britain's major imperialist rivals had either been defeated or overwhelmed by revolution, or, in the case of the US—economically already the most powerful country in the world—had limited its imperial ambitions to South America and the Pacific. Britain's imperial reach had, however, out-stripped its grasp. The British state in the period between the two world wars did not have the economic or military resources to securely hold the territory it now occupied. A combination of grow-ing popular unrest in the occupied countries (the great Palestinian revolt of 1936-39 and the Quit India revolt of 1942 were examples of this) together with the emergence or re-emergence of imperialist rivals (Nazi Germany, fascist Italy, imperial Japan and the Soviet Union) was to fatally compromise the British Empire.

The Second World War posed a massive challenge to British imperialism, almost overwhelming it. The empire was forced into an uneasy alliance with two of its rivals, the Soviet Union and the US, in order to defeat the threat posed by the others—Germany, Italy and Japan. The war left the British state exhausted, virtually bankrupt and dependent on the US. This was the situation in July 1945 when a Labour government, with an overwhelming parlia-mentary majority, was elected into office.

LABOUR AND EMPIRE

Clement Attlee's Labour government was absolutely determined that Britain should maintain its position as a great imperialist power, as one of the world's three superpowers, alongside the United States and the Soviet Union. In the circumstances that existed in the post-war period this involved what amounted to a revolution in strategy with regard to both the dimensions of British

It was the 1945-51 Labour government that took the decision in January 1947 to develop a British atomic bomb

imperialism. Let us look at the competitive relationship with rival imperialisms first.

In the post-war years the US remained a rival to the British Empire. The American intention was to bring about the liquidation of the British and other European empires so that the newly liberated territories could be incorporated into America's own emerging informal global empire. Despite this, British policy was to ally with the US in order to confront the more dangerous imperialist threat posed by the Soviet Union. This unequal alliance was to involve the Labour government in historically unprecedented developments that have since become naturalised and taken for granted. It is time to revisit them.

Labour's part in the creation of the modern welfare state is, of course, well known, but more important as far as the British state was concerned was the contemporaneous creation of the modern warfare state. It was the 1945-51 Labour government that took the decision in January 1947 to develop a British atomic bomb. In the words of the then Labour foreign secretary, Ernest Bevin, 'We have got to have this thing over here whatever it costs... We've got to have a bloody Union Jack flying on top of it.' This decision was taken in secret without the House of Commons, let alone the British people, being consulted. Interestingly enough, it was not so much aimed at Russia, but was regarded as vital if Britain was to maintain some sort of equality with the US. Later on that same year (April) the government decided to keep military conscription as a peacetime measure. Initially conscripts served one year, but in 1950 it was increased to two. This was at least in part to make up for the loss of Indian troops occasioned by withdrawal from India.

Even more dramatic was the decision in July-August 1947 to allow the US to establish bases for B-29 bombers in Britain, to convert Britain into Orwell's Airstrip One. This began the permanent establishment of foreign, that is American, military bases on British soil. This was something without any historical precedent. By 1950 the US was basing bombers carrying nuclear weapons in

Britain. And in April 1949 Britain, more particularly Ernest Bevin, was instrumental in establishing the North Atlantic Treaty Organisation (Nato), which involved the permanent stationing of British forces on the continent, another unprecedented development. Nato was, of course, to become one of the most important international organisations through which US imperialism exercised its power.

In 1945 British troops crushed a popular Communist-led insurrection in Saigon and fought a bloody war against nationalist rebels in Indonesia

The Labour government's commitment to the American alliance saw preparations for a third world war with the Soviet Union in 1950. Prompted by the Korean War (Labour sent a Commonwealth division to fight alongside the US in this bloody, murderous affair), the government proposed a massive increase in military expenditure. War spending was to be increased first to £2.3 billion, and then this was increased to £4.7 billion or 14 percent of GNP. This was to be paid for by cuts in the welfare state, splitting the Labour government at a time of economic difficulty, and returning the Conservatives under Winston Churchill to power.

What of the other dimension of British imperialism—its rule over conquered lands and subject peoples? Labour is usually credited with granting independence to India. This is seriously misleading to say the least as far as the Labour government's colonial policy was concerned. In the immediate aftermath of the Second World War the Labour government not only reoccupied those territories that had been conquered by Japan but sent strong military forces to restore French rule in Indochina and Dutch rule in Indonesia. In 1945 British troops crushed a popular Communist-led insurrection in Saigon and fought a bloody war against nationalist rebels in Indonesia. The heroic resistance that the rebels offered to the British forces attacking the city of Surabaya is still celebrated as Indonesia's national day.

In India the Labour government was confronted by a militant mass movement demanding independence. To have resisted this demand would have provoked revolution, a revolution in which the Indian army was expected to side with the rebels. The Labour government still hoped to keep India within Britain's informal empire, maintaining military bases in the country, making use of Indian troops to police the rest of the empire, and controlling the country through a puppet government. Nehru's Congress government refused to play this role, and the British state was too weak to insist. Britain withdrew from the country in 1947.

Elsewhere the Labour government actually increased its control over and exploitation of the colonies. In Malaya this provoked rebellion, leading to a 12-year war against Communist guerrillas. When Malaya finally became independent in 1957, the intention was once again that the country would remain part of Britain's informal empire. By the end of the 1960s British economic and military weakness had made even that prospect an imperial daydream.

SUEZ AND AFTER

The futility of the British state's attempt to pretend that its relationship with the US was one of equality was brutally demonstrated by the Anglo-French invasion of Egypt in 1956. Britain had first occupied the country in 1882, and British troops were only finally withdrawn in 1954. Once they were gone, Egypt's nationalist leader, President Nasser, proceeded to nationalise the Suez Canal. This provoked an outraged response from the British prime minister, Anthony Eden, who saw Nasser as a threat to both Britain's formal and informal empire throughout the Middle East. Inevitably Nasser was described as a new Hitler, and Eden even ordered his assassination. Britain joined with France and Israel in a conspiracy to overthrow Nasser. What this involved was the Israelis attacking Egypt, and the British and French subsequently occupying the country, ostensibly to protect the Suez Canal. The problem was that this had not been agreed with the US, which had moreover no wish to see the position of British imperialism strengthened in the Middle East. The US had every intention of replacing British influence in the area.

The outcome was complete humiliation. The Anglo-French forces occupied Egypt, but the US then used its economic muscle to force their withdrawal, leaving Nasser stronger than ever. This decisively ended any British pretensions to equality with the US. What is particularly significant, however, is the different ways that the British and French states responded to this demonstration of American power. The British resolved to never again get out of step with the US. Britain was to become one of US imperialism's most loyal satellites. As far as the leaderships of both the Conservative and Labour parties were concerned, from this time on, in all fundamentals, America's interests were Britain's interests. France, however, refused to accept this satellite status and instead determined to build Europe up as a counterbalance to US power.

Why this difference? It would be easy to see it as deriving from the sort of gutless poodlery exemplified by Tony Blair today, but this is not an explanation. The British state's embrace of satellite status derives from British capital's global interests, interests that are more extensive than those of French capital. British capital has more need of a protector with a global reach, and now that the British state cannot play that role, it looks to the US state instead. This is of course something of an overgeneralisation, because important sections of British capital looked to Europe or to Europe and the US, but in essence it explains the servile relationship that developed between the British state and US imperialism after 1956.

Another crucial instance of British dependence on the US is provided by the fate of Britain's 'independent' nuclear weapons. As we have seen, Labour had initiated the development of a British bomb in 1947, but it had not been delivered until late in 1952. American and Russian development of the hydrogen bomb made this obsolete, and it was not until the early summer of 1957 that Britain was able to explode its own hydrogen bomb. By now the problem was that Britain's delivery system, the V bomber, was obsolescent, as was its proposed replacement, the Blue Streak missile that was still in development. As far as Conservative prime minister Harold Macmillan was concerned, it was absolutely vital that Britain should be armed with nuclear weapons. In 1960 Blue Streak was cancelled, and he negotiated the purchase of American Skybolt missiles (still in development), which could be delivered by the V bomber force. In return the US was given the Holy

In many ways US imperialism is in a similar situation to British imperialism at the end of the First World War Loch submarine base for its Polaris submarines. When Skybolt was cancelled late in 1962, Macmillan went cap in hand to beg President Kennedy for Polaris. He warned that refusal might actually lead to the fall of his government and its replacement by Labour. In April 1963 the US agreed to let Britain have Polaris. To put it bluntly, Britain's continuing Great Power pretensions derive from the possession of 'dependent' nuclear weapons that are in the gift of the US. Without any doubt, British refusal to play the role of loyal satellite would see this gift withdrawn, something that no Labour or Conservative government could contemplate.

The Conservative governments that held office from 1951 to 1964 presided over the withdrawal from much of Britain's formal empire. Britain's African empire was liquidated with considerably less violence than it had been established with one important exception—Kenya. In Kenya the Mau Mau rebellion that broke out in 1952 was crushed by the British state with a degree of violence and brutality that was only equalled by its conduct in Ireland in 1798 and in India in 1857. In the course of the repression some 77,000 Kikuyu men, women and children were interned without trial (thousands more were imprisoned with trials that made a mockery of justice). Over a million people were forcibly resettled in new villages that were placed under armed guard. Torture and summary execution were used as a matter of routine. And before the rebellion was crushed over 1,000 rebels had been hanged, including over 40 for the crime of administering illegal oaths.

According to official figures over 11,000 rebels were killed in the fighting, but a more realistic estimate puts the figure in the region of 50,000. The number of white settlers killed was 32. What this demonstrates is the incredible violence that the British state was prepared to inflict on virtually defenceless people, violence that was acceptable in good part because the victims were black. This did not happen in the 1790s or in the 1850s, but in the 1950s. Many of the men responsible are still alive, honoured former servants of the Crown.

The British state successfully covered up the atrocities for which they were responsible by demonising the victims.

STATE AND EMPIRE TODAY

Since the end of the Cold War the US has successfully established a military supremacy that is without historical precedent. Nevertheless, in many ways US imperialism is in a similar situation to British imperialism at the end of the First World War—its reach is outstripping its grasp. The US's military superiority is not matched by an equivalent economic superiority, which means that in the long run it will not be sustainable. This has already presented serious problems for the British state, and these problems are likely to increase. On the one hand, it has committed itself unreservedly to a satellite relationship with US imperialism. No British political leader has ever been as open and unashamed about this as Tony Blair. Europe, however, pulls in a different direction. The tension this creates within British politics reflects the interests of different sections of British capital. While the emergence of a European imperialist rival to the US is still in the formative stage, it arguably played an important part in the downfall of Margaret Thatcher, and one suspects it will play a similar role in the downfall of her New Labour heir, Tony Blair. More important in deciding his fate, however, will be the protests of the anti-war movement on the streets.

John Newsinger is a writer and activist. He has written a number of books, including the acclaimed *Orwell's Politics*, *Dangerous Men: Myth, Masculinity and the SAS*, and *British Counter-Insurgency: From Palestine to Ireland*

he British state used every method to hold on to its empire—here a rebel in Burma is
tured. Burma finally gained its independence in 1948.

Bush's proposed military budget for 2003 is $396 billion. Only $25 billion has been proposed for international aid

ARMS TRADE
MARK PHYTHIAN

The export of arms is a highly political act, because the arms trade is utterly different from all other types of commerce. It involves the transfer of the means to kill and repress, to sustain oppressive systems in power, and to wage aggressive wars.[1] While these exports tend to be justified in terms of providing 'friends' with the means to defend themselves—invoking Article 51 of the UN Charter—exporters cannot control the uses to which their arms are put once they are exported, or anticipate political developments which alter the political context into which they are being sent. The act of exporting arms is also a recognition of the political legitimacy of the recipient (and also, implicitly, of any courses of action it is then engaged in), while the withholding of arms is an acute expression of political disapproval and punishment.

In the post Cold War world, one state dominates this arms trade—the United States. Arms trade statistics are gathered and published by various bodies and tend to employ slightly differing methodologies. However, all agree on this absolute US dominance. The most recent figures from the Stockholm International Research Institute show that in the period 1997-2001 the US enjoyed almost 45 percent of the trade in major conventional weapons.

TABLE 1: Leading suppliers of major conventional weapons, 1997-2001[2]

Rank	Supplier	Value (US$m)	Percent of total
1	United States	44,821	44.5
2	Russia	17,354	17.2
3	France	9,808	9.7
4	United Kingdom	6,699	6.6
5	Germany	4,821	4.8
Total of top five		83,503	82.8
Total		100,732	100.0

In terms of arms sales to the developing world (approximately two thirds of all the world's legal arms traffic), the Congressional Research Service tells a similar picture of US market domination.

TABLE 2: Leading suppliers of arms to the developing world, 1994-2001[3]

Rank	Supplier	Value of deliveries (US$m)
1	United States	74,928
2	United Kingdom	37,000
3	France	23,300
4	Russia	19,900
5	China	4,900

The value of this global market fell in 2001, and consequently so too did the value of US arms exports. However, as a proportion of all arms exported, its market share held up well (falling only marginally from a 46.3 percent share in 2000 to a 43.6 percent share in 2001). Increasingly the US *market share* is immune to challenge, because of the large number of countries that now operate US weapons systems and regard the US as their armourer of choice. They regard the US in this way for a range of political and economic reasons. No other supplier can offer such largess in the guise of a range of military aid programmes to facilitate the purchase of its arms. Also, these countries generate an ongoing demand for US upgrades, spare parts, munitions, training and support services. The above factors together account for a significant proportion of the dollar gap between the US and its nearest arms supply rivals.

It should come as no surprise that US defence companies are the largest in the world. In fact, seven out of the world's ten leading defence companies in the year 2000 were American, and five of the top six, as Table 3 shows.

TABLE 3: Top ten defence companies, 2000[4]

Rank	Company	Country	Defence revenue (US$m)
1	Lockheed Martin Corp	US	18,000.0
2	Boeing Company	US	17,000.0
3	Raytheon Company	US	14,033.0
4	BAE Systems	UK	13,247.5
5	General Dynamics Corp	US	6,542.0
6	Northrop Grunman Corp	US	5,600.0
7	EADS	France	4,559.8
8	Thales	France	4,261.5
9	United Technologies Corp	US	4,130.0
10	TRW Inc	US	4,000.0

There are very good reasons to expect the US share of the global arms market to increase in the immediate future, and to continue to do so for as long as the 'war on terror' remains the dominant prism through which the US frames its approach to foreign policy. One reason lies in the fact that the supply of arms is one highly visible way of rewarding or recognising partnership in the post 11 September 'war on terror'—especially for states where involvement may carry a domestic political price, but where US arms supply can satisfy institutional requirements around arms. In addition, long-existing insurgencies, relabelled as far-flung expressions of the global 'war on terror', qualify the states combating them for increased military aid and arms sales. To take a few recent examples, Colombia (where the nearly 40-year civil war waged by the Farc is now being classified in 'war on terror' terms), Georgia, Indonesia and the Philippines have all benefited in this manner. Elsewhere, Israel's deft linkage of the ongoing violence between Israeli forces and the Palestinians to the 'war on terror' has helped to pave the way for the US to agree to continue to sell Israel advanced weaponry to be used in that conflict.

In these instances, various interests and principles compete to influence policy, just as they have in earlier arms export decisions. Broadly speaking, there are three types of interest and principle involved: (1) geo-strategic interests; (2) domestic interests (whether industrial/commercial or in terms of foreign policy lobby groups); (3) principles/norms of international conduct, for exam-

Prior to 1999 the US was the principal supplier of arms to the Suharto regime, despite the fact that from late 1975 Indonesia was in illegal occupation of East Timor

ple regarding human rights, arms control, and non-proliferation. While these do not have to be mutually antagonistic, because of the way in which the US defines and seeks to pursue its national security, they rarely tend to pull in the same direction. Moreover, the 'poor relation' in these three sets of interests has been that which emphasises norms around human rights and arms control. The response to 11 September and the 'war on terror' has in fact allowed the US to pursue arms sales regardless of these norms. It has done so in a way that contributes significantly to the erosion of these norms by embracing a language where, at a global level, US national security is explicitly prioritised over individual rights. Earlier adherence to these norms offers one explanation for a supposed erosion in US security.

However, just as the unilateralism of the Bush administration was clearly evident prior to the events of 11 September, only to be codified in the policy of pre-emption in its aftermath, so there is a sense in which the 'war on terror' has allowed the US to arm friendly states where there was evidence of a pre 11 September desire or disposition to anyway, but where international norms had to be overcome or bypassed.

Take the case of Indonesia. Prior to 1999 the US was the principal supplier of arms to the Suharto regime, despite the fact that from late 1975 Indonesia was in illegal occupation of East Timor. The invasion of East Timor was given a 'green light' by US President Ford, who stopped off in Indonesia on the eve of the Indonesian invasion. In the early 1990s—as a result of atrocities carried out principally in East Timor using US-supplied arms, such as the 1991 massacre in the capital, Dili, conducted in part with the use of US M-16 assault rifles—restrictions were placed on US arms sales. This culminated in the Clinton administration's moratorium on all US arms exports in the aftermath of the slaughter that accompanied the August 1999 East Timorese independence referendum.[5] However, Indonesia's geo-strategic importance, and fears for the consequences of its break-up, meant that the re-establishment of close ties with the Indonesian military was always going to be a priority. This process was clearly under way prior to 11 September. On 30 July 2001 the Bush administration announced plans to push for the step by step restoration of US military ties with Indonesia, in part responding to fears that Indonesia might buy the Russian SU-30 fighter aircraft, and that consequently the US may begin to see its market grip weakened.[6] However, the post 11 September climate has seen the Bush administration accelerate this push for a renewal of military aid—to forces that its own State Department accepts are continuing to engage in widespread abuses of human rights in Aceh and Papua. For example, in the 2001 human rights report on Indonesia (released in March 2002) the State Department noted:

> The government's human rights record remained poor, and it continued to commit serious abuses. Security forces were responsible for numerous instances of, at times indiscriminate, shooting of civilians, torture, rape, beatings and other abuse, and arbitrary detention in Aceh, West Timor, Papua (formerly known as Irian Jaya), and elsewhere in the country. TNI personnel often responded with indiscriminate violence after physical attacks on soldiers. They also continued to conduct 'sweeps' that led to killing of civilians and property destruction.[7]

In short, Indonesia represents a clear case where the Bush administration's 'war on terror' paradigm allows it to override ongoing human rights concerns to re-establish or cement military relations with states important to the US via the provision of US arms or military training.

The 'war on terror' has also impacted on the climate of US military support for Israel. In the past decade the US has sold Israel $7.2 billion in arms, given it arms and ammunition for free under the Excess Defence Articles programme, and underwritten the development of its domestic armaments industry. Inherently controversial, US arms sales to Israel came under heightened criticism in the context of the intifada, and their high profile deployment in intifada-related Israeli operations. As Amnesty International reports, two years on from the start of the intifada:

The imperatives of the 'war on terror' have also required loosening restrictions on the supply of arms, spares and military training

> There appears to be no end in sight to the human rights crisis... Some 1,800 Palestinians have been killed, most of them unlawfully, by the Israeli Defence Forces (IDF), who routinely use F-16 fighter jets, helicopter gunships and tanks to bomb and shell densely populated Palestinian residential areas. The victims included more than 300 children and some 80 individuals killed in targeted state assassinations.[8]

During 2002 there were a number of reported instances of US-supplied arms being used in Israeli attacks in which civilians were killed. To take just three, on 8 March, the *Washington Post* carried a report of an incident in Bethlehem where:

> ...the Israeli military almost immediately launched more missiles and opened fire with gunboats at official Palestinian buildings in the Gaza Strip, where there were heavy casualties. Israel also sent dozens of tanks and armoured personnel carriers into Bethlehem, two adjacent Palestinian refugee camps and a pair of neighbouring West Bank towns, bringing full-scale military action to the suburbs of Jerusalem. The bark of heavy machine guns atop Israel's armoured vehicles echoed throughout Bethlehem, considered the birthplace of Jesus, and US-supplied AH-64 Apache helicopters fired into the Aida refugee camp between Bethlehem and Beit Jala.

The following month, on 18 April, the *New York Times* carried a report from Jenin, observing that:

...the decaying body of Mr Khurj's sister appears to be one of the clearest examples to date of a civilian having been killed in an Apache helicopter missile attack. There is an enormous hole in the wall of her bedroom and a two foot wide crater in the floor. Shards of a missile, including one with labels in English describing 'firing temperature' and 'cooling temperature', littered the floor. Near the hole in the wall was a pool of dried blood. Mr Khurj said the missile struck in the middle of the night on the third day of the attack. It killed his sister instantly.[9]

On 23 July, in a Gaza City apartment complex, Hamas leader Salah Shehadeh was attacked using US-supplied F-16s, resulting in the deaths of at least 15 (including nine children), leaving a further 140 injured, and flattening three apartment buildings. President Bush merely described the attack as 'heavy handed'. Human Rights Watch labelled it 'part of the Israeli government's policy of assassinating individuals it considers responsible for attacks against Israeli civilians and military targets'.[10] Under the terms of US arms export control legislation, the use to which US arms should be put after export is limited to self-defence and internal security, and any

> The value of UK military export licences to Israel almost doubled from £12.5 million in 2000 to £22.5 million. During this time the peace process broke down and Israel began its military campaign. The irony is that the UK government agree that the Israeli occupation of Palestinian land post 11 September is illegal by international law, yet they fund Israel's campaign against the Palestinian uprising that is a response to this situation. In July 2002 the UK government drew up new guidelines allowing it to bypass its own export criteria and authorise the sale of UK manufactured components to the US that are then incorporated into F-16s bound for Israel.
> CAMPAIGN AGAINST THE ARMS TRADE www.caat.org.uk

excesses in the use to which US arms are put should be monitored by the executive branch and reported to Congress. In practice, the 'war on terror' and Israel's adoption of the language of the 'war on terror' make it easier for the administration to override the norms that might dictate investigation and condemnation, and continue its military support for Israel's approach to ending the intifada.

The imperatives of the 'war on terror' have also required loosening restrictions on the supply of arms, spares and military training to a host of states where international norms had previously dictated that their behaviour merited the imposition of sanctions or a more restrictive approach to military relations. Foremost among these were Pakistan and India, despite the fact that contemporaneous tensions over Kashmir were pushing the region to the brink of nuclear war. Sanctions had been imposed on both after their 1998 nuclear weapons tests. As with Indonesia, with regard to India in particular there is clear evidence that the Bush administration felt the costs of applying the sanctions were outweighing the benefits well before the events of 11 September, but lifting sanctions also provided an immediate and highly visible way of rewarding the Musharraf regime for its support for the 'war on terror', vital to its prosecution in Afghanistan and in attempts to round up key Al Qaida and Taliban figures.

Keen to reward now-key players with dubious human rights and proliferation histories, the administration included a provision in a draft anti-terrorism bill that would have lifted all restrictions on military aid and arms exports for up to five years. It considered doing so would help fight terrorism or other threats to US security. However, strong criticism from Congress and campaigning groups led to the proposal being reduced to a request to lift the remaining sanctions imposed on Pakistan for two years. Other

Blair's government supplies Israel with chemical warfare technology, including PCPs, which can be turned into sarin nerve gas. After nuclear weapons, it is the most feared weapon of mass destruction.

beneficiaries of this approach, being rewarded for their cooperation in the 'war on terror', have included Azerbaijan, Kyrgyzstan, Tajikistan, Turkmenistan and Uzbekistan." According to the US State Department, all have poor human rights records, and yet all now stand to enjoy the legitimacy—and even receive the arms that could further aid the repression of their populations—that the US proposes to bestow on them as the 'war on terror' comes to be prioritised over international norms of respect for human rights and tolerance of political dissent. To take just a couple of examples, the most recent (2001) report on Uzbekistan explains:

> Uzbekistan is an authoritarian state with limited civil rights... The government's human rights record remained very poor, and it continued to commit numerous serious abuses. Citizens cannot exercise the right to change their government peacefully; the government does not permit the existence of opposition parties. Security force mistreatment resulted in the deaths of several citizens in custody. Police and NSS forces tortured, beat, and harassed persons. Prison conditions were poor, and pre-trial detention can be prolonged. The security forces arbitrarily arrested and detained persons, on false charges, particularly Muslims suspected of extremist sympathies, frequently planting narcotics, weapons or banned literature on them.[12]

The most recent report for Tajikistan notes how:

> ...the government's human rights record remained poor, and the government continued to commit serious abuses. The February 2000 parliamentary elections represented an improvement in the citizens' right to change their government; however, this right remained restricted. Some members of the security forces committed extrajudicial killings. There were a number of disappearances and kidnappings. Security forces at times tortured, beat and abused detainees and other persons. These forces also were responsible for threats, extortion, looting and abuse of civilians. Certain battalions of nominally government forces operated quasi-independently under their leaders.[13]

There is now a widespread dispersal of US military equipment across many states previously disqualified from receiving it on a combination of human rights, non-proliferation and non-engagement grounds. This shows clearly how the lessons of the recent past regarding 'blowback' have simply not been absorbed. That is, the way in which present day policy involving the supply of military equipment or know-how, especially where provided on the basis of the 'my enemy's enemy is my friend' calculation, can return to haunt the US in the future. This is particularly worthy of note given that the classic expression of blowback to date relates to the groups and culture that grew out of the US experiment in arming the anti-Soviet Mujahadeen in Afghanistan during the 1980s. One of the most under-reported stories of the entire 2001-02 US campaign in Afghanistan concerned the number of US Stinger missiles, which the CIA could not buy back at any price during the 1990s, which then turned up in weapons searches in places like Kandahar.

In short, the lease of life that the post 11 September US security environment has given to US arms sales is unlikely to encourage compliance with the kind of norms that international society should be most concerned with—around human rights, non-proliferation and so on. Instead it will reward strategically valuable allies regardless of their reputations, undermine norms, and increase the pool of arms liable to being traded illicitly. At the same time it will be extending US military influence to new areas and cementing the US role as by far the world's dominant arms producer and armourer of choice. As Michelle Ciarrocca has argued:

> Washington's policies must promote, rather than undermine, human rights and democratic institutions abroad. The narrow, military focus of the Bush administration can be seen most vividly when comparing the FY [financial year] 2003 military budget request of $396 billion to the $25 billion requested for international aid. The administration's unwillingness to increase spending on diplomacy or foreign economic aid underscores the extent to which it is treating the war on terrorism as primarily a military enterprise, in which the US rounds up a series of ad hoc 'posses' to go after the enemy of the moment. This go it alone attitude is at least as dangerous as the military build-up that is being justified in the name of fighting terrorism.[14]

Currently there seems little prospect of such a message permeating the corridors of power in Washington, DC.

Mark Phythian teaches politics at the University of Wolverhampton. He has written widely on aspects of the arms trade

NOTES

1   When exported to non-state actors arms also facilitate challenges to state power. However, transfers to non-state actors are almost invariably illicit (although sometimes referred to as 'grey' market transfers). This chapter deals only with the US role in the legal arms trade.

2   Derived from data at http://projects.sipri.se/armstrade/appx8a2002.pdf Values given are at constant (1990) prices.

3   Richard F Grimmett, *Conventional Arms Transfers to Developing Nations, 1994-2001*, Congressional Research Service, 6 August 2002, data from Table 2F, Available at www.fas.org/asmp/resources/govern/crs-rl31529.pdf. Values are in 2001 US$ millions.

4   Source: *Defense News*, 30 July-5 August 2001.

5   For a summary, see *Arms Sales Monitor* 41 (October 1999), p1, available via www.fas.org/asmp/

6   *Arms Sales Monitor* 46 (September 2001), p4, available via www.fas.org/asmp/

7   US Department of State, *Country Reports on Human Rights Practices 2001: Indonesia*, available at www.state.gov/g/drl/rls/hrrpt/2001/eap/8314.htm

8   http://web.amnesty.org/web/web.nsf/pages/IOT_home

9   Both of these accounts are taken from William D Hartung and Frida Berrigan, 'US Arms Transfers and Security Assistance to Israel', Arms Trade Resource Center Fact Sheet, 6 May 2002, available at www.worldpolicy.org/projects/arms/reports/israel050602.html

10 Human Rights Watch, 'Israeli Airstrike on

Crowded Civilian Area Condemned',
available at http://hrw.org/press/2002/
07/gaza072302.htm

11 See *Arms Sales Monitor* 47 (January
2002), p1, available via www.fas.org/asmp/

12 US Department of State, *Country Reports
on Human Rights Practices 2001:
Uzbekistan*, available at www.state.gov/
g/drl/rls/hrrpt/2001/eur/8366.htm

13 US Department of State, *Country Reports
on Human Rights Practices 2001:
Tajikistan*, available at www.state.gov/
g/drl/rls/hrrpt/2001/eur/8353.htm

14 Michelle Ciarrocca, 'Post-9/11 Economic
Windfalls for Arms Manufacturers',
Foreign Policy in Focus, vol 7, no 10
(September 2002), available at
www.fpif.org/briefs/vol7/v7n10arms.html

Anti arms trade protesters take direct action outside a BAE Systems annual general meeting in London. BAE Systems has

WORLD MILITARY SPENDING IN 2000:
$839 BILLION

ANNUAL COST OF UNIVERSAL PROVISION OF BASIC SERVICES IN DEVELOPING COUNTRIES:
$80 BILLION

ANNUAL US MILITARY RESEARCH BUDGET:
$75 BILLION

ANNUAL COST OF PROVIDING HEALTHCARE AND NUTRITION FOR EVERYONE IN THE WORLD:
$15 BILLION

STEALTH BOMBER PROJECT:
$48 BILLION
COST PER BOMBER:
$1.5 BILLION

TO PREVENT 500,000 MALARIA DEATHS IN A YEAR:
$1 BILLION

Ecuador—IMF policies take their toll on the poor

IMF AND WORLD BANK
GEORGE MONBIOT

What's the first thing that people should know about the functioning of the IMF and World Bank, and how are these international institutions connected to corporate power?

The key issue is that the World Bank and IMF are controlled exclusively by the rich nations and work exclusively in the poor nations. They set economic policies for those poor nations and effectively deny the governments of those nations from making a serious attempt at setting their own economic policies—and therefore their own political prescriptions.

So you have a straightforward refutation of democracy taking place here. You have the poor world being governed by the rich world, almost exactly as if we were still living in colonial times.

The result is that very often we see decisions made which appear to favour not the interests of the poor world—which supposedly these two institutions are trying to help—but the interests of Wall Street brokers, foreign multinationals, big business based in the rich world. The rich world has done very well out of World Bank and IMF decisions, while the poor and less developed world have done very badly.

Take the principal emergency packages from the IMF over the past few years. These have involved enormous bailouts, whose prime purpose is to allow foreign 'investors'—which really means speculators—to get their money out before the economies of poor nations collapse.

There have not been any substantial bailouts at all for such essentials in the collapsing countries as health and education, the welfare of the poor who lose their job as a result of the crisis, the government institutions which can't function anymore. The bailouts seem to be aimed exclusively at securing the investments of these foreign speculators.

More profoundly than that, many of the crises—the Asian financial crisis of 1997-98 and now the Argentinian crisis are very good examples—were caused as a result of, principally, IMF policy that was aimed exclusively at pleasing the financial community in the United States.

So, for instance, in Asia, we saw the IMF demanding the removal of all capital controls and financial controls, which exposed Asia to this incredible speculative flow of what's called hot money—short-term funds—allowing the Wall Street brokers to launch ferocious speculative attacks on the currencies of the Asian countries and bring those countries to their knees.

The removal of all regulations, which the IMF demanded, had nothing whatsoever to do with the welfare of the nations concerned. The only possible reason for the stringency of its demands is that it was being lobbied to make those demands by Wall Street. The only beneficiary of those policies were the brokers who made a very large amount of money after the South East Asian collapse.

We see this pattern repeated time and again, and you have to ask after a while, 'Who is driving this?' The only possible answer that comes to mind is that these very exclusive financial interests in the West are driving this.

And they are systematically destroying economies all over the world.

One of the messages coming out of the United Nations Earth Summit in Johannesburg was that institutions like the IMF and World Bank were recognising past mistakes and trying to be more inclusive. What do you think of this?

There are two problems with the idea. The first is that it's impossible to see how they can reform themselves if they continue to refuse to acknowledge the scope of the mistakes they have made in the past. Neither institution has done that.

They've acknowledged certain minor errors. They've acknowledged errors of implementation. They've acknowledged that they've gone a little bit too far in some respects. But they haven't faced up to the systematic failure of their policies—and the fact that their policies have been, in many cases, far more destructive than beneficial to the interests of the poor.

Until they can do that, why on earth should we trust them when they say that they will do better in the future?

The second issue here is that both the World Bank and the IMF are constitutionally destined to fail. Partly, this is because they are controlled by the rich world, working on the poor, so they are as undemocratic as you can get. And in the absence of democracy, one can only expect failure. Also, because they are effectively enforcing a debt-based global financial system, which can only lead to more debt.

The IMF and World Bank were created in response to the failure of the original proposal before Bretton-Woods, made by the economist John Maynard Keynes, for a self-correcting international financial system, where both creditors as well as debtors were obliged to clear both imbalances of trade and international debt.

That was thrown out, principally because of lobbying by the US, which was at the time the world's largest creditor. And a wholly inadequate system—namely, the World Bank and the IMF—was put in its place. However much you tinker with that system, it will remain wholly inadequate.

The US government's 'war on terrorism' has had a big impact on the global justice movement, especially in the US. How do you see the relationship between the war and global justice issues?

I think these are intimately connected, and I take a lot of heart from the fact that many people who previously were campaigning exclusively on issues of corporate power have widened the scope of their campaigning to take a powerful stand against war.

There's no question that these interests are connected. It's partly because of corporate power that you have a president called George Bush at all. We know the extent to which campaign contributions help to steer the result in American elections.

It's partly because the administration feels the need to secure oil reserves that we have this prospect of war. And one of the reasons it feels that need is that it's an administration run by oilmen and heavily influenced by oilmen.

It's also mindful of the extraordinary power of what Dwight Eisenhower called the 'military-industrial complex'—the amazing lobbying power that the defence industry has in the US, and indeed in other countries such as Britain. While that's not the whole reason why George Bush wants to go to war, there's no question that it's part of the reason.

So it's intimately connected with the struggle that those of us in the global justice movement have been involved in already.

How do you think 'global justice' can be achieved?

I'm working on just this myself at the moment—and looking at just what democracy would look like if it were applied to international relations.

What would a democratic world order look like, as opposed to the ultra-undemocratic world order we have at the moment—the World Bank and IMF controlled by a few rich nations, the G8 nations bringing a great deal of weight when they get together in their meetings, the UN Security Council controlled by the world's five biggest arms traders, the World Trade Organisation effectively controlled by shadowy teams of corporate lawyers who are utterly unaccountable to the public?

I'm looking at what the alternatives might look like, and I'm writing a book at the moment that will be out in June called *The Age of Consent*. And I'm saying that what we need to work towards is a global economic order based on consent, rather than the current one based on coercion.

So I have various models that I'm currently developing with that in mind.

What role does the grassroots organising of the global justice movement play in all this?

If you read the book by Joseph Stiglitz, *Globalization and its Discontents*, you will see that he—the man who was previously the chief economist of the World Bank—makes a very clear case that it's only because of protest that these issues are on the agenda at all in the rich nations.

Protests—like the ones that were seen in Seattle, and Prague and Genoa, and Washington in previous years—have alerted the rich world to the appalling injustices being meted out by institutions such as the IMF and the World Bank. And that raising of consciousness is the first step toward political change.

So I would say that the protests are absolutely essential step towards creating a just world order.

George Monbiot has become one of the leading voices of the global justice movement worldwide. He is a regular columnist for the *Guardian* and author of *Captive State: The Corporate Takeover of Britain*. This interview was taken from *Z Magazine*: www.zmag.org/weluser.htm
www.monbiot.com

PROTEST & THE GLOBAL ECONOMY

In 2001 alone the World Development Movement reported protests in 23 countries, charting 77 separate incidents involving millions of ordinary people. Over a third of these countries hosted protests directly against the IMF and World Bank. About 18 of the protests ended in brutality from the police or army. The arrests and injuries ran into thousands.

Decisions in the World Trade Organisation are made by voting or consensus. It is dominated by rich countries, especially the 'quad' countries, consisting of the US, Canada, Japan and the EU countries together. These 'quad' countries often make important decisions in meetings closed to others. Roughly 30 WTO member countries cannot afford an office in Geneva. Hardly any representatives from developing countries can attend the 40 to 50 important trade meetings held in an average week.

WTO rules are enforced through the Dispute Settlement Process, where countries are allowed to challenge each other's rules if they violate WTO rules. Cases are decided by a panel of three trade bureaucrats who rarely care about government responsibility to protect workers, their human rights and the environment. Poor countries do not possess the economic power to challenge richer nations when they fail to fulfil their commitments.

WORLD DEVELOPMENT MOVEMENT www.wdm.org.uk

THE UN ESTIMATES THAT POOR
COUNTRIES LOSE $1.3 BILLION
PER DAY DUE TO UNFAIR TRADE
RULES—14 TIMES THE AMOUNT
THEY RECEIVE IN AID

70 PERCENT OF WORLD TRADE
IS CONTROLLED BY
MULTINATIONAL CORPORATIONS

THE POOREST 49 COUNTRIES
MAKE UP 10 PERCENT OF THE
WORLD POPULATION—BUT
ACCOUNT FOR ONLY
0.4 PERCENT OF WORLD TRADE

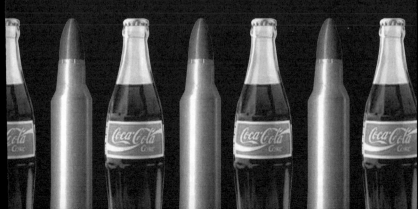

Vietnam, 1967. Photos like these helped shift public opinion against the war. The US government has since been determined to control media access to war zones.

MEDIA

PHILLIP KNIGHTLEY

The United States wants to wage war on Iraq because the Iraqi leader, Saddam Hussein, is a mad, bloodthirsty tyrant who sponsors international terrorism. Or does the US want to wage war on Iraq to make the Middle East safe for Israel? Or does it want to wage war on Iraq because Saddam Hussein wants/is developing/already has weapons of mass destruction that threaten world peace? Or, finally, does the US want to wage war on Iraq to steal its oil? This could go on indefinitely. There are as many theories as there are American hawks. But none of them carry conviction. There are lots of tyrants around who might or might not be sponsoring international terrorism. So why single out Saddam Hussein?

Israel will never be safe while it denies the Palestinians a state of their own. Other countries have weapons of mass destruction, and one has even used them—the US, back in 1945. So why single out Iraq? With so many new sources coming on-line, why should America worry about Iraqi oil? The real answer is much less complicated. America plans to wage war on Iraq because it is top dog, the most powerful nation in history, and its government can do whatever it likes to whoever it dislikes. Professor Noam Chomsky supports this view, and his argument is very persuasive. The way he sees it, you do not get to be top dog overnight. The British Empire was top dog for centuries. Then the Second World War came along, and in just five years it had been replaced by the US and the Soviet Union. They battled it out for more than half a century, and then Moscow surrendered and Washington was left in sole charge of the planet. Neo-conservative American int-

Chomsky compares the new international order with the criminal world. Like the Mafia, you have to establish that other people cannot get out of line

ellectuals think a lot about such matters, and one of the first things that occurred to them was that up until now, no top nation has avoided the fate of eventually being replaced by another, tougher dog. Was this inevitable or was there some way the US could dominate the world forever?

'Easy,' thought the think-tankers, and promptly coined a phrase to describe their idea—full spectrum dominance. The US must adopt policies that would enable it to dominate the rest of the world not just in military power, but in every field of human endeavour—military, industrial, commercial, cultural and, significantly, public information. It must not wait until another country begins to flex its muscles and think of becoming a rival to the US. It must crush any possible competitor the moment it shows the slightest sign of getting uppity. Chomsky compares the new international order with the criminal world. Like the Mafia, you have to establish that other people cannot get out of line. The US government therefore must make sure that other nations are scared shitless of them. Chomsky argues that politicians sometimes dress up this policy by claiming that it is America's manifest destiny, or creed, or moral duty to play world policeman. The Mafia don feels the same way, Chomsky says. It is his moral duty to keep his territory under control.

So the generally agreed plan of the neo-conservative nationalists in the US is to dominate the world through absolute superiority, especially military superiority. They may differ over tactics but their basic aim remains steadfast, even among the so-called doves. Do not forget that it was Colin Powell who, as chairman of the Joint Chiefs of Staff, said back in 1992 that the US needs sufficient power to deter any challenger from ever dreaming of challenging them on the world stage.

Although the US might try to justify a war against Iraq by the line that the road to Middle East peace lies through Baghdad, the real reason for attacking Iraq is simply to frighten the rest of the world with American military might. Then, with everyone else cowed into submissive silence, the American nationalists can turn their attention to what they see as the biggest challenge of all—China.

Anatol Lieven, a senior associate at the Carnegie Endowment for International Peace, Washington, DC, argues in the *London Review of Books* (3 October 2002) that what radical US nationalists have in mind is either to contain China by overwhelming military force and the creation of a circle of American allies or, in the case of the real radicals, to destroy the Chinese Communist state, just as the Soviet Union was destroyed. As with the Soviet Union, this would presumably involve breaking up China by liberating Tibet and other areas and, under the guise of 'democracy', crippling the central Chinese administration and its capacity to develop either its economy or its army. In the past the president and his supporters might have felt the need, to use Chomsky's phrase, to 'manufacture consent' for such an idea long before it could become policy. But the events of 11 September have done that for them.

'You are either with us or with the terrorists,' says Bush, and the few Americans who are brave enough to disagree are labelled as terrorist supporters. As confirmation of this, you only have to note the change in attitude among prominent American civil liberties lawyers. Alan Dershowitz, professor of criminal law at Harvard University, says he sees nothing wrong with torturing a terrorist suspect for information that could prevent another terrorist outrage. In fact, it might be moral cowardice not to torture a suspect, and a legal framework to allow torture should be set up. A London academic lawyer told me of a meeting he had with an American colleague, a friend of many years, who he could not bear to name. His friend is a leading civil rights lawyer, a man respected around the world for his adherence to the rule of law, belief in the presumption of innocence as a principle, the right of suspects to call upon the help of a lawyer, habeas corpus, and all the machinery of a fair justice system. He now says all this was a mistake, that it gives an impression of American weakness. 'I don't give a damn about that any more,' he said. 'Anything, I repeat anything, we have to do to get these bastards is OK by me.'

More than any other conflict in history, the war against terrorism is a war for information and its suppression

The only other professional group that should have been able to keep the neo-conservatives in check, the media, has been marginalised. Most of the media giants are on side, anyway, and the administration treats the others with contempt. One reason for this is a personal one. Vice-president Dick Cheney dislikes the press 'big time'. But the other reason is the development of a new approach to the media which should worry every journalist. More than any other conflict in history, the war against terrorism is a war for information and its suppression. This is the most information intensive war you can imagine. One military officer involved in the planning of the war openly told Howard Kurtz from the *Washington Post*, 'We're going to lie about things.' The Pentagon's growing fondness for a military discipline called 'Information Operations' (IO) certainly suggests that the military officer was not exaggerating. Ten groups together function to cover areas ranging from public affairs (PA) to military deception and psychological operations (psyops). In practice, what this means is that those military people whose job traditionally has been to talk to the media and divulge what they are able to say about conflicts now work hand in glove with those whose job it is to support battlefield operations with misinformation. In short, the media risks becoming an unknowing pawn in military strategy.

Maud S Beelman, director of the International Consortium of Investigative Journalists, Washington, DC, and a former Associated Press war correspondent in the Balkans, recently gave an example of what this could mean. The Pentagon has a fleet of EC-130 'Commando Solo' aircraft which can insert radio and TV programming into national broadcasting systems against the wishes of those systems and without their prior knowledge. The programmes may include video images created and/or altered electronically in a manner that cannot be detected. Journalists monitoring local media in a war zone would have to constantly question whether what they were receiving was genuine or US military misinformation. Beelman asked the American military officers who explain all this if, when it occurred, they would take the reporters into their confidence to spare them from spreading misinformation. The officers replied that they would not. Journalists are to kept in the dark.

Even more chilling is the warning issued by US Deputy Assistant Defence Secretary for Public Affairs, Rear Admiral Craig Quigley, to those sections of the media not fully on side. It can be summed up as, 'Don't get in our way or we'll bomb you, too.' This is of particular significance because the main American TV networks and the BBC have been planning to cover a war against Iraq not only from the American side but—as they did in the first Gulf War— from the Iraqi side as well.

The BBC, concerned that one of its correspondents was nearly killed when an American shell hit the corporation's newly reopened bureau in Kabul on 12 November, sought assurance from the Pentagon that these were accidents. There was a similar strike a few hours later on a compound occupied by the Arabic TV network Al Jazeera. It was not an accident, according to the Pentagon. The targets had military significance—which the Pentagon refused to define—and, in any case, the US military command makes no effort to distinguish between legitimate satellite uplinks for broadcast news communications and the identifiable radio or satellite communications of whoever it defines as the 'enemy'. Put bluntly, the Pentagon is saying to the world media that want to cover a war against Iraq, 'Stay out, or assume that your technology will make you one of our targets.'

There is another reason behind this new attitude towards the media. The neo-conservatives are determined to avoid a repetition of Vietnam where the media, free of restrictions, were able to report what was really happening there. This, according to the American military establishment, cost the US the victory it desired. With the American media pulled into line by accusations of a lack of patriotism, Bush's 'with us or with the terrorists' rhetoric, and the warnings given to the foreign media wanting to cover the war, the neo-conservatives believe that they have ensured that images of bloody battle will not erode public support for the war.

But what about the risk of the public seeing soldiers coming home as a long line of body bags at US airports? Will that not make them think again? The advantage of using 'hawks' is that the military believe they can wage war in the 21st century with minimum American casualties. Other casualties do not count. New war technology and the use of mercenaries have transferred the risk of being killed in a US-run war away from US servicemen to others.

Who are these others? At the beginning of the 20th century about 90 percent of all casualties in war were soldiers. At the beginning of the 21st century 90 percent of all casualties in war are civilians.

President Bush says that America is already involved in a war, but that it is now simply more at war than before. Since the Second World War US governments have either invaded, bombed, or both, the following places: Korea, Vietnam, Laos, Cambodia, Guatemala, Honduras, Panama, Cuba, Grenada, Haiti, Lebanon, Libya, Iraq, Somalia, the Balkans and Afghanistan.

They may describe these operations as 'containing Communism', 'restoring democracy', 'spreading freedom and the American way of life', 'humanitarian intervention', 'playing international policeman' or 'waging war on terrorism', but they are all part of the grand American plan of keeping the US top dog for at least the rest of this century.

Phillip Knightley is the author of many books. He is best known for *The First Casualty*, a history of war correspondents and propaganda

...testing against the media's distortion of the truth on an anti-war demonstration.

The effects of civil war in Somalia. UN intervention only worsened the situation. UN Somalis from all over the world committed atrocities against Somali people

UNITED NATIONS

JOHN BAXTER

On 8 November 2002 the UN Security Council passed Resolution 1441. Superficially, the resolution only refers to attempts to disarm Iraq, removing weapons of mass destruction. In reality the resolution gives Bush a green light to declare war. There had been speculation that the United States would have difficulty getting a resolution it could accept. France, Syria and Russia seemed unlikely to back down from their earlier opposition. But the US managed to bribe and threaten Security Council members into voting unanimously for the hardline resolution. Russia and France have been promised a share of the Iraqi oil industry. It was made clear to Russia that there will be no opposition from the US to further military action against Chechen rebels. Syria was threatened with being declared a 'terror state' if it did not vote for the resolution, and offered the hope of a deal to regain the Golan Heights, taken by Israel in 1967. The tiny island state of Mauritius was under threat of losing aid from the US African Growth and Opportunity Act.

For the second time in recent history, it appears that the US will be slaughtering Iraqi men, women and children with the backing of the UN. In 1991 America's first war on Iraq was launched after Bush Sr managed to win Security Council backing in much the same way. In reality, that war never ended, as UN sanctions and the US and British air strikes continue to kill tens of thousands of Iraqis each year.

Despite the United Nations' role in the slaughter of Iraqis, many in the anti-war camp see it as a potential force for peace, if only it could be reformed. The United Nations Charter, signed by the founding states in 1945, certainly commits the UN to goals which are hard to disagree with. They resolved:

The UN is, and always has been, the creature of the imperialist powers

> ...to save succeeding generations from the scourge of war, which twice in our lifetime has brought untold sorrow to mankind, to reaffirm faith in human rights, in the dignity and worth of the human person, in the equal rights of men and women and of nations large and small, to establish conditions under which justice and respect for the obligations arising from treaties and other sources of international law can be maintained, to promote social progress and better standards of life in larger freedom.[1]

However, it is wrong to mistake the laudable rhetoric which so often emerges from the UN for its real purpose. The UN did not emerge out of people's hopes for peace, but from the machinations of the major powers as they existed at the close of the Second World War. The UN is, and always has been, the creature of the imperialist powers. For the last 60 years the US has been the most powerful imperialist nation, and as such it has dominated the organisation.

THE BIRTH OF THE UNITED NATIONS

The UN was launched in 1945 at the close of the Second World War. Officials within the US State Department had been planning for peace from as early as 1941, and by 1943 the formation of the United Nations was a declared objective of US foreign policy. The closing years of the war saw rounds of conferences at Tehran, Yalta and Potsdam as the three major powers, the US, Russia and Britain, horse-traded for influence. The launch of the UN was part of this process.

The shifting alliances and splits between and within the ruling classes of the different countries founding the UN were complex. But, put simply, Russia and Britain saw their interests as being to maintain the pre-war system of spheres of interest, acting as largely independent trading blocs. For Britain this reflected the desire to hold on to empire and to develop a trading block in Western Europe. For Russia it reflected the desire to develop a sphere of influence in Eastern Europe. Russia and Britain were lukewarm about the prospect of the UN, but were not prepared to openly oppose it.

The US emerged from the war the most powerful nation, with more than half of the world's industrial capacity, almost two thirds of the world's gold reserves, and a military capacity which dwarfed that of other states. The desire to prevent damaging wars was no doubt important to US strategists, but only in so far as wars damaged US interests. Those interests were reflected in a desire to see free trade throughout the world, so as to provide open access for America's powerful business interests. The creation of the UN would provide a forum in which the US could use its weight to hold back the aspirations of its former allies to create trading blocs resistant to American influence.

Whilst at times the US had to make compromises in order to keep the Allies on board, it was always American interests which dominated in the negotiations. What emerged was a UN system dominated by the Security Council, which was in turn controlled by the five permanent members, each with the right to veto any resolution. The five represent the balance of power as it existed at the close of the war—the three Allies with France and China.

At the launch of the UN, as today, other countries had to be satisfied with membership of the General Assembly, a talking shop which has passed thousands of resolutions but has no real power. Even so, at the founding of the UN, America wanted to ensure that the assembly would not pass anything embarrassing, and made sure it was packed with powers sympathetic to the US. The criterion for membership was a declaration of war on the Axis powers. The US pressured its previously neutral allies in South America to declare war by the deadline of 1 March 1945. The success of this strategy can be judged from the fact that in the first seven years of the General Assembly (1946-53), of the 800 resolutions adopted the US was defeated in less than 3 percent, and in no case were important US interests involved.

THE UN DURING THE COLD WAR: 1945-89

Within two years of the founding of the UN the Cold War had begun. America and the USSR held back from direct conflict at the heart of the system, but instead fought their wars largely by proxy at the edges of the system. Between 1945 and 1989 there were 138 wars, resulting in 23 million deaths. All were fought in the so-called Third World. The Korean War killed 3 million, the Vietnam War 2 million. Military interventions not classified as wars, like those in Hungary in 1956, Czechoslovakia in 1968 and Grenada in 1983, claimed thousands of lives.

The US attitude to the UN General Assembly changed during this period. In the early years, when it could count on a majority in the assembly, it was particularly keen on using the assembly to promote its initiatives and, if necessary, to bypass the Security Council. However, during the 1960s, as decolonisation gathered pace, a seat in the General Assembly was seen as a confirmation of nationhood, and the number of members soared. By 1961 the numbers had grown from 51 to 100, and US dominance was destroyed. On more than one occasion the Assembly has condemned US actions, for example in 1983 when it described the invasion of Grenada as 'a flagrant violation of international law'. The difficulty in controlling the assembly votes forced an uneasy alliance between the USSR and America to re-establish the role of the Security Council, and since 1961 all UN military action has been authorised by the council. This recalcitrance on the part of the assembly also explains why at times both countries were unwilling to pay their full financial contributions to the UN, leading to a crisis in funding.

The period of the Cold War is recognised by even the most sympathetic liberal commentators as a period in which the stand-off between America and the USSR prevented the UN from acting as an effective peacekeeper. In the major conflicts (with the exception of Korea) the UN stood back and let the superpowers get on

In the major conflicts (with the exception of Korea) the UN stood back and let the superpowers get on with it

with it. America and the USSR could slaughter with impunity in Vietnam, Hungary, Czechoslovakia, Afghanistan and Cambodia, sometimes monitored by UN observers. The other permanent members did not tend to involve themselves in conflicts where their interests could clash with those of the US. On the one occasion when France and Britain did, in Suez in 1956, America was able to bypass their vetoes on the Security Council and push a motion through the General Assembly calling for their withdrawal. Britain and France had to bow to their economically superior ally. But where the US had no interests, the other permanent members could intervene without fear of interference from the UN: France was able to launch brutal wars to defend its colonies in Algeria and Indochina; China invaded Tibet; Britain murdered and tortured thousands to crush the so-called Mau Mau rebellion in Kenya in 1953. Countries outside of the Security Council elite have also been able to get away with slaughter when it has not been in the interests of the permanent members to intervene. The UN did nothing when Indonesia took advantage of the withdrawal of Portuguese troops from East Timor in 1975, launching an invasion in which over 200,000 were killed.

THE UN AFTER THE COLD WAR

For many the end of the Cold War seemed to offer the possibility that the UN could finally act as a force for peace. But any hope that the UN would come into its own was quickly demolished.

The UN-sanctioned war against Iraq in 1991 showed exactly the form that post Cold War cooperation would take. Russia's weakness after the revolutions of 1989, its desire to secure US investment and its own strategic interests in the region meant it was prepared to give its backing to the Gulf War. China too was anxious to develop trade links with the US and abstained when, on 30 November 1990, the Security Council passed a resolution sanctioning the use of military force. Within weeks Russia was repaid when Bush authorised the shipment of $1 billion worth of food to the USSR, while the ban on high level US-Chinese meetings, imposed after Tiananmen Square, was lifted.

The reason given for launching the first Gulf War was that Iraq had broken international law by invading a sovereign country, Kuwait. In fact Saddam Hussein had every reason to think he could resolve his border dispute

UN soldiers from all over the world committed atrocities against Somali civilians. Internal UN documents openly referred to Somali civilians as the enemy

with Kuwait by military means. The UN had said nothing when Iraq invaded the sovereign state of Iran in 1980, launching the Iran-Iraq war, which would last eight years. It suited US and Soviet interests to see Iran and Iraq tied up in a war of attrition. It was only after seven years of slaughter, when it appeared that Iran might win the war, that the Security Council finally determined that there had been a breach of the peace between the two countries. America could not afford to see its arch-enemy in the region strengthened by victory, and so joined the war on the side of Iraq. The intervention was the key to changing the balance of forces, and gave Iraq its victory.

The fact that Saddam Hussein murdered and tortured his opponents didn't matter when he was fighting Ayatollah Khomeini. However, when the monster the US had created got out of hand, Saddam Hussein was branded the 'new Hitler' to justify the onslaught against Iraq. In reality the war was necessary for two related reasons. The first was that the US was not prepared to see a huge proportion of world's oil reserves fall under Saddam Hussein's control. The related strategic reason was that the US was determined to construct its new world order, to stamp its authority on the world, and to banish forever the spectre of the Vietnam syndrome.

The American victory under a UN flag was followed by a second US-led intervention in Somalia. The US government claimed that military intervention would save 2 million people from certain starvation and death. In fact, while one optimistic report suggested that between 10,000 and 25,000 lives may have been saved, US troops alone claimed 10,000 casualties in a six month period in 1993.

UN soldiers from all over the world committed atrocities against Somali civilians. Internal UN documents openly referred to Somali civilians as the enemy. Pictures which appeared in the world's press showed Belgian troops roasting a Somali boy over a fire. The troops involved were brought to trial but were acquitted because the Somali child had never brought a complaint. When an American gunnery sergeant shot a boy dead for allegedly trying to steal his sunglasses, his punishment was the loss of one month's pay and demotion. Italian troops looted refugee camps. Malaysians beat up hospital staff. Pakistanis and Nigerians shot unarmed protesters.

By the mid-1990s the unanimity on the Security Council had effectively ended. It had become clear to the Russian ruling class that the US was not going to step in and solve its economic problems. Russia was again prepared to use its Security Council veto to thwart US plans. In its attempts to impose its will on the Balkans, America found it necessary to conduct operations under the flag of Nato. However, the UN was still a part of the strategy. In Bosnia and Kosovo multinational Nato forces, in reality US-dominated, were used to provide overwhelming firepower in order to impose the US's will on the ground. Once America had imposed its preferred solution, the UN was used to provide legitimacy to the settlement. In both cases UN administrations were used to provide a fig leaf for what were essentially colonial administrations.

THE UN AND ISRAEL

The very first act of the United Nations was to recognise the state of Israel, legitimising the ethnic cleansing of the Palestinian people, who had been driven from their lands to make way for Israeli settlers.

The UN General Assembly has passed resolution after resolution condemning the criminal behaviour of Israel, but no action has ever been taken and no sanctions have ever been enforced. The US veto on the Security Council has kept Israel safe from anything worse than harsh words from the assembly.

There was one occasion on when the Security Council passed a resolution critical of Israel. In 1967 Israel invaded Egypt, Syria and

Jordan, occupying Gaza, the Golan Heights and the West Bank. Israel's victory was welcomed by the US—it was, after all, a crushing blow to Arab nationalism, which had been threatening American oil supplies. But for the US this

The US and the other countries on the council are not going to allow change unless their predominance is protected

also led to problems—not least from the USSR, which felt threatened by US/Israeli advances in the region. A diplomatic solution emerged, in the form of Security Council Resolution 242. This called for a withdrawal to pre-1967 borders and recognition of the territorial rights of all existing states. There was no mention of the Palestinians.

Many see Resolution 242, suitably amended, as offering some hope for a just peace. But the US has consistently blocked any attempts to act on 242, whether amended or not. In 1976 Arab states on the Security Council introduced an amendment calling for the incorporation of a Palestinian state in the Occupied Territories. The amendment of course fell when America exercised its veto. Israel responded to the tabled amendment by boycotting the session and launching a bombing raid against Lebanon, killing 50.

> In September 2002 the UN passed Resolution 1435 asserting that Israel must 'immediately cease measures in and around Ramallah, including the destruction of Palestinian military and security infrastructure', and withdraw to pre 11 September positions. The resolution was passed 14 to zero, with one abstention from the US. Israel ignored the resolution, and no action was taken.

If Resolution 242 does have any part to play in the future of the Middle East, it will be on US/Israeli terms. They have already made it clear that if there is to be any Palestinian state, they are determined it will be a series of Bantustans.[2]

IS REFORM AN OPTION?

Many would agree with the bulk of my criticisms of the UN. Their argument is not that the UN has been a success story, but that it can be reformed. However, there seem to be as many proposals for UN reform as there are commentators. It has been argued that

Britain and France should give up their seats in favour of a single European Union representative. Others have argued that any one of a number of states deserve the status of permanent membership, including Japan, Germany, Indonesia, Brazil, Nigeria and India. The Commission on Global Governance called for the expansion of the Security Council, the phasing out of the veto, and an increase in power for the General Assembly.

Denis Halliday, the UN Commissioner for Humanitarian Aid to Iraq, was one of a number of UN officials who resigned in disgust from an organisation which proclaims humanitarian ideals but oversees genocide through sanctions in Iraq. He sees the Security Council as the root of the problem, contrasting it with the General Assembly:

> This is where democracy applies—one state, one vote. By contrast the Security Council has five permanent members who have veto rights. There is no democracy there. It does not in any way represent the real world. Had the issue of sanctions on Iraq gone to the General Assembly it would have been overturned by a very large majority. We have to change the United Nations, to reclaim what is ours.[1]

It would be harder for the US and Britain to bribe and threaten enough members of the General Assembly to get their own way, but not impossible, as we have seen from the experience of the UN's early years. But even if we wanted to transfer power away from the Security Council, we come up against the brick wall of the veto. The US and the other countries on the council are not going to allow change unless their predominance is protected. Even if we could reduce the role of the permanent members, who would we replace them with? We cannot point to any country in the world that will do anything other than represent its national interests, or more accurately the interests of its ruling class:

> Each member of the UN tries to use its membership to further its own interests. States have not joined out of respect for the 'UN idea', or with a view to creating a stronger organisation by transferring some of their powers to it. Rather they are in the UN for what they can get out of it. Of course, some states may see it as in their

interests to increase the deference which is paid to the opinions of the UN—as expressed, particularly, in the resolutions of the General Assembly. This is likely to be much more true of the weaker than of the stronger members... But even weaker states show little sign of wanting to endow the UN with any general authority.[4]

There is no possibility of creating a neutral force standing above the states of the world while those states are wedded to a system based on economic and military competition with one another. The world is made up of capitalist nation-states, all dominated by ruling elites who are prepared to stop at nothing to hold on to their power. The representatives they send to the UN are hand-picked to represent the interests of those elites. They don't turn into radical democrats when they walk through the doors of the General Assembly.

The United Nations was a tool designed by and for US imperialism, with the collusion of the other victors, at the close of the Second World War. That was a different time. History has moved on, and we should not be surprised that there many occasions when elements of the American ruling class find the UN more of an irritation than a useful tool. There are other times when the UN still proves its worth. As I write, it appears more and more likely that Iraq will fail the loaded test of weapons inspection. It would be very useful to Bush and Blair if elements of the anti-war movement muted their criticisms as a result of supposed UN legitimisation.

It may seem that denigrating the UN is a counsel of despair. Rather it is a call for more determined action. Ruling classes around the world have been shaken by the size of our anti-war movement. The battle for peace will be won on the streets, not in the United Nations.

John Baxter is a member of the Socialist Alliance (www.socialistalliance.net)**. He is a staff tutor at the Open University**
j.s.baxter@open.ac.uk

NOTES

This chapter is an abridged, updated version of my article 'Is the UN an Alternative to Humanitarian Imperialism?', *International Socialism* 85 (Autumn 1999). Further references can be found in that work.

1   Charter of the United Nations available from www.un.org
2   Noam Chomsky, 'Introduction', in Roanne Carey (ed), *The New Intifada: Resisting Israel's Apartheid* (London, 2001).
3   Quoted in John Pilger, *The New Rulers of the World* (London, 2002), p97.
4   A James, 'The United Nations', in D Armstrong and E Goldstein (eds), *The End of the Cold War* (London, 1990), p187.

THE CAIRO DECLARATION

AGAINST US HEGEMONY AND WAR ON IRAQ AND IN SOLIDARITY WITH PALESTINE. DECEMBER 2002

The international meeting organised by the Egyptian Popular Campaign to Confront US Aggression was convened in Cairo on 18 and 19 December to launch the International Campaign.

We, the participants, reaffirm our resolve to stand in solidarity with the people of Iraq and Palestine, recognising that war and aggression against them is part of a US project of global domination and subjugation. Solidarity with Iraq and Palestine is integral to the internationalist struggle against neoliberal globalisation. The Cairo meeting is not an isolated event, but an extension of a protracted international struggle against imperialism, from Seattle and Genoa to Lisbon and Florence, to Cordoba and Cairo.

The US provides unlimited support, and even justification, to the Zionist perpetrators of genocidal crimes against the Palestinian people. The suffering of the Iraqi people under a regime of genocidal sanctions lasting over a decade, and the aggressive militarism which they face today, is but a logical outcome of the structures of power asymmetry of the existing world order.

The suffering of the Arab people and the US's unwavering support of the system of apartheid imposed on the Palestinian people will undoubtedly fuel conflict and lead to the escalation of violence in one of the most sensitive areas of the world. Such danger can easily extend to neighbouring Europe, Asia and Africa. Continued preparation for war on Iraq in spite of its acceptance of a UN resolution of aggressive inspection of its armaments, as well as civilian industries, signals a predetermined intent to control the Arab region, its oil and indeed the entire world supply of oil.

The Cairo conference against war on Iraq and in solidarity with Palestine represents the launching of an international popular movement that creates effective mechanisms for confronting policies of aggression. The participation of international activists who are prominent for their struggle for human dignity, rights and justice, as well as intellectuals, authors, unionists, human rights workers, journalists and artists—from Egypt and the rest of the Arab world, Africa, Asia, Latin America, Europe, and the United States—will no doubt accelerate this noble endeavour in spite of the numerous obstacles that we have to confront.

It is important that this international popular initiative of solidarity with Iraq and Palestine proceed according to an action plan which includes clearly defined priorities:

1 Condemnation of US military presence on Arab land along with pressuring the Arab governments that allow US military bases on their territory to close them down, and not to provide air, naval or land facilities.

2 Develop cooperation among popular organisations of the South to reinforce solidarity in confronting the policies and practices of neoliberal globalisation and US hegemony.

3 Work towards cooperation with the international and anti-globalisation movement of the North and South, and participation in activities and meetings organised by this movement.

4 Under the banner 'Together against globalisation and US hegemony' add Iraq and Palestine to the agendas of international progressive meetings, particularly the next social forum at Porto Alegre.

5 Prepare to send human shields to Iraq

6 Introduce a boycott of US and Israeli commodities in solidarity campaigns.

7 Elect a steering committee to follow up on the implementation of the Cairo Declaration, and coordination among organisations which commit to its principles, and enhance awareness through appropriate actions raging from the preparation of posters to organising marches and demonstrations in solidarity with Iraq and Palestine.

For the full declaration go to www.stopwar.org.uk

Young Muslim women have played key roles of political leadership in the anti-war movem

ANTI-WAR MOVEMENT

LINDSEY GERMAN

It is something of an irony that London, the city which was built as the hub of an empire on which the sun never set, is now the scene of huge demonstrations against that latest imperial venture—the war with Iraq. The multiracial and multicultural elements in Britain, which are at their most accentuated in London, are well represented on all the demonstrations. People of all ages, races and nationalities, people from every background, have come together to oppose the drive to war with which Britain is identified as the second most bellicose country in the world.

There have been many anti-war movements in recent times—Vietnam, the big CND protests against cruise missiles in the early 1980s, the movement against the first Gulf War in 1990-91. But the present movement organised by the Stop the War Coalition is different.

It is much, much bigger. This was true even before the astounding turnout of 15 February. The demonstration of 400,000 on 28 September 2002 was bigger than all the demonstrations against the Vietnam War combined. The demonstration on 15 February was simply the biggest ever in Britain. Two million people marched in a huge movement of protest against the war. A *Guardian* poll estimated that at least one person from each of 1.25 million households had attended. Motorway service stations were gridlocked, trains crowded and West End streets packed. The Oxford Street department store John Lewis reported a 40 percent drop in sales on the Saturday.

The demonstration marked a turning point in British politics, and a challenge to the establishment—represented in parliament, Whitehall and the media.

The Stop the War Coalition is more diverse than any previous movement. Whereas the traditional peace movement has been identified as a white middle class movement, this is not true of the Stop the War Coalition. The demonstration on 15 February was undoubtedly the largest gathering of black and Asian people on a political march ever in Europe.

It also expresses a new politics. The huge public meetings which have taken place—200 in Gloucester, 300 in Swindon, 400 in St Albans—are not simply among the largest gatherings ever to have taken place in these towns, let alone on such a political issue. They also have the feel of true participatory democracy, with young and old, black and white, gay and straight all having an equal voice.

The politics are of course varied, but there are a number of key themes. There is a sense of betrayal over the fact that a Labour prime minister can be taking us into a war. There is a linkage between the war drive and the cuts in public services such as education and health. There is a dislike of the priorities of global capital, which lead to misery for so many, and the way in which war is used as the big stick when poor countries do not comply with capital's priorities. There is a very sophisticated understanding of a whole range of international policies over the Middle East, weapons sales and the effect of past wars.

Most important in the run-up to 15 February, however, was a sense that people in Britain have a historic opportunity to stop the war. The turnout for the demonstration was definitely increased by the feeling that those who opposed the war had a duty to turn out and try to break Blair from Bush, since the general understanding was that Bush would then find it impossible to go to war.

Increasingly the arguments at meetings have also turned on longstanding Labour Party members asking how it is possible to kick out a prime minister, activists querying where we are going after the anti-war campaign, and a broader feeling that we need to build democratic political alternatives.

The movement is so big that it has become its own story. The press now wonder how you get so many people on the streets spontaneously. In fact most of the mobilisation is not spontaneous—it is the product of activists around Britain booking coaches, selling tickets, leafleting, postering, demonstrating, holding public meetings and, above all, arguing with those around them. The events of 15 February tapped a political mood, but they did not just come from nowhere.

The Stop the War Coalition has been able to build a mass movement because it has taken a number of important decisions at its outset or in the course of its existence which helped to increase its strength. It has built a broad and diverse grouping bringing together various key elements—the left and the peace movement, the trade union movement and the Muslim community. It has therefore been able to become a genuinely multiracial mass force, which has made it easier for each grouping to go beyond its traditional constituencies. It always understood that the main enemy for those fighting the war against terrorism in Britain had to be the British and US governments. Therefore calls to equally condemn the Taliban, Saddam Hussein, etc, have always been rejected—not because of any support for, or illusions in, such regimes, but because it was felt that such demands could only play into the hands of pro-war elements here. It rejected a specifically anti-imperialist programme, arguing that all those who opposed the war, racist attacks and attacks on civil liberties were welcome to join. To limit membership of the coalition to those who had an understanding of imperialism would have been to cut it off from a genuinely broad level of support.

At the same time, much of the leadership of the Stop the War Coalition was comprised of people who defined themselves in some way as anti-imperialists. This meant they had a strategic understanding of what was happening with US imperialism, and that they could link up the various wars of the past decade as part of an overall onslaught. The coalition always tried to keep focused on what it was possible to do and what was the next step in the campaign.

The Stop the War Coalition was formed after the events of 11 September 2001. It was launched at a meeting in London's Friends Meeting House which attracted so many people that there were

Time and again, young Muslim women have played key roles of organising and political leadership, belying the conventional view

two overflow meetings, including one in the street. Its first organising meeting the following week attracted 500 people and voted to adopt policy against racism and in defence of civil liberties, as well as to oppose the 'war against terrorism'. The coalition mobilised large numbers for a CND demo shortly afterwards, which had the bombing of Afghanistan as its focus. The Stop the War Coalition demo against the Afghan War on 18 November attracted 100,000—even more remarkable given that the war looked like it was drawing to a close. Perhaps the most striking element of this protest was its multiracial nature. It was held during Ramadan, and when the time came for Muslims to break their fast this took place in Trafalgar Square, with Muslims and non-Muslims alike sharing food and drink.

The demonstration attracted many black and Asian people who were non-Muslims as well. There were people of all nationalities and ages coming together to protest at war. It was a landmark in protests in Britain and throughout the world, and was the beginning of Britain being seen as one of the centres of the anti-war movement internationally. Muslim involvement created major arguments with some on the left in Britain, who echoed much of the European left in believing that any Muslim who defended their clothing, culture or religion could not be an ally but must in some way be 'fundamentalist'. The Stop the War Coalition always welcomed and valued Muslim involvement, which in many areas has been the backbone of coalition activity. Time and again young Muslim women have played key roles of organising and political leadership, belying the conventional view.

With any campaign it is important to assess its ups and downs, and why it is possible to mobilise on issues at any one time. Clearly, after the Taliban regime was overthrown and a pro-

Western regime installed, the government and media declared that there were no problems left and that peace had broken out.

Although these views were strongly contested by most anti-war activists, there was little possibility of mobilising the huge numbers who had turned out while the bombing was still taking place on a daily basis. At the same time, the war was still continuing in a more general sense—in Afghanistan itself, possibly exploding into Kashmir or Palestine, and of course the main thrust of US military might was increasingly aimed at Iraq. How could we keep the Stop the War Coalition going when we didn't know the speed or scale of where the war would strike next?

There were a number of suggestions and competing calls on the Stop the War Coalition's resources. We held a 1,000-strong demonstration over Palestine outside the Israeli embassy at the end of January 2002, and also decided to organise a national demonstration over the war for early March. This was somewhat controversial. Many on the left claimed that few would mobilise for it, and there was obviously less interest among the Muslim community and peace campaigners than there had been the previous November. However, those of us organising the coalition felt it was important to show that we were still there, to rally our supporters and, most crucially, to tap into an anti-war mood within wider society. This we did very successfully, with 20,000 demonstrating, and with a strong anti-imperialist core. The trade union conference season brought some real successes for the coalition, which held a number of important fringe meetings and won union support.

Events in Palestine erupted in the spring, when the coalition gave its support to two very substantial demonstrations which took place within a month of one another. It was soon after these that we took the decision to mobilise for a demonstration around the theme of 'Don't attack Iraq' in the run-up to the Labour Party conference at the end of September 2002. The organisers of the April demonstration over Palestine, the Muslim Association of Britain, had called a demonstration on the second anniversary of the Al Aqsa intifada, and both sides felt that rather than have two competing demonstrations the events were sufficiently connected to be able to mobilise one large protest. The demonstration therefore became about two issues—Iraq and Palestine. There was some scepticism in the early summer over whether Iraq

Ron Kovic, Vietnam veteran and author of *Born on the Fourth of July*, e-mailed us to say, 'You have inspired the world'

would be an issue. We were as certain as it was possible to be, given that we can't see into the minds of Tony Blair or George Bush (thankfully), that invasion of Iraq was very much on the agenda. This had been the key aim of the Bush administration following 11 September, and there was a fairly rigid timetable worked out in Washington. Although the situation in Palestine, especially the events round Jenin, deflected the US administration for a time, they clearly did not alter its basic trajectory.

Our analysis was borne out over the summer, as Iraq became the main political question of the day and it became clear that the British government was prepared to act alongside George Bush, regardless of the wishes of the people in Britain or indeed the rest of the world. The drive to war provoked opposition at the TUC, where a large minority opposed any war against Iraq; at meetings up and down the country, where speakers such as the Labour MP George Galloway attracted huge audiences; in schools and colleges where we are seeing the beginning of a mass protest movement among young people. All this came together in the 28 September demonstration, which had reverberations around the world.

Ron Kovic, Vietnam veteran and author of *Born on the Fourth of July*, e-mailed us the following day to say, 'You have inspired the world.' We were inundated with requests and messages from anti-war campaigners as far away as Japan and the US.

In Britain the demo gave a new impetus to existing activists and pulled in new ones. The 'Don't attack Iraq day' on Halloween was a success in bringing the anti-war protests home. School assemblies, workplace meetings and student occupations all draw attention to the heightened war drive. The Europe-wide demonstration in Florence in November attracted a million marching against globalisation and war. The Stop the War Coalition played a major part and also helped organise an international day of action on 15 February. This was also taken up at the Cairo conference in December 2002, and in Porto Alegre in January 2003. The result was a coordinated international protest involving tens of millions. The call for demonstrations in every town and city the day war breaks out has also been taken up internationally.

Our movement has also avoided the trap of elitism. Many different parties, MPs and celebrities have now sponsored it, but it does not simply rely on those at the top—it is a genuine grass-roots movement whose strength lies in unity in action across the different components of the movement. The Stop the War Coalition has shown that not only can it match anyone in the size of its demonstrations, but that they are also the most multiracial and mixed in every sense.

Nor does it rely on a small and self-appointed elite to carry out the protests. One tradition of the peace movement has been moral protests carried out by the few to represent the views of the masses. When we talk about direct action and civil disobedience we mean mass direct action which can involve large numbers of trade unionists, students and peace campaigners. If small groups of people want to go off and do their own thing, or spend time training in non-violent direct action techniques, that is fine, but they should not try to impose this elitism on the rest of us. Instead we should be building the movement outwards, by establishing groups round workplaces and unions, and organisations such as Out Against the War, which aims to organise gays and lesbians, Artists Against the War and many more.

Tony Blair is still desperate to get a UN resolution phrased in terms acceptable to the US. Some people will no doubt believe that this gives any war an authority which US and British involvement alone does not give it. However, a war which is wrong in every respect before a UN resolution does not suddenly become right because the US bribes and bullies the other members of the Security Council—including Vladimir Putin, who has just used chemical weapons against his own people. We have the potential to stop war, and millions of people now believe this following 15 February. Bush and Blair have set a determined course, and they will not allow one demonstration to stop them. But we have shaken them, and we have the power to keep shaking them until they are forced to retreat, as they did over Vietnam. That will take a deepening of the movement here, and a determination to keep going until we win.

Lindsey German is convenor of the Stop the War Coalition (www.stopwar.org.uk) **and editor of *Socialist Review*** sr@swp.org.uk

NO WAR
ON IRAQ

Picture: Paola Desiderio

DIRECTORY

AMNESTY INTERNATIONAL
Worldwide campaigning human rights movement. The website has information on breaches of international human rights law in countries such as Israel, the US and India (especially since 11 September 2001).
▣▸ www.amnesty.org

ANTI NAZI LEAGUE
The ANL is a broad-based mass organisation. Anyone who wants to stop the Nazis can join, regardless of political belief, religion or creed. Its aim is to stop the Nazis reaching a wider audience and growing. The ANL fights the Nazis by use of propaganda, demonstrations and counter-mobilisations. It has organised hugely successful anti-racist carnivals through its Love Music Hate Racism campaign.
▣▸ www.anl.org.uk

ATTAC
Was founded in France in 1998 by a group of citizens, associations, trade unions and newspapers. Attac advocates the imposition of a Tobin Tax, which is a tax on speculative transactions in the exchange market proposed by the Nobel Prize winning economist James Tobin. It works to ban currency speculation, tax capital revenue, punish fiscal paradises and 'recapture the spaces of democracy lost to the financial sphere'.
▣▸ www.attac.org

BERTRAND RUSSELL PEACE FOUNDATION
Formed in 1963 to further the cause of peace and to assist in the pursuit of freedom and justice. Its publishing imprint, Spokesman Books, publishes among other titles the *Spokesman* journal which was founded by Bertrand Russell near the end of his life.
▣▸ www.russfound.org
▣▸ www.spokesmanbooks.com

BOOKMARKS
The socialist bookshop. Sells a broad and exciting selection of anti-imperialist books (including this one!), in addition to books on a variety of subjects. Regular book launches and events are held at the bookshop. Bookmarks also has a publishing department—Bookmarks Publications.
▣▸ www.bookmarks.uk.com

CAMPAIGN AGAINST DEPLETED URANIUM
Launched to organise for a global ban on the manufacture, testing and use of depleted uranium weapons.
▣▸ www.cadu.org.uk

CAMPAIGN AGAINST SANCTIONS ON IRAQ
Provides information about the humanitarian situation in Iraq, and its context. It aims to raise awareness of the effects of sanctions on Iraq, and campaigns on humanitarian grounds for the lifting of non-military sanctions. CASI does not support the government of Iraq.
▣▸ www.casi.org.uk

CAMPAIGN AGAINST THE ARMS TRADE
Campaigns for the reduction and ultimate abolition of international arms trade. CAAT encourages policies to reorientate the economy away from military industry, and towards civil production.
▣▸ www.caat.org.uk

CAMPAIGN FOR NUCLEAR DISARMAMENT
CND campaigns non-violently to rid the world of nuclear weapons and other weapons of mass destruction and to create genuine security for future generations. CND's major campaigns are to scrap Trident, oppose Nato, prevent National Missile Defence (NMD) and halt the Plutonium Economy.
▣▸ www.cnduk.org

CAMPAIGN FOR PALESTINIAN RIGHTS
Launched at a London rally in January 2001, where Paul Foot, Tony Benn, Susannah York and many activists were determined to shift public opinion in Britain, look honestly at Middle East politics, and demand justice for the Palestinians.
▣▸ www.palestinian-rights.com

COMMITTEE TO DEFEND ASYLUM SEEKERS
The CDAS demands the right to work for asylum seekers, income support for asylum seekers, the abolition of detention centres, no forced dispersal, full legal rights and representation for asylum seekers, no deportations, and the scrapping of the UK Asylum and Immigration Act. The website has information about the group's numerous campaigns. Individuals and organisations can join.
▣▸ www.defend-asylum.org

DROP THE DEBT
Formerly Jubilee 2000. They have called for deeper debt cancellation for more countries, including 100 percent debt cancellation from the IMF and World Bank for the poorest countries in Africa, Latin America and Asia. Supported by Oxfam, Unison, WDM and others.
▣▸ www.dropthedebt.org

EUROPEAN NETWORK AGAINST THE ARMS TRADE
Umbrella group for European anti-arms and peace organisations.
▣▸ www.antenna.nl/enaat/

FASLANE PEACE CAMP
Began in 1982 with the arrival of anti-nuclear protesters who pitched camp on a small strip of land opposite Faslane's Gare Lock in Dunbartonshire, Scotland. They are there to alert the public to the four nuclear submarines now berthed in the beautiful and historic loch. The nuclear submarines are only 30 miles away from Scotland's second largest city, Glasgow.
▣▸ dspace.dial.pipex.com/cndscot/camp/

FOOD NOT BOMBS
The first Food Not Bombs group was set up in 1980 by anti-nuclear activists. It is an all-volunteer organisation committed to non-violent protest against war and poverty throughout the Americas, Europe and Australia.
▣▸ www.foodnotbombs.net

FRIENDS OF AL AQSA
A non profit making organisation concerned with the defence of the basic rights of Palestinians and the protection of the Al Aqsa Mosque in Jerusalem. The Al Aqsa Haram Sharif is under threat from building proposals made by Zionists to demolish the sacred mosque.
▣▸ www.aqsa.org.uk

GLOBALISE RESISTANCE
An organisation that brings together direct action activists and organisations from many strands of anti-imperialist and anti-capitalist movement. They have organised actions against George Bush's warmongering, the patenting of Aids treatments and Gap's

sweated labour, and has been part of the organisation of the recent anti-imperialist social forums worldwide.
⊟▸ www.resist.org.uk

HOUSMAN'S BOOKSHOP
Specialises in radical books and periodicals. Also sells anti-war T-shirts and peace diaries.
⊟▸ www.apogee.com/Housmans/order.mv

INDYMEDIA
A network of collectively run media outlets for 'the creation of radical, accurate and passionate tellings of the truth'. Indymedia has networks all over the world, and centres even in politically sensitive areas such as the Middle East. It is an invaluable source of independent media coverage, and the website has extensive information on the different regions of the world affected by imperialism.
⊟▸ www.indymedia.org

INTERNATIONAL CAMPAIGN TO BAN LANDMINES
A network of a huge number of non-governmental organisations in 60 countries, working for a global ban on landmines.
⊟▸ www.icbl.org

LIBERTY (NATIONAL COUNCIL FOR CIVIL LIBERTIES)
One of the UK's leading human rights and civil rights organisations. Its principal work is the campaign to defend and extend civil liberties. They undertake some advice and training work, and have their own lawyers. Liberty has been taking legal action against the curtailment of civil liberties that has taken place as part of the 'war on terror'.
⊟▸ www.liberty-human-rights.org.uk

LABOUR ACTION FOR PEACE
An organisation of Labour Party members and trade unionists working for peace, socialism and disarmament, and seeking to keep these issues to the forefront of Labour Party policy at all times.
⊟▸ www.labour-peace-action.org.uk

LABOUR AGAINST THE WAR

Aims to mobilise opposition to war throughout all levels of the Labour Party and the affiliated trade unions. You can join LATW either as an individual or as an affiliated organisation.

▷ www.labouragainstthewar.org.uk
▷ latw@gn.apc.org

MEDIA WORKERS AGAINST WAR

Run by volunteers working in different types of media. They have different ideologies, but are an independent organisation united by their opposition to the so-called 'war on terrorism'. They are also opposed to the mainstream media's support for aggressive action against innocent civilians under the pretence of 'anti-terrorism'. The organisation was originally formed in response to the last Gulf War, but reformed in September 2001. The website holds a plethora of articles and reports that counter the misinformation in the mainstream media.

▷ www.mwaw.org

N-BASE NUCLEAR INFORMATION SERVICE (SCOTLAND)

The N-Base Information Service has a 10,000-record database of newspaper articles and publishes weekly briefings on the UK nuclear industry, reprocessing and plutonium production at Sellafield and Dounreay, nuclear transports, waste, pollution and other environment and health issues. Searching the database and 200 archived briefings is available free.

▷ www.n-base.org.uk/public/index.html

PALESTINE SOLIDARITY CAMPAIGN

The PSC was established during the build-up to the Israeli invasion of Lebanon in 1982. It organises protests and political lobbying, and tries to raise public awareness of the Palestinian cause.

▷ www.palestinecampaign.org

PEACE PLEDGE UNION

One of the main secular pacifist organisations in Britain. It produces white poppies and is a British affiliate of WRI (War Resisters International).

▷ www.ppu.org.uk
▷ info@ppu.org.uk

REFUGEE ACTION

An independent national charity that enables refugees to build new lives in the UK. Provides practical advice and assistance for newly arrived asylum seekers and a long term commitment to their settlement through community development work.

▷ www.refugee-action.org

RELIGIOUS SOCIETY OF FRIENDS (QUAKERS)

An anti-war Christian group. Organises peace vigils and is concerned with the protection of human rights worldwide. They have human rights observers in Palestine and work with other anti-war groups.

▷ www.quaker.org.uk

SCOTTISH SOCIALIST PARTY

The SSP aims to replace capitalism with an economic system based on democratic ownership and control of the key sectors of the economy. It would like a system based on social need and environmental protection rather than private profit. The SSP is Scotland's youngest and fastest-growing party, which campaigns inside and outside parliament for social change.

▷ www.scottishsocialistparty.org

SOCIALIST ALLIANCE

An electoral alliance offering a left alternative to New Labour, challenging the government on everything from its scapegoating of asylum seekers to Blair's imperialist warmongering. The Socialist Alliance is made up of ex Labour Party supporters, and individuals and organisations from Britain's radical left.

▷ www.socialistalliance.net
▷ www.welshsocialistalliance.org.uk

SOCIALIST WORKERS PARTY

The biggest revolutionary party in the UK. It is a member of the Socialist Alliance, and many of its members are involved with the Stop the War Coalition and Globalise Resistance. The SWP is a member of the International Socialist Tendency, which is a network of revolutionary socialist organisations throughout the world. The organisation stresses the need for the mass mobilisation of ordinary workers to fundamentally change society, and put 'people before profit'.

▷ www.swp.org.uk
▷ www.socialistworker.co.uk

STOP THE WAR COALITION

The national coalition for organisations and individuals in Britain to campaign against the 'war on terror' was formed on 21 September 2001 at a public meeting of over 2,000 people in London. It campaigns under the slogans 'Stop the war', 'No to a racist backlash' and 'Defend civil liberties'.

Has been responsible for organising several enormous anti-war demonstrations in Britain including the biggest ever protest of 2 million people on 15 February 2003. Affiliated organisations include several national trade unions including Unison, CWU, NUJ, FBU, RMT, Aslef, TSSA, PCS, Natfhe, Napo and the NUM, and numerous other organisations including the Muslim Association of Britain, Just Peace, the Muslim Parliament and Fed Bir (Kurdish organisation).

⊟▶ www.stopwar.org.uk
⊟▶ office@stopwar.org.uk

TRIDENT PLOUGHSHARES 2000

Trident Ploughshares is a campaign to disarm the UK Trident nuclear weapons system in a non-violent, open, peaceful and fully accountable manner. The organisation brings together people from all over the world pledged to disarm Trident in this way. Upholds international humanitarian law and exposes the illegality of the Trident system.

⊟▶ www.tridentploughshares.org

UK AMERICANS AGAINST WAR

A network of UK-based Americans who oppose the war agenda of the US government. The group is a forum to network and pass on helpful information of relevance to members.

⊟▶ groups.yahoo.com/group/ukamericansagainstwar/
⊟▶ thedishbench@yahoo.com

VOICES IN THE WILDERNESS US/UK

A joint campaign inspired by the principles of Gandhi that opposes the development, storage and use by any country of weapons of mass destruction. Also campaigns to end economic sanctions on the people of Iraq.

⊟▶ www.nonviolence.org/vitw (US)
⊟▶ www.vitw.freeserve.co.uk (UK)

WOMEN'S INTERNATIONAL LEAGUE FOR PEACE AND FREEDOM

Active in 45 countries worldwide, including Palestine and Israel. WILPF was founded in 1915 and works towards a peaceful resolution of conflict and total, universal disarmament. It campaigns on peace, human rights and economic justice issues.

▷ www.ukwilpf.gn.apc.org
▷ ukwilpf@hotmail.com

WORLD DEVELOPMENT MOVEMENT

Tackles the underlying causes of poverty, and lobbies decision makers to change policies that keep people poor. The website has extensive information about protests in countries across the world (including Latin America, Africa and Asia) against IMF and World Bank policies. The WDM work alongside people in the developing world standing up against injustice. It is against economic systems that keep powerful countries in control of global economics. The WDM is for sustainable development, the reform of the WTO, and against the power of multinationals.

▷ www.wdm.uk.org

ZAPATISTAS

The Zapatista National Liberation Army carried out an armed occupation of the state capital in the Chiapas region of Mexico in 1994, on the very day that Nafta's launch was announced. The Zapatistas have become an important symbol of resistance against neoliberalism on a global scale. There are a huge number of organisations and activities associated with the Zapatistas, but a guide can be found on their website.

▷ www.eco.utexas.edu/faculty/Cleaver/zapsijcyber.html

ANTI-IMPERIALIST ESSAYS AND ARTICLES CAN ALSO BE FOUND ON THE FOLLOWING SITES:

▷ *Z Magazine*: www.zmag.org/weluser.htm
▷ The films and writings of John Pilger: http://pilger.carlton.com
▷ Noam Chomsky archive: www.zmag.org/chomsky/index.cfm

Mass rally in London after the 2 million strong demonstration on 15 February 2003

TO ORDER MORE COPIES OF THIS BOOK CONTACT

Our overriding purpose, from the beginning through to the present day, has been world domination—that is, to build and maintain the capacity to coerce everybody else on the planet, non-violently if possible and violently if necessary. But the purpose of US foreign policy of domination is not just to make the rest of the world jump through hoops—the purpose is to facilitate our exploitation of resources.

Ramsey Clark, former US Attorney General